Other books by Joanna Devrais

Allergy Free Eating

Hearthstories

A Modern Woman's Quest for the Essential Self

Joanna Devrais

iUniverse, Inc.

New York   Bloomington

iUniverse books may be ordered through booksellers or by contacting:

iUniverse
1663 Liberty Drive
Bloomington, IN 47403
www.iuniverse.com
1-800-Authors (1-800-288-4677)

Because of the dynamic nature of the Internet, any Web addresses or links contained in this book may have changed since publication and may no longer be valid. The views expressed in this work are solely those of the author and do not necessarily reflect the views of the publisher, and the publisher hereby disclaims any responsibility for them.

ISBN: 978-1-4401-6397-5 (sc)
ISBN: 978-1-4401-6398-2 (ebook)

Printed in the United States of America

iUniverse rev. date: 09/01/2009

~ To all seekers

Contents

Acknowledgments

First I would like to thank my editor, Hal Zina Bennett, for his guidance, wisdom and support. A beginning writer needs a guiding hand and respectful presence. He gave that and more. Thank you to Emily Hanlon who carried me deeper, to Jan Allegretti who spent many hours editing and refining, and to Dan Barth who carried the copy editing to peaceful completion.

Thank you to my Irish and Scottish ancestors whose spirits guided and led the journey from the thresholds of their world; to Princess White Feather, who taught me about the mystery and sacredness of life; to my family, who gave support, love and patience; and to Sula, cat muse and companion.

Foreword

By Hal Zina Bennett *

This is a memoir of journeying, covering several years of the author's personal *pilgrimage*. It is a feminine quest in which the author seeks purpose and meaning in terms of her own womanhood, sharing insights that help to bring us each to ourselves. It is filled with stories of both inner and outer discovery and growth that rise out of experiences as immediate as enjoying tea in the garden with a friend and as far-flung as visiting Black Madonna sites in England and Ireland.

There are particular passages from the book that come to mind as I write this. One of them is Joanna's description of her "Ireland pilgrimage." It takes place as she is waiting to board the train for Oban. It was easy to identify with the restlessness she was experiencing as she waited. It is a subtle description of the kind of uneasiness that so often comes with waiting, when our anticipation of what is *yet to be* is more compelling than our ability *to be* fully present and conscious of the moment. In these passages, the author reminds me that this ability to be present is a challenge to each of us not just in traveling to places unfamiliar to us but in our everyday lives—to be aware and be able to take in each moment, to be responsive and open to the *now*.

As the author waits for the train, she keeps checking the time, impatient as she considers the long day of travel that's still ahead of her. And then, suddenly conscious of what she is doing, she allows herself to settle down, to become more present. She takes out her journal, her pen, and begins to turn inward, contemplating where she is and what she is doing right now. I don't recall whether she writes this down or simply reflects on it, but she has the insight that even while she was feeling impatient and eager to begin her trip to Oban, she also knew that "being in the moment allowed the journey to come to me."

While the book at times reads like a travelogue, it more importantly chronicles the author's spiritual life, a journey of heart and mind and soul that unfolds on many levels. As a chronicle of the spiritual journey, it is filled with everyday stories that in their simplicity, subtlety and *everydayness* often remind us to pay attention not only to the more dramatic or sensational outer events of our lives but to our more familiar sense of being connected and responsive to those more everyday events. I am here reminded of something the author Eudora Welty said of spending all her life in a small Mississippi town: "I am a writer who came of a sheltered life. A sheltered life can be a daring life as well. For all serious daring starts from within."

While Joanna journeys far beyond the confines of small town living, she keeps her stories focused on those vital interior moments each of us can relate to—whether it is in our own kitchen preparing a special dinner, an insight that comes to us during a walk in nature, shopping at a local farmers market, waiting to board a train in a strange land, or gazing at a mysterious icon in an ancient cathedral. The author's stories, like all stories, are inner markers of personal evolution that are intimate and lucid. Without the stories, we might miss the journey altogether. In the end, that is the purpose of all story-telling, whether imaginative, mythological, or reportorial.

The stories contained in these pages often take the author, as well as us, her readers, into strange lands and experiences that are beyond the familiar and comfortable. But ultimately, this is a memoir of the journey home, of the author coming into herself, returning to the *hearth*. Though the author's experiences may be unlike our own, the passage she reports, going out into the unknown and circling back to the familiar, is a journey we all share as we seek self-knowledge and comfort in our own skin.

 ✦ Hal Zina Bennett is the author of more than 30 books, including *Write From the Heart: Unleashing the Power of Your Creativity*.

Introduction

While each of us is unique, we also belong to the great one-ness of life. This book is about the quest to honor the spark of our individual journey even as we participate in the one-ness.

It is summer as I write these final pages and prepare to send *Hearthstories* off to the publisher. I look back over the years of this writing, noting that I have traveled as a hermit much of the time. However I wasn't alone. I shared my life with a tabby cat named Sula, beautiful in her grey, warm orange and white coat. She personified the unique *catself*, owning who she was. She spoke her mind in *cateze* and never let me stray far from my writing path. She had the gift of swatting me back into presence.

Sula died as I completed my preparations for publishing. I felt a great loss, yet her death reminded me that all endings—all destinations in our lives, even death—are also new beginnings. Sula left me the gift of a new beginning, a reminder to reconnect and appreciate relationships which I had often taken for granted. A writer spends a lot of time alone. I woke up to the importance of companionship. Those who companioned my writing include friends and family, summer coreopsis, birch, and the call of hawks. The gifts of the feminine quest for healing asked me to walk the spirals of the labyrinth, to treasure my passion for farmers markets and cooking, and to learn that every day is a quest.

Our lives are spirals. I began this book as I turned sixty, when I sought more depth, aliveness and presence in my life. I sought a new blueprint for living. The quest asked me to stop my frantic pace, to stop and listen and allow life to flow toward me and to include what I loved each day. I discovered a soulful hand who guided me to new territories, both inner and outer. My outer travels took me to France to explore the invitations of the Black Madonna's and the labyrinth at Chartres Cathedral. The last year of my travel took me to my roots in Ireland and to Scotland where I fell in love with the sacred isle of Iona.

The book is woven with the sacred fabric of everyday life in the beautiful Sonoma valley. You will find hearth stories, recipes and riches of exploration. Please read this book as a conversation, knowing that our lives are journeys. Each day we have the opportunity to craft new dreams, open new doors, and meet new teachers. Each day is a special time to share trust and explore.

I began that first winter of the book sitting quietly by the fire, to restore and nurture my physical body and listen to an inner calling. Once quiet I found I could tend to my dreams, longings and listening. I made time to walk regularly in nature. As I opened to the matrix of Mother Earth's wisdom I fell in love with the seasons again, found my personal rhythm in the day and fed myself well with both physical and spiritual food. I gave myself a life with gentleness and a slow pace.

The winters brought unexpected emotional upheavals and study in the exploration of my Celtic roots. The springs brought house cleaning of the old, creative explorations and sacred travel. The summers opened me to play, to expand my life by facing fears and walking through them. The falls were times of celebrating the harvest of the year, of stocking and preparing for the inner times of winter. Labyrinths invited me to walk deeply in my body. The mysteries of the divine feminine drew me into new spiritual paths and challenged old thinking, opening me to the surprises of meeting Black Madonna's in France.

I always returned from inner and outer travels to my hearth. So I invite you to come and sit by the hearth for this story. I offer up the warmth of sharing.

Prologue

An ancient woman sleeps. Fabric woven 2,000 years ago wraps around Her body and hides Her black face. The world's religions know Her as Tara, Isis, Sophia. Few remember Her names.

I must unwrap Her and bring Her back from Her sleep deep inside me and the Earth. She waits for me to remember Her, to become Her archaeologist. Although I do not know exactly what mysteries she will reveal, I must mount the ancient camels and travel to Her place of knowing. I must dare to become a new pilgrim calling up old treasure from beneath my feet. I must dare to speak from her ancient tongue.

She has called me. She calls from longings, and she hands out invitations to Her world—to Her womb of being. When I have taken the time, I have found marks of Her presence in places such as wells, islands, meadows, labyrinthine circles, ancient shrines, and sacred geometry. I have met Her in places where I have listened for Her presence. She awakened me in sacred islands and in my garden. These places remind me that I can bring forward the very essence of Her knowing. My own tradition of Christianity would name Her Wisdom. The instinctual call of Her being is now upon us, but I must choose the process to arrive in Her presence.

This is my story of quest, discovery, and reclaiming the sacred feminine face of God.

Year One

Winter

"In a way winter is the real spring, the time when the inner thing happens, the resurge of nature."

—Edna O'Brien

Auntie's Gift

My yellow and rose comforter, a tried and true friend, fell to the floor as I stepped from the warmth of a late morning sleep-in. I checked the clock and found it was eight a.m., two hours past the time I usually wake up.

Nothing felt the same that day. My cat Sula, my other comforter, crept out of the bedroom to be about her morning of bird watching. She favored the sunlit sill of the living room window. A black journal lay on the floor where I'd left it that night. Not a word had marred its pages.

That October morning was different because of a death. I had recently returned from my ninety-one-year-old aunt's funeral in San Diego. My sister and I had given her a beautiful California sunset goodbye. We both mourned her deeply. Aunt Annie's death had turned my head and my heart. Death has its way of opening us.

It was after my return from her funeral that I sat one afternoon and faced my own death. Like others I had avoided death. Yet at the time, I knew facing it was necessary. After all, I was about to turn sixty, no longer mid-life. My forehead wrinkled as I realized that facing death also meant facing life. Had I been living *my* life? The "my" stuck in my mind. If not my own, whose life was I leading, or for whom, and why? Waves of anxiety and grief met in my heart. Had I left parts of my life unlived? I looked back at my aunt's life. She had been a renegade, of sorts. I loved

3

her adventuresome nature and her pioneer spirit. Long ago she had met my Uncle Edwin, married and then driven across country to live in California. She was a pilgrim of outer journeys, and I was embarking on an inner spiral.

Was I willing to leave my known world and become a pilgrim in search of my true self. Was I willing to just stop and take stock of my life, make time to look deeply? I longed to say yes, but in that moment I needed to feel the grief. I had become good at not recognizing or connecting with feelings, especially sad ones. Sitting intimately with myself was foreign. For days and weeks that followed I made tea, wept, and wrote in my journal. It soon became obvious that I was grieving more than Annie's death. Journaling became a container, a place to let go and feel safe to express myself. I learned to listen to myself. The reward gained was the opportunity to review my life. It felt natural at my age to sort and harvest experience. My father had died some years before. My mother was soon to turn eighty-one. Questions hounded me. Had I lived my life fully? What held meaning for me now that I was about to turn sixty? What if I were to die in a year? Empty-nest blues, menopause, and general concerns about aging were all part of the mix.

Winters in northern California wine country mean moderate temperatures and rain. Each year I hope the rains come early, but our seasons are unique. From late spring to October or sometimes into November there is no rain at all. When winter arrives I welcome the relief and change from hot and dry sunny days.

That winter I had my wish, and the rain did come early. I had not always loved the grey overcast, the dark days. But in recent years I had come to enjoy them. Winter certainly was the season that invited introspection. It felt essential to make time to stay with the questions, follow the twists and turns of an inner labyrinth.

I knew the gift of walking spiral labyrinths in the outer world. My introduction to them came through my friend Alyssa. She herself loved the labyrinth, and had been trained as a facilitator at Grace Cathedral in San Francisco. Inspired by her many experiences teaching others to walk the spiral, she had one painted onto a canvas, so it was portable. I had made the hour's drive to San Rafael that Saturday to help her set up; a group of us unrolled it onto the floor of a small church. The experience of walking that canvas spiral calmed and centered me. Soon after my experience with Alyssa, I discovered a beautiful outdoor labyrinth near my home in Sonoma. The labyrinth sits nestled in a redwood grove at Trinity Episcopal Church, seven spiral paths lead you to a center circle. The paths are defined by beautiful river rock.

Winter invited me to listen, to slow down. If I didn't stop, when would I find answers to my burning questions? I felt like a mountain lake whose waters shift seasonally. Two times a year the nutrients that lay at the bottom of the lake rise to the surface, the layers churned by changes in temperature. My life waters, too, seemed to stir and turn. A northern wind with frigid temperatures had touched me. I felt a catch in my throat, and a feeling of sadness moved like a wave through my heart again and again; I felt the loss of something essential, but I did not know what.

The grief from that loss would set me on my journey.

I padded my way to the living room and found Sula curled on her window ledge. She turned to me with her clear eyes, and made her plea to go outdoors with a word that I swear sounded like "out." I opened the front door and off she scurried. I watched her leap across tuffs of grasses. Would I ever start the day with such joy?

I walked to my desk and pulled out a notebook of quotes I had kept for years. I leafed through the pages, and stopped at "when inner things happen." Yes it was time to listen and evaluate. I had no idea what an inspired life would look like. Wasn't it time to give myself permission to find out?

Striving wasn't helping me gather back my truths. A different life called which challenged old roles. I had played the role of a "pleaser," which meant seeking approval as a good mother, friend, lover, cook. I'd come to feel I was acceptable in the eyes of others. But I was afraid to be myself, which would ultimately mean being different. As a child of the fifties I was expected to be anything but myself. That was my experience, at least. I was afraid to be myself. I suspected I was actually an artist at heart. But the play-it-safe part of me had never let go. How could I release the old? A labyrinthine maze lay ahead.

What did the essential part of me look like? Like many women I had not stopped to make time to find out, felt guilty considering it. I feared being labeled selfish almost as much as being labeled a bitch. Was I willing to turn toward myself and find my own authority?

That inner search seemed too large a task.

First I would have to find out who I was and what I wanted. What I hadn't given myself was time, time to enjoy my life and find out what I loved. One afternoon I set to planting tulips and daffodils, something I hadn't taken time for before. Suddenly I stood up. What I wanted was clear. "I want to stop working!"

Something inside me shouted back, "What? We can't do that!"

I had never imagined not working.

I had worked at several different professions since I became single in the early nineties. In the mid-nineties, out of my love for cooking, I had birthed a small catering business called Heart Cuisine. Its inception emerged from my experience as an art therapist, when I used art to support women as they explored their struggles to love their bodies and find peace in their relationships with food. It was, of course, my own issue, as well.

My business took me down new paths and grew my relationship with food and creativity. But over the course of those ten years I eventually began to burn out. Heart Cuisine was mainly a five-day-a-week dinner delivery service, and also included small parties and seasonal events. The business required multitasking—menu planning, ingredient purchases, food prepping, cooking, packaging, billing, and delivery. When I thought of everything I did I was exhausted. Besides, I had always been troubled by performance pressure. I loved the creativity but not the pressure, and in the last year, as I aged I felt exhausted.

Yes, I was tired. What if I rested and out of that rest found a larger story for my life. I had money in the bank. Why shouldn't I stop? I owned my business. All I needed to do was give notice to my clients. I had only one part-time employee, and I knew she was ready to move on to different work. My mind wanted to be practical and stop me from changing my life. The fear chatter went on. Fear had run my life, anxiety had driven decision making for too long. But that day I knew I had to risk.

Letting Go

I sat with the anxieties of closing my business for many days. But winter slowly helped me settle in and relax. Gathering a stack of books was a favorite winter pastime. I had already set one close to the fire. Four of the books in my stack included two volumes about my Celtic heritage, a book about pilgrimage, and *Pilgrim at Tinker Creek* written by Annie Dillard, my favorite author. I noted my interest in being a pilgrim. I picked up Dillard's book ready to settle back in my chair when I realized that I felt cold. I had not put socks on, had forgotten my morning tea and I'd neglected to build a fire. Too messy, lugging the logs I had thought. I needed a fire. It was clear I had not been listening to my body. In fact, I was overriding my needs. Wasn't the idea of taking time off to notice such things? It was time to warm myself.

I got up from my chair and walked on the chilly wood floors toward the fireplace to prepare the fire. As I crumpled the paper and stacked wood, my eyes wandered inside the hearth to the blackened stone. I felt a sense of emptiness as I saw the dark smudges. Dark smudges, fires past. How often had I listened to my need of warmth, inspiration, and connection? I lit the match and set the fire blazing. As I stood in front of the blaze I began to feel warm. The fire drew me to its beauty, comfort and inspiration.

As my outer skin warmed, I went to make that tea I had forgotten. I heated the kettle. My rusty red kettle had seen its day; I still loved it and wouldn't trade it. Next I chose my tea. Did I want my Irish Breakfast Blend or a more soothing herbal, perhaps mint?

Tea always conjures up feelings of connection and love, time spent with my grandmother. I lifted one of her cups, white with a delicate blue rim, from the shelf. I recalled my Nana serving up cups of afternoon tea in bed while we browsed the photograph album. Tea was always served with milk and sugar and lemon cookies.

When the kettle boiled and my mint tea steeped I returned to the living room, where the fire had warmed the open space. I was happy to sit and look about me. The room had two large windows. The light was welcomed in the low dark space. The accompanying art room / office had another window. Two French doors opened off the living room into the yard where I could see a persimmon tree. The orange lanterns of fruit hung from bare branches, the leaves long gone. Something about the bare branches engaged me. The bright orange color of the persimmons contrasted with the green of the pine tree that rooted itself on the far edge of the inner yard. Color always feeds my soul. As I sat appreciating

I saw the gifts in slowing down. This was a clue to the life I wanted to live; I wanted to appreciate the richness of life, breathe into the day, feel the breeze.

It was time to give myself the small joys of life. I sat down with my tea. Just sipping the tea brought me back to myself. I realized how my anxiety to accomplish drove me. I had abandoned myself somewhere at the side of the great get-it-done highway. I could barely breath as I spoke the word *abandon*.

As I drank tea by the fire I remembered an old diary resting on my bookshelf and went to get it. I took it off the shelf and read from it. My entry from a year ago read: "I feel tired today, tired of trying so hard, struggling. Will I ever get to rest?" I know I had felt tired for a very long time. Speeding along, going from one thing to the next, keeping busy was the way. I felt guilty when I rested. This entry helped me revisit my truth. I knew I wasn't alone in the speed. But I knew my answer was clear: Yes, it was time to stop working.

But then what would I do if I stopped working? I would have open time, time to face truths. I was not sure I wanted to open that door. A swamp of fear engulfed me. Did I want to soften into myself? Could I find out what I needed? Could I learn how to nourish, how not to exclude myself? I got up to stoke the fire and realized how late it had gotten.

While my plan to close my business became more real there were steps to be taken. The first step meant giving a one-month notice to my clients. It was the beginning of the week, my workload was light, but it was time to turn from musing to work. I dressed and gathered my food list and went to market. I hauled my purchases inside to my state-approved kitchen. In rote fashion I gathered my pots and knives and started cooking. Twelve carrots chopped, ginger peeled, apple juice poured, chicken sautéed, potatoes chopped. I stopped chopping and felt tired. I did want to stop. I finished the cooking for the day, delivered the food and headed home.

It was natural to feel fear as I contemplated stopping my work. Cooking was who I was...or was it? I had been a woman at her stove for many years. I owned my own business and worked hard. I had become rigorous and harsh with myself. I never allowed a generous balance to my life. I wanted more *being* in my life. My body was tired and at the bottom I knew I struggled to accept my aging.

At the end of the week I finally did call long-time clients to say I would be closing Heart Cuisine. Then I called Susan, my employee, and did the same. I felt good that day.

My home turned out to be ideal for what was to come. I normally love light in my homes, but that year I found the large wood beams and cave-like quality appealing to me. The location was perfect; my home on Seventh Street enabled me to walk to town. Sonoma is a small piece of paradise. The town square offers history, wine tasting, and wonderful restaurants. A visitor can speak to wine merchants or offer a carrot to our favorite Clydesdale horses whose pasture is just off the square. My favorite living close to- town- joy is walking to farmers markets on Fridays. Lovall Valley Road is edged in grapevines, often offering free harvest of walnuts or figs.

The house I lived in sat back from the road. The front of the property housed artists' studios. It was a perfect nest for me. Its funky entrance was enticing to the imagination, but horrifying to my traditional upbringing. Since it was once an industrial property there was an unexpected order to its hodgepodge structures. The house was solid and spacious and overlooked an old walnut orchard and open fields. The cave-like quality of the house was balanced by the spacious feeling of land about it.

The property included structures with rough, tin roofs and warped boards. It is a dilapidated but charming place. The back of the property invited me into arched concrete pylons. Once I stepped through the arches I was transported to the ruins of an Italian countryside. Liz, another renter, had woven her magic between the arches with small gardens, each arch led to another retreat space where second-hand artifacts, spider plants, old bottles, and whimsical statues of fairies and gnomes graced the walls and small tables. It was a place for dreaming.

A large field flanked the southwest boundary of the property. Here a band of ruffian goats chomped their way through the day, calling to each other when they found themselves separated. I often carried table scraps to them; much horn butting ensued over carrots and celery. They became neighbors, each day teaching me to kick up my heels and to expand my idea of community. It was fun to think in bigger pictures. The stay-on-task part of me would never allow time to converse with goats.

But my home was unique for its quirkiness, unusual in its contrasts. The charisma of the neighborhood also included a family of peacocks who roamed from house to house. The history of their appearance on Seventh Street is a mystery. At some point in each day, the great indigo blues and greens of their bodies and their wild piercing calls startled me into the moment.

As I began to nest into my new life after letting my business go, I committed to revisit creative efforts. Watercolor painting was one of them. My love of writing was another. I had kept a journal for many years but never took writing seriously. Living among artists, glass blowers, and painter gave me creative mirrors. The creative mirrors were calling, calling me to grow.

As the month unfolded I felt the light withdraw and darkness come early. The quiet would help me surrender to the unknown road. I felt like a plant whose energy retreated into the "place of the root and the bulb and the seeds hugged tight." I loved the image, written so beautifully by Mara Freeman. I had begun to explore her writing about Celtic spirituality. Like a bulb, I needed to rest in the dark. It would be new to me, but I would learn to allow the darkness to grow in me.

Most women worry during the dark season of the year. Our moods suffer. But there was a part of my being that loved the dark. Could I be a pioneer into the unknown, take the risk of descent? What did I love about the dark? Was it because I could hide? Or did I, too, need to wrap the cocoon of darkness about me to grow? I revisited the notion that the dark was often considered evil. But I was drawn to it to explore.

The prospect of inner questing challenged me. I stepped willingly with one breath and then retreated with the next. I wanted to be brave in the unknown. If I accepted this invitation to become a pilgrim to my own center there was no turning around. No journey was taken without the rough road of exploration and inquiry—and what would they bring? What would I discover about myself? I had not come this far to turn away. Yes, I felt fear as I approached the tight bud of an essential me.

In my heart of hearts I knew that our lives had cycles, I needed to stand face to face with aging and death. New seasons, transitions, and change are not easy. I was comfortable with the inquiry part of the journey. I had some ground of understanding about the gifts of self -exploration and meditation. I had committed before to healing through various therapies. This work was part of my generation's life process. For most of my life I had felt something was wrong with me, felt I needed fixing. Like many women, I have brought with me the wounds of childhood sexual abuse. Unresolved feelings lay just below the surface. I wanted to claim my joy and power.

Making time for exploration meant having no schedule. My body felt the signal to slow down and rest. When my tense, get-it-right self could relax, I knew I would be more connected to the flow of life. A month passed quickly and the last day finally arrived. It felt strange to be preparing Heart Cuisine's final meals and put up my knives, cookbooks, and pots. I felt loss and relief at the same time.

Several days later I looked around me and began to feel happy, like a vacationer. What to do? I wanted to just sit and stare out the window, which I did for days. One morning I woke up and looked around the house feeling a desire to create more of a home for myself. Beauty was a gift I gave in my food, but did I give it to myself? No.

I looked about the room and realized that I loved the challenges of an empty canvas. I noticed the large beams. There were two, one toward the front third of the room, the other toward the end. At the east end of the living room a high counter separated the large area from the galley kitchen. Down the hall was a small bathroom paved in Mexican tiles, and beyond it was the bedroom. Tucked in the back of the house, it had just one large window. The light in that room was dim because of the porch overhang. It became the ultimate cave room.

What feeling was missing in the room? Softness I thought. I knew immediately that I needed fabric. Where I wasn't sure, but fiber and texture and color were my joys. It took only a few days to find several pieces of fabric. I considered drapes, but then realized that I needed to break the rules. I decided to drape the fabric from the beams. One was a thin gauzy fabric, the other a red and gold Indian sari that had been given to me by my friend Carol. Draping these fabrics meant expressing myself in that moment. I let down into my creativity. Living in a structure that had little surface conformity to it gave me permission to step outside the usual boundaries.

I had already broken some internal rules about appearances by moving into the funky art setting. When I entered the compound from Seventh Street, what came into view were old cars in various stages of repair, a very dusty drive, not a stick of proper landscaping, large loading docks, and at the back of the drive a large adobe and wood home. I could become an artist, dress like an artist, whatever that meant, maybe even become the lost parts of myself. I could turn toward the parts of me I had abandoned. The dress-for-success part of myself had a rather strict form to it; there was drive and perfection in it. Could I let go into a messy wild self, a self who didn't obey the rules, a self who was waiting?

I went to my file draw and pulled a file of pictures I had torn from magazines. They included things I wanted to buy, pictures of beautiful gardens, food photos, places I wanted to visit and more. Just looking at the photographs stimulated my senses and opened my creative eyes. I had new dreams and doorways to walk through, doorways to a richer and deeper, more satisfying life.

One file folder contained images from an art history class I had taken years before. The class was particularly interesting to me because it had included several lectures on early goddess images. My teacher, Margaret, had returned from recent trips to Crete and early goddess sites, so she shared photographs of bare-breasted women, spirals, and other symbols of ancient life. I began to realize that while taking that class, I was standing at the beginning of a larger spiral. My interest in exploring the sacred feminine began. I became inspired by the writings and teachings of other women artists, writers, and anthropologists like Maria Gambutas. Many of these women were on journeys to recover the sacred feminine through imagery, history, art, and religion.

More recently in the nineties I had come upon the icon of the Dark Madonna. The Dark Madonnas were images unknown to me until I read China Galland's *Longing for Darkness*. I felt longing to connect to a feminine face of divinity and heal the split between my body and spirit. These aspects of healing were needed, but the time had not yet come for my journey to begin.

As I stepped into my new life which offered me more space to listen, it became clear that the years of trying to balance the pressures of work with the process of inner pilgrimage had allowed me to commit to neither. While I missed the joy of the process of cooking, I did not miss the demands. As I took the first tiny steps toward releasing the pressure, I could feel my mind let go. I left behind a schedule, a plan for my days. I felt the unknown in front of me. I had been used to gulping coffee and gearing up to a high pitch every day. Without a plan I had no clue how to relax or slow down. But I found myself wracked with feelings of guilt. It was easy to imagine a hunched woman in tattered clothes shuffling across the Safeway parking lot with her bags—yes, for sure I would become a bag lady. Often the fear drove me to pace back and forth in front of my fireplace. But I knew I was following my truth.

My thoughts often turned back to menopause and to the day I found myself with an empty nest. When I was honest with myself I saw that I had not paused for any of it. Clearly it had been time for my son Matt to set out on his own life path. I applauded his steps and yet felt the emptiness in my heart. In that letting go I'd had to face where I was in my own life.

Thoughts of aging lead me to death and my aunt's passing again. I considered her life. She had lived a long life of ninety-one years and was loved by my sister and me for her maverick, humorous self. My aunt was feisty and clear-headed when she died. Could I become like her? When I thought about doing what I truly wanted, I hesitated.

The things I hadn't done filled pages. I had not made time to dream. For years I had tentatively considered my desire to travel, go back to painting, perhaps take my writing more seriously. I loved writing, had kept a journal for many years but had never taken it seriously. Why hadn't I made more time for self-expression? I felt guilty, plain and simple. I had put what I loved on a back burner. The front burners had been turned on to get somewhere. All of them were not helping me feel happy or fulfilled. What if in fact I had only one year to live?

I took several mornings to sit and imagine what I would love to do with my days. Perhaps I could take trips to the museums in San Francisco. That thought sparked my though of painting again. I had not picked up a paintbrush in a long time. One thought followed another. Writing was a lost love. I had been a "sort –of-'writer for years. Like many women I struggled with feelings of unworthiness. After all, who would care to hear what I had to say? It was easy to source that comment: "Who do you think you are young lady?" My mother's words are familiar to many women of my generation. I felt uncomfortable being full—full of life, full of myself, full of worthwhile things to say. "Being full of myself" denoted selfishness, or arrogance. Expressing myself from deep inside was just plain unknown territory. There would be so many doors to reopen.

Where to begin? What I had done was journal; I had often recorded dreams. However, I didn't always honor the messages shown to me in dreamtime. Adding up my daily accomplishments seemed much more important. Was my value to be measured in the things I did? for I had already identified my need to please.

The more I sat with myself the more I saw what I had known but ignored. I spent more time with my critic than I did with self care. I also became aware of my need to please others, to give up what I knew supported a fulfilled life.

There were unmet parts of me who wanted to speak. I longed to meet 'the stranger," myself. I had read Derek Walcott's poem, *Love after Love*, and put language to the disconnection I felt. To reconnect meant facing my truths and meeting the past. My friend Emily had given me a poem called "The Warrior." Hafiz says, "The warrior tames the beasts in their past so that the night's hooves no longer break the jeweled vision in the heart." I longed to live the heart's knowing.

Questions kept coming; I needed containers to hold the process. So I began recording my dreams and taking my journaling more seriously. My journal became the place I met myself. As I listened more closely I dreamed more deeply and asked for dreams to guide me. My requests for dreams were answered.

One morning I woke with a start. The dream was actually a form of guidance. It went as follows:

> I found myself walking through a hole into the underground. I walked in dark, earthen passageways with a flaming torch. In the passages I passed an occasional rabbit. I kept walking. After some time I saw a light and a stairway. I left the torch behind and walked up a spiral stairway, stopping on several landings to catch my breath. After what seemed like forever, I reached the top and stepped out into a large cathedral. It felt ancient, and was made of stone. I walked toward a large altar and pews of stone.
>
> Near the end of the altar I saw three aunts coming to greet me. The aunts were my mother's sisters. They included my recently deceased Aunt Annie, Aunt Jane,

and another aunt who married into the family who is also called Aunt Jane. All of them had passed away. My Aunt Annie being the last. I was glad to see them.

My aunts suddenly motioned for me to follow them. They lead me to the back of the cathedral and instructed me to climb over the pew and then sit backward, turning away from the altar. I was amazed to see the rear of the cathedral open to a numinous night sky. I then turned just in time to see my aunts leaving. I sat gazing out at the black void and felt a deep peace. Time passed slowly.

At some point in time I stood up and left to begin my journey back down the stairs where I finally arrived in the underground passage. There, I took the torch to light my way back down long tunnels to the end. Then I found my way back through the hole where I began.

Gathering Hearth

After waking from that dream I felt anxious, yet a sense of awe and a deep knowing passed through me. The dream was a lovely sign, one that encouraged me to take the journey into a deep, black, spacious altar. I felt the presence of my aunts as ancestors who would guide me in the new territory. I took comfort in the dream and realized I would have companions for the journey, unseen but known to me. My ancestry held clues and offered comfort.

I spent hours pondering the dream, the meaning of such vastness, and the guidance in the dream. To begin, I knew that the deep presence of darkness was an altar. If my female ancestors were my guides, I could look to my Celtic roots. I already had been drawn to reading several books. So I sat in my favorite wicker chair and mused by the fire. *Rekindling the Celtic Spirit* by Mara Freeman often rested at the top of my pile. One day I opened the book, again, to the beginning. On the first page was the phrase "buried treasure." I felt joyful as I contemplated the search for buried treasure; yes, I could consider my pursuits as a mystery adventure. Perhaps my lineage would offer me other touchstones to nurture my journey. Treasures recovered meant inner gains.

I continued reading, turning page after page, then stopped at the word "hearth." I felt a deep round, heart sound fill my body. I imagined a burning hearth and reconnected with the knowledge that the hearth was the sacred center of home, the hearth fire was a place of gathering, storytelling, and cooking. Warmth spread through my body and I smiled. I loved the feelings it evoked as a place of nurturing. A quiet chuckle slipped through my lips—it seemed I couldn't get away from the stove and the fire.

The feminine quality of the hearth was not lost on me, nor was the fact that I had already been living a life guided by hearth and home. Again I felt affirmed on my path. I realized I could take the aspects of hearth I knew and expand them. As I continued to read, I took in Mara's writing and imagery, which drew me back to a time when everyday life was lived from a sacred center. Daily tasks, the work of tending crops and animals, were woven with seasonal celebrations and the cycles of the year. The reading reminded me to find my center and seek the qualities of interrelatedness and respectfulness. I did not live in those ancient times; I lived here in the twenty-first century. Still, I wanted the gifts of sacred attention.

What was a hearthful life? I turned to my day and knew that part of what was lost to me was joy and fun. Food still came to mind. What was comforting and hearthful I thought. I loved rituals, without my cooking every day I saw how I needed to put back some of the passion I felt for cooking. I loved the season of winter for its comfort foods. Something I normally did in fall was stock my pantry. But I was late that year, and without my business why stock the pantry? Here was the old story, don't cook or nurture self. Yes, I would stock it for myself! Happily I grabbed paper and contemplated what really I wanted to buy. The winter foods I loved included black beans, sweet potatoes, squash, and leeks. Other winter staples included chickpeas and lentils. I stopped and realized it was Friday, farmers market day. Instead of lists geared to work life, I realized I could go and meander my way with joy as focus. I let go of pantry stocking.

I wrapped my shawl around me, put my market basket over my arm, and strolled off with simple joy. Arriving at the farmer's stands, I saw ruby pomegranates first. The rich visuals of the offerings at that time of year—the pomegranates, wreaths, potatoes of all colors, bright carrots, and the yellow of squashes—all increased my joy. Our Sonoma Friday market was and still is small enough that one can stop and visit with friends without pressure. Meeting others laden with fresh local produce gladdens my "hearth heart." I began to use these words to wake me up to a new quality of appreciation.

Over the counter of squash, I bumped into my friend Carol. As we often do, we shared culinary tips. Carol asked, "What's on the stove today?"

I smiled and responded, "I haven't decided. What are you planning?"

"A leek and potato soup," she said.

I was happy for the leek connection, so I took her clue and searched my memory archives for a recipe similar in comfort food ingredients. I recalled my butternut squash recipe and pickd up a beautiful deep yellow squash, green cilantro, and onions. I waved goodbye as Carol wandered off. We promised each other a seasonal soup feast in one of our homes. As I strolled home with a full basket, I smiled and planned the butternut squash soup. The soup is an easy one, a comfort food soup. It is an excellent winter meal with a spinach salad. First I cook the squash with apple juice. I then sauté several onions till just lightly browned, combine the cooked squash, onions, and apple juice in the blender. I puree everything until smooth, or the consistency that warms me at the moment. That day I anticipated the ease of heating it for dinner in the days to come.

When I sat with my bowl of creamy soup that evening and reviewed my day, I remembered feeling happy. I had actually enjoyed myself.

Holiday Surprises

A few weeks later I sat with a cup of tea and an egg salad sandwich with pickles, and just stared out the window at the descending darkness. The Thanksgiving holiday was approaching and I felt the loss of family. The egg salad sandwich sparked memories of my childhood. Thoughts of past Thanksgivings flowed though me. I remembered the luscious smell of turkey roasting, and the stress my mother felt cooking for a large gathering. Our house always looked beautiful, fresh with holiday greens and chrysanthemums. Looking in on our family from the outside, one would think we had an ideal life. It was gracious. We lived in house where everything was spit and polish, everything in its place.

And yet, as a child I remember feeling stifled and contracted, afraid to disturb anything. I felt unwelcome, and tiptoed through the house ever so carefully. Hearth and home it was not. Holiday celebrations became events filed with tension. Perfection was required in everything from table settings to the food. Getting it right with proper dinnerware and dress-up clothes meant creating something akin to a movie set. Camera, action, performance! Of course, I longed for connection. But no amount of wanting made it happen. I often fantasized that I was sitting at my neighbor Diane's table. Real life in her house meant joyful noise, the dog running back and forth, warm smells, hugs, and smiles. I wanted the kitchen where cookies were baked and warm scents flooded the house every day.

Holiday preparations were sometimes fun, but as the day approached the stress began. What I did love about those times was the beauty my father created with flowers and potted plants in the indoor window box of our den. Of course, there was also the beauty of our best china, silverware, and cut glassware. Somehow that beauty was cold and crisp, never comforting. The bar was always well stocked. Before-dinner cocktails continued through the meal and after. But then, as voices got louder and people became more and more disconnected, I retreated. I felt unseen in the alcohol glaze, except when I was expected to pass the potatoes or fill water glasses. After the good china and the silverware were put away and the glasses of alcohol downed, unwanted footsteps came down the hall, with prodding fingers and unwanted need, all overshadowing celebration.

I felt unsafe in my home anytime of the year, but holidays were especially confusing to me. I was certainly a lucky child, my mother would remind me. At the dinner table I sat quietly, holding my breath, being "seen but not heard." I was never sure what would happen: loud angry words, a pounding fist, or polite empty conversation? I looked forward to escaping to the kitchen to clean up, before the crème de menthe and other after-dinner drinks were served.

Those memories belonged to the past, I told myself. What about now? As a single woman for many years, I had worked to create alternative holidays with friends. The previous year had been one of those satisfying and simple get-togethers. Three of us—my friends Nan and Richard and I—enjoyed a delicious meal together. The gathering was special because we all shared the love of the labyrinth. Our meal was simple and quiet. What followed after desert was the best part of our holiday; Nan danced to a piece of music called *Winter Solstice*. Putting out her arms she twirled and move with incredible grace. It was a dance of thanksgiving. Our meal, the dance and a walk at the labyrinth made the gathering special. Our shared walk with prayers added to the feeling of true thanksgiving. After that holiday, I made a mental note to include more thanksgiving prayers and dancing.

The question, then, was how was I to spend the coming holiday? My son had left eight months before to live and work on the east coast. There he connected to the roots of his father's family. I felt the loss of his physical presence. My nest was empty. I couldn't deny it. With my son gone, I felt a deep sadness. His absence was accentuated by the emptiness I felt from giving up my familiar routine of work.

I diverted my attention to the rain that dripped from the upstairs porch. The day before, I had taken the morning to gather walnuts from the orchard. I had fun retrieving the large nuts. Some were still caught in their hard green husks. Scavenging untended orchards was fun. Bringing myself back to the moment, I noticed how I had moved away from my feelings. It was uncomfortable to stay with the sadness I felt about the truth of my life. Diversion was a way of avoiding the pain. I let the feelings go and went to the kitchen.

It was the day Carol and I had chosen to make good on our plan for a soup feast. About a week before, I'd become curious about the origins of soup. I found that the modern-day word "soup" derived from the old French word "sope" and "soupe." In the middle ages soup was considered a nutritious liquid served in a bowl with a piece of bread to sop it up. Much later, it became a first course in restaurants. But soup was often served as a dinnertime meal, leading to the word "supper." Soup was certainly one of my favorites, especially in winter.

I thought about all the different varieties of soup, which included soups with vegetables, meats, pasta, fish, fruits, and more. My favorite season for soups is winter. The weather outside was blustery that day, so I looked forward to the hearty fare on our menu. Carol and I had decided we'd each prepare a different soup. Preparations meant adding the remaining touches to my Sweet Potato Soup; Carol had made her Leek and Potato. We both agreed that potatoes, as usual, felt comforting.

I showered, threw some of the walnuts in a bag, grabbed my soup and my coat, and headed for Carol's house. I turned off Seventh on Lovall Valley Road. Nostalgia filled me. It still felt like home to begin the hilly part of the road. Did I want to walk through that door of the past? It had been the road home for thirteen years of my marriage. How many times did I drive it during that time? My blue Toyota was often packed with precious cargo, which included my son Matt, our two Labrador retrievers, groceries, and plants for the yard. I loved turning up the hill and winding along its sharp curves. A rushing stream banked the narrow road on one side. Lovall Valley Road ends in a loop, which in those days hosted only a few homes. Our home sat at the edge of the valley that ended in that loop. It was a quiet place. Those days of my marriage, the birthing of dreams, and the birth of my son were in the past. New dreams needed honoring. I felt the curve of a new cycle, but nostalgia gripped me.

I almost overshot Carol's driveway as I reminisced. Her leaf-green house with chartreuse trim sat at the rear of the drive. As I turned in, I noticed a few beets and some chard growing in her garden. Her pear tree was bursting with beautiful fruit. I carried my still warm pan and walked up the stairs to the door. Carol greeted me with a spoon in her hand. I love the colors in Carol's house. So I passed slowly under the arch of her soft yellow living room, then through a vivid blue sitting area. The smells of soup drew us into her Cheeto orange kitchen with dark green trim.

Both hungry, we sat at the table for the first course. Carol put steaming bowls of her soup on the festive table, which was spread with an orange cloth and purple napkins. We dipped our spoons in and sighed. I was glad to have reconnected with Carol. I only knew her in passing, as a friend of Claudia and David's, who shared our land. We had gotten to know each other more since my move to Seventh Street. She visited my neighbor Liz often. The three of us shared an occasional summer dinner and glass of wine in the outdoor garden area. Later we had started walking together in Bartholomew Park.

I enjoyed having a friend along on my walks. Carol had an artist's eye like mine, and we noted colors, shapes, and seasonal changes. She pointed out mushrooms hiding on a log; I noted the sound of the wind scraping branches overhead. We shared family stories while hiking, as well as our passion for food.

As we sat enjoying Carol's Leek and Potato Soup, conversation turned to David and Claudia. David and Claudia were friends who had moved away many years ago; Carol told me she was going to visit them for Thanksgiving. She paused and suggested I come with her, with Claudia and David's approval of course. I said no at first. Later in our conversation I reconsidered saw the fun in visiting them in Oregon, see their bed and breakfast. I'd heard news of them over the years, but hadn't stayed in touch.

Carol carried our soup bowls back to the stove. She then brought a beautiful salad of her homegrown pears and endive to the table. I was delighted, for I had looked longingly at the pears as I drove in. I served my soup next. It proved to be a great contrast to the velvety smoothness of Carol's leek soup. The sweet potatoes and beans provided texture, while the curry spices sparked our palate and warmed our bellies. An unconventional lunch, we both agreed, laughing, but glad to have shared our joy of cooking and eating. After our meal I headed home.

I sat musing over the lunch later in the day. Our visit was heartfelt and warming. While we were both gourmet cooks, the meal was hearthful. The beauty of her home and the sharing of our food had a quality of communion, not haute cuisine.

Later that evening Claudia phoned, "Please, please come for the holiday. We would love to have you." I felt welcomed, but still questioned whether I wanted to visit. Not only had I not seen them for many years, but I also identified them with the past. I hesitated but said yes.

I called Carol to tell her I would be going to Oregon with her. Although it was late to be booking a flight for the holidays, we scheduled a flight from Oakland to Portland. The day we would depart was the Tuesday before Thanksgiving.

Our day of travel was a day of anticipation. We carried treasures of wine and cheese from Sonoma valley, and sighed with relief when our Southwest plane took off on time. Once we arrived we picked up our rental car and headed south in a drizzling rain to the tiny community of Independence where David and Claudia lived. Years ago they had bought the house and converted it into a small café and bed and breakfast. I'd heard from Carol that many repairs had been made, the rooms opened and floors replaced. I looked forward seeing the fruits of their hard work.

We drove into the early evening toward Independence with a low mist obscuring our view. Carol had been to the house before, but we seemed to have missed a turn. Stopping at the side of the road for a moment we realized that we were closer than we thought, and soon pulled up to a well-lighted old house.

As we walked the path to the front entryway, we could see Claudia through the smoked glass in the upper part of the door. Wearing a green vintage apron, she greeted us with hugs. David followed behind her; I recognized a gray sweater from days gone by. But it was eighteen years later and we were in Oregon, where a toasty fire burned in their fireplace.

I had developed a slight cold a few days earlier and was glad to arrive. Traveling during the holidays with a cold was not my idea of fun. Claudia showed us to our rooms and said dinner would be ready in fifteen minutes. I headed upstairs for a quick shower. I took out a fresh sweater from the suitcase and headed for the bathroom. The hot steaming water offered relief from my stuffy cold. Letting the water fall over my shoulders, I drifted back to memories of my home in Lovall Valley. This would be my first visit with David and Claudia, my one-time neighbors there, since my divorce. It was strange to be thrown back in time.

I recalled our home on Lovall Valley Road. Our five acres included our house, several outbuildings, a barn, and a beautiful ancient oak tree. Our small business was opened during the craft renaissance of the late sixties. Stephen and I worked together turning our love of fibers, textures, and color into a small but successful enterprise. The business has evolved and thrives to this day under his care. Looking back, I thought about the woman I was in those years we were together. I had headstrong reasons for leaving the marriage. In retrospect I could see that the most important need I had was to find out who I was. I felt lost when I left, unsure of why, but knowing I had to.

Standing in the shower in a strange house in Oregon recalling the past, I suddenly felt drawn into the heart of deep grief, and quiet sobs rose from my belly. I was shocked at the strength of the emotions and knew that more lay beneath. Could I admit to myself that I had not made time to feel my life? It was easier to live from my mind, where I felt safe. My heart had not spoken for a long time. I needed to listen, that was sure. My tears joined the water falling over my body; if I had been at home I would have let out my large piercing cries. I certainly did not feel safe from my childhood history where feelings were denied.

I couldn't bear to continue the conversation with myself, so I just cut off my feelings. I knew I was expected for dinner so I finished showering. I stepped from my shower, feeling vulnerable. Uncomfortable with myself in truth, I was glad to have my cold, which could justify my red eyes and droopy mood. The trip seemed to be opening the floodgates of emotion. But dinner waited.

I struggled to dress and put on some sort of sociable face. Carol, David, and Claudia waited for me in the kitchen. Once in the kitchen I helped carry our meal of salad and quiche to the table. We settled in front of the fire and toasted our reunion and the holiday with a glass of Sonoma Zinfandel. We bit into a delicious spinach and red-pepper quiche. David and Claudia brought us up to date with stories of their renovations to Buena Vista House over the previous year.

I made it an early night, excusing myself because of my cold. I thanked my hosts for the meal. Carol, Claudia, and David stayed downstairs. Settled in my upstairs room, I crawled into the crisp sheets and warm comforter. I fell asleep, hearing my companions' laughter filtering up through the walls of the old house. I felt left out.

We woke to a rainy morning and the smell of fresh scones baking. All of us sat down to a breakfast of pastries and fruit, delicious strong coffee, and fresh orange juice. Claudia handed out sheets of paper so we could add or subtract from the menu we had discussed earlier. She made a list of the foods we needed. With our bellies full and fueled for the road, we set out to forage for ingredients for our Thanksgiving Day meal. David, Claudia, Carol, and I piled into their van. I sported a box of Kleenex. My cold had worsened, and shopping was the last thing I felt like doing. However, the sooner done, the sooner I could come back and nurse my cold. I realized I did not feel safe. I felt like a little girl who set off on an outing, thinking it would be fun, but who now just wanted to be at home. I retreated by falling asleep as they made stops for fresh cranberries, salad makings, pears, blue cheese, and fresh quail from a local farm. The gathering of our festive foods felt in contrast to my withdrawal and desire for sleep.

I longed to go home and curl up under the covers, to nurse my body and my fearful heart. I found myself longing for my old self, the one who was polite and able to maintain casual conversation regardless of the truth I felt inside. At the same time I had a compelling new desire to be authentic. But I didn't know how to speak from my truth; I had no practice and feared telling my truth.

Returning to David and Claudia's home, we unloaded the car and emptied our bags of goodies. Food for our feast covered the counters. Every surface was filled with pears, salad makings, butter, milk, onions, mushrooms, quail wrapped in white butcher paper, cranberries, and blue cheese. Beside our purchases, there was homemade plum juice, pumpkins recently harvested, and hazelnuts gathered from the tree that learned over the kitchen garden. Not an inch of space remained for making lunch. I begged off and headed upstairs to my room for a nap and escape.

Memories from my married days still swirled around as I settled under the quilt. At first I couldn't sleep, for I felt lost and confused as I negotiated two worlds—the world downstairs with friends and the world of memories and feelings in my own consciousness. So much life and so many changes had come and gone since those years. But I knew the path I had stepped on would free me. I finally fell asleep and dreamed of the home on Lovall Valley Road.

When I awoke from my nap I still felt displaced, weaving past and present into an awkward tapestry. The light had faded into dusk as I pulled myself out of the past. Though I didn't feel well and would have preferred to remain alone in my room, I went downstairs. Carol and Claudia had started to prepare dinner. I fixed some black tea to caffeinate myself. It was going to be a long night. As we begin dinner preparation, a tattered looking man with a rough beard appeared at the back door, smelling of the earth. Claudia explained it was her neighbor Ken, who often stopped by. Today he brought more mushrooms, hand picked chanterelles.

Claudia's description of him as a true man of the woods was accurate. As he handed Claudia the mushrooms, he told tales of poachers in his mushroom territory. "I got a few shots off at those buggers," he said.

I moved to the other side of the kitchen.

When he left, Claudia explained that Ken had inherited his mushroom-hunting territory and made a good living with his harvest. The mention of guns put me in a flashback to my well-dressed dad returning from hunting forays with carcasses of deer. My stomach turned and I left the room.

My recollections burned in my body. The image together with the pop of a wine bottle cork sent my stress soaring, and I left my body. Old fears related to alcohol lived in my flesh. Still, the level of anxiety I was feeling in that moment seemed irrational, since only the first glass of wine was being poured. I was emotional, traversing a raw edge and having trouble sorting out the past from the present. I ate quickly and excused myself early. I hoped for an easier and gentler tomorrow, and was surprised I fell asleep so easily. I stayed asleep until the morning when I heard pans rattling in the kitchen below.

Thanksgiving morning was cold and rainy, but the wood stove had warmed the dining room. I felt better having sorted through some of my feelings. I also feel better because I knew I would return home soon. Cooking would also lift my spirits. Claudia, Carol, and I started our breakfast. As we looked at the counters piled high with food, we decided to spread out our courses over the whole day instead of gorging at one big meal. We wanted to savor each morsel. Breakfast included chanterelle mushrooms gently folded into eggs. We squeezed fresh grapefruit, orange, and tangerine juices to spark the palate. Claudia made us her strong coffee with steamed milk. As we sat down to our meal we lit a candle and offered prayers of gratitude for our abundance, for the gift of friendship. We toasted the beginning of the day together.

Sully, a large sweet Newfoundland, slept stretched out on a braided rug nearby. I noticed the finches outside the window searching for seed fallen to the winter soil—their Thanksgiving meal. Looking past the birds to the south, I noticed sheep standing with their backs to a strong wind. Low clouds settled on the hills and wisps of ground fog drifted like ghosts. I felt the storms of the past still swirling inside.

Closer to lunch the sweet scent of soup called: It was time for Claudia's wonderful ambrosia of pumpkin and coconut milk. A delicious salad with Gorgonzola cheese and pears finished the generous lunch. I loved the smooth creamy texture of the cheese, contrasting with the crisp lettuces. The pungent taste of the cheese also set off the delicate flavor of the sweet pears.

We finished lunch with small ginger cookies, and then all agreed it was time for a walk to stretch our legs. We quickly stacked dishes in the sink and turned off anything still simmering on the stove. Gathering warm coats and hats we set off, with Sully bringing up the rear. We headed toward the hill where the sheep had huddled together. The rain paused long enough for us to enjoy our walk. On our way to the hill we spied a cherry tree at the edge of a large empty lot. We smiled to each other as we saw perfectly dried cherries hanging from the tree. Without hesitation we gathered some to add to our dried plum stuffing.

As we walked on, the fresh smells of grass, earth, and rain woke us up. It felt good to move and stretch in spite of the rawness of the day. After climbing the hill and greeting the sheep, David and Claudia suggested we go explore a cemetery we saw in the near distance. The cemetery was filled with gravestones of pioneers. We wandered through the cemetery and imagined what it must have been like for those settlers. We knew in our hearts that the abundance of our modern table was not what they had sat down to. I wondered back in time to facts from my history classes. What foods did early pioneers carry on the Oregon Trail? I only recalled that the staples carried on wagon trains included corn, dried meats, flour, and sugar. How had I managed to remember these details and yet become so adept at denial? Bravery must have been the rudder on pioneering expeditions. In that moment I found it reassuring to remember that any new adventure requires a willingness to take a risk.

We soon returned home by way of River Road. As we were walking along its banks, Claudia told us about the evening they took a summer cruise on a paddleboat. She described a warm Oregon weekend when they had closed the café early. I identified with the rarity of a Saturday evening when a cook isn't cooking. Both David and Claudia worked very hard. That evening must have been a special respite and a treat. I enjoyed listening to the story; it lifted my spirits. As we turned away from the river, the afternoon light suddenly faded into dusk. We walked the short distance home in silence.

Back in the kitchen after the refreshing walk, all our spirits were up. We began preparing for our evening feast. Carol, Claudia, and I joined forces to make the stuffing. We shelled and chopped the hazelnuts. I washed the cherries and chopped them while Carol chopped the plums. Claudia sautéed onions in generous quantities of butter. The kitchen smell divine after. We cut the bread and sautéed it. Then we combined the bread with sweet dried fruits turned with sage and rosemary. The result was like nothing any of us had tasted before. The house began to smell like Thanksgiving. Our preparations continued as we stuffed the quail and cleaned the asparagus. Claudia broke into a favorite song and Carol and I joined in. I began to feel more at home. I was amazed that three women could negotiate space in the medium sized kitchen. Claudia had set up the area well; the room was efficient, yet homey. So our communal chopping and preparations went more smoothly than could have been expected from three temperamental chefettes.

The fire that David had tended all day in the large dining room glowed with bright embers. Since the café doubled as their dining room, several tables fill the space. We choose a table close to the fire for our dinner. I started to set the table, then paused to watch the firelight reflected on the hardwood floor. I thought about other wood floors, fireplaces, and times in my life. It was easy to recall the light of the sun hitting the eighteenth-century floors at Quaker meetings in my hometown in New Jersey. The reflected gold light from times past infused good into that afternoon. I remembered that I only had to be myself. I returned to the table, making sure to set out the wine glasses for the special reserve bottle of cabernet sauvignon. Carol had opened it in the morning to breathe so it would be ready for the celebration.

Soon the stuffed quail, roasted asparagus, hazelnut and dried plum and cherry stuffing, and sweet potatoes drenched in maple syrup were all paraded to the table. The hours of work had paid off, for this bounty of delicious and beautifully presented food was a sight to see. We again said a prayer of gratitude for the best thanksgiving food any of us had had in a long time. The meal was not only a visual delight, but rolling eyes and silence also proved how scrumptiousness it all was. We agreed the stuffing was magnificent. I loved the savory and sweet combinations of the dried fruits and fresh thyme in the dressing; the added sweetness of our cherry raid was a gift. The just right cooking of the quail satisfied our love of crisp skin and moist flesh. Not a morsel remained on the table when we finished. We groaned, stretched, and waited for our bellies to settle down. Together we cleared the table, and then waited only briefly before serving Claudia's delicious cheesecake and other sweets of chocolates and dates. David poured the special port, which we had brought from Sonoma. Its dense, musky flavor balanced the richness of everything that went before. We took our glasses and dessert plates to the kitchen and began the cleanup. Between the soapsuds and clinking of dishes we agreed it had been a meal we'd all remember for years to come.

Once the kitchen was spotless we all fell happily into bed. Carol and I woke early enough to grab some coffee. On our way out the door Claudia handed us a care package of her famous scones and small wrapped packets of dried plums. Our return drive to the airport in Portland proved to be easier in the light. As we headed north Carol and I reminisced over the extraordinary food. We agreed it was a joy to have three foodies as chefs for celebrations. Before long we pulled into the car rental return lane and unloaded our luggage. There was a snake of a line of travelers ahead of us as we checked in at Southwest Airlines. But with bellies still full, we waited patiently.

Our flight arrived in Oakland on time; I was glad when Carol dropped me at home. I felt the joy, sadness, and intensity of the review I'd taken of my life over those past days. I had mixed feelings about my trip, but still appreciated the sharing of food and old times, the weavings of Thanksgivings past and present.

I was glad to sleep soundly in my own bed. I looked forward to my morning ritual of tea in bed with Sula curled at the bottom of the bed. The morning brought the smell of rain. A light mist covered the valley when I awoke. The new rain refreshed me. My cold lingered, so I stayed tucked into bed and felt a dull pain just under my skin. I knew my Oregon revelations could only be handled in small portions. Even in retrospect the feelings were overwhelming. Awareness comes in waves. Compassion was key, if I could remember it. I knew that it was time to face the old so I could live alive in the here and now. My soul had spoken, had urged me to claim my truth.

I stayed in bed and mused about the holiday trip. Besides my unexpected emotions, I felt unsettled. I realized that most people would hear the story of my time shared with friends and consider it ideal. Who would argue with the delicious abundance and creative menus we all prepared, the setting with grazing sheep, the small-town-America feeling? I felt grateful to Claudia and David for their hospitality. But somehow I felt a sense of loss. Something was missing, and quite frankly I felt wrong for having such questions. I was still looking for that feeling of connection which I was unable to touch just yet. That place was in myself.

With that thought I jumped from bed, pulled on thick wool socks, and went to the living room to warm myself at a fire. I bent over the hearth, crumpled paper, and stacked kindling. I put a match to the kindling and then stacked a log on top. Slowly the fire caught and slowly began to warm the room. I felt happy sitting there, and followed the thread of images sparked by the fire.

The thread was tied to a quality of hearth and home. I felt kinship with the idea of belonging to a tribe of fire people. What that meant, exactly, I did not know. But it conjured not only the hearth itself, but hearth keepers. I remembered I had a file of photographs of hearths, some from Irish cottages. I pulled them out and sat enjoying them.

As I looked at the picture I wove my life and work with the image. I realized that what my friend Barbara had said was true; I was a Hestia women. Hestia is the Roman goddess of the hearth. I realized I wanted to be a modern day hearth keeper. I recalled reading in my Celtic literature that women had been the keepers of the fire. Women created ceremony and offered prayers around lighting and tending fire. This practice invoked a sacred focus in their homes. In community life of ancient times, central fires were built to honor and celebrate the seasons. The celebrations marked different phases of the year. I knew I wanted to grow back into sacred relationship with fire. Fire became a symbol of much needed connection, of humanity and healing.

I put down my thoughts and pulled a favorite book from the shelf, *Serving Fire* by Anne Scott. During my ten years of cooking I had gathered cookbooks and other food related stories. I loved reading recipes, but also developed an interest in the spirituality of food and cooking. As I thumbed through the pages my eyes fell on a line where the author asks us to look for "the needs of the soul." She defined hearth as a symbol for "the knowledge of the sacred relationship between inner and outer worlds."

Another passage from the book, however, disturbed me. Anne cautioned, "The modern hearth is disconnected from the transformative power of the feminine and of the fire. Yet when we form a conscious relationship with the inner world of the feminine, we restore that which has been neglected." She explained how the gifts of the inner life and the relationship between the feminine and fires have been overshadowed. Her words gave me new language for the search for the balance between male and female.

The book continued on a positive note, saying, "The hearth is a symbol of the feminine that nourishes our soul and embraces our body. Rather than pushing us to transcend ourselves, the divine aspect of the feminine leads us into ourselves, and we are nourished by this journey." Yes, I was on a path that would lead me to my inner world. I had focused outwardly and out of my body. As I read about the sacred symbol of the hearth, I became more aware of my disconnection. The feminine brought me back into a relatedness that nourished and reconciled.

When I thought back to my relationship with the physical world, I reminded myself that cooking had been my first step to healing my disconnection. I really had never thought of it that way. I had worked with food and nurturance, but never saw how my work had been healing to myself as well as others. There were many new ways to look at the sacred everyday and bring the feminine principles into my life fully. Anne Scott's writing opened me to a deeper longing for nurturing presence and self trust. My mind still wanted control and I struggled to let go into my body.

My life continued to take new turns as I faced by true feelings. The process carried me back to the original fears. My sister and I were called "crybabies." She reminded us, "I'll give you something to cry about!" Yes, those were the days when a child didn't talk back or were allowed opinions. No wonder I stopped feeling, stopped saying my truth. If I was humiliated and threatened for opening up, why would I continue to do so? Silence became a weapon and a defense. After so many years those tactics were blocking my life flow, my ability to communicate. I knew the dull pain that lay deep inside me.

Passivity had become a way of life for me. I agreed with others, saying yes, accepting their truth above my own. I also had trouble establishing boundaries. But change was need. I knew I must creep out from my hiding place.

At that point I became anxious. I closed my thoughts; perhaps it was time to get up. A walk would help me ground my feelings and bring me back into my body. I pointed the car in the direction of Bartholomew Park, my favorite place to commune with the natural world. Once there

I parked my car and headed in my usual direction. But first I stood appreciating the grapevines, stands of eucalyptus and the villa which stood on the slight rise.

I choose my known route left to the deer gate which separated the woods from the vineyard and picnic area. As the gate clicked behind me, I walked with the curiosity of a small girl looking for adventure. Soon the fresh air and bird sounds brought me into the moment. I felt more lighthearted and invited the spirits of the woods to spark me.

As I headed uphill toward the steps I noticed a small path off to the right that I hadn't seen before. I stopped and studied it for a moment. Was it a dead end? I went forward to investigate, and discovered that it took a sharp turn past a tall redwood and then opened to the stream. Spotting a safe crossing downstream, I trekked across slippery rocks and rushing winter rainwater. Finding my way through dense trees, I entered a clearing. The hill rose abruptly ahead of me.

A tree burnt by a lightning fire caught my eye as I walked. Only part of the scarred trunk and a great mass of roots remained. A tangle of root arms arched downward to cover a cave. The rich brown earth had been washed out over time by the water runoff. The long arms served as hosts to green, velvety moss. My childlike eyes saw a green castle rise in front of me, perhaps a place where fairies lived. It was a strange dreaming place. I realized in that moment of delight that I had been missing magic and adventure. My imagination was sparked; I would return there to muse.

I had taken an unknown path and met mystery. I felt exhilarated and full of enthusiasm. I knew my enthusiasm was a testament to the gifts of that day. I knew this was the language Mother Nature was teaching me. Ancient Mother had led me into the woods to recover her treasures.

I returned to the main road again and climbed the roughhewn stairs to the upper path. At the top of the hill I breathed in the gift of the giant redwoods which rose just ahead of me. I then started down the stairs. As I negotiated the slippery moss covering the redwood plank steps, I realized my mind wanted to get up and over—to just get it done. I turned my attention to my next step. I looked about, smelled the bay and redwood, and took time to breathe more deeply. I noticed my legs were tired, so I sat and rested on a large rock.

As I sat I felt the cold, hard rock beneath my seat. I turned my attention to all the sensations of my body sitting on the rock. I had spent so little time feeling that deeply into my body. No wonder I felt fear. How could I feel safe living outside myself.

I left my perch on the rock reluctantly and began walking again. But I continued a conversation most women know, the struggle to accept our bodies My relationship with my body was mirrored in the culture. I often felt like a "packaged commodity," trying to live up to some standard of physical beauty that had nothing to do with who I was. I was more than my external looks. I realized how on some level it became more problematic as I aged, because I was not so likely to starve myself to maintain a youthful figure. I had spent too many years of my life being disciplined about food. I never gave myself dessert. I often denied even simple joys related to food. All of my withholding had been in the service of maintaining a thin body. To think I was a good chef, in the context of all that self-denial, was amazing.

But I knew I had a choice. I chose to be healthy, and battled fear of rejection when I gained weight as a result. I recalled the writings of Marion Woodman, author and Jungian therapist, whom I had been reading for many years. Her writing gave me language to understand my experience. Her word "embodiment" suddenly made more sense to me. I wanted to be connected to myself. My body was different from others. I needed to live from my own values, my own standards of thin or thick. Marion Woodman's description of embodiment was the opposite of living my life in my head, abstracting, distancing, and pretending to be something I was not. I was not a mannequin to be dressed and told to "sit straight, be seen and not heard." I gagged at the thought of how many years I had spent enslaving myself to image. I had yet to free myself completely. When was I going to do that?

I stopped and closed the gate behind me and entered back into the manicured gardens past the gazebo. I caught myself pulling my hat down and straightened my clothes. I was shocked at how I automatically returned to the need to put on a face. Why was I still struggling with appearances? As a child and young adult I had felt the pressure of never having a hair out of place, no flaws, no dirt on my clothes, never wearing a face of anger or unhappiness. Any kind of messiness was discouraged.

I felt the restrictions of childhood. Looking good was connected to control. The body was to be controlled and avoided. Don't let out those messy feelings, don't be too loud, too full of yourself. Longing for integration and freedom I picked up a large stick and scraped it along the dirt, making marks along the path—marks that meant I had walked there.

At the parking lot I unlocked my car and recalled a line from David Abram, whose book *Spell of the Sensuous* I had recently read. He suggested we connect with our natural, human self. That human self was animal, that human self offered presence. I wanted to feel my humanity, be more compassionate with myself, and love my body. I appreciated David's writing which reminded us "to affirm our solidarity with this physical form, is to acknowledge our existence as one of the earth's animals, and so to remember and rejuvenate the organic basis of our thoughts and our intelligence." The animal body as I had known it was sinful; the natural world was somehow at odds with righteousness and cleanliness. I was happy to be given words that supported change. I couldn't help but connect the dots and pull the thread of the feminine, Mother Nature through my being.

Driving home that afternoon I felt rejuvenated by the joyful mirror of nature and relieved to bring awareness to my truths.

Falling Into My Body

A week later I woke to a new day with the sun shining through the slats of my shades. I wanted to return to Bartholomew Park. Staying indoors too much in contemplation can lead me to depression. I was glad for the sunlight. I pulled on my heavy blue sweater, hopped in the car, and parked up the hill closer to the winery.

As I unlatched the gate and turned uphill I felt the warm sun on my back. Morning light caught drops of dew sparkling from bare branches. My walks provided welcome invitations. My artist's eye became awake again, but then the exquisite beauty was always there to be received.

I wound my way up the stairs across the path and then headed down the stairs which lead to the stream. Judy and I had walked them several weeks ago. Our visit was long overdue; we had not seen each other for three months. As I was reminiscing about that visit, I lost my step. All of a sudden I found myself smack down on the ground. I had slipped and fallen on the wet stairs. I had forgotten the danger of falling, exactly what I had warned Judy against weeks ago. I picked myself up, my pride wounded but with no physical bruises, just a slightly sore back.

I walked on gingerly, giving attention to legs and a pelvis that felt a bit wrenched. As I crossed the stream I walked slowly across the slippery rocks. Suddenly I felt more vulnerable, a reminder that I was aging. I walked more slowly finding my way to the pungent smell of bay laurel which drew me to the last gate. I shut it behind me.

I arrived home, showered, and changed clothes. As I started to dry off after the shower, I noticed blood running down my leg. I looked to find a cut, but there was none. With a bit of shock, I realized that I had begun to bleed again. It had been years since I'd had a period. The sight of blood triggered my fear. I was years into my menopause, and suddenly the return of the "curse"—such a strange word for our bleeding. I remember leaving my body. It was an automatic response, one I knew well, for it often accompanied times of stress or fear. The leaving my body signaled a habit I began early in life, core to those early fears was the sexual abuse. My body was the enemy, in a way. I could not trust it, especially "down there." The insides of my body were unseen, so why bother?

I suddenly felt hatred for my body. How inconvenient, I muttered to myself. The quick fix was to label bleeding "down there" as female problems. I can still feel the disrespect I had for myself. That language was rooted in the story that begot my shame. Would I ever be free and happy in a female body? I also knew that this avoidance of my instinctual body wisdom was a generational issue—currently being rewritten, but still powerful all the same.

Days later when I visited the doctor, she discovered a fibroid growing in my uterus, not uncommon at my age. She scheduled a biopsy. The bleeding still frightened me. I also realized that I felt out of control. My body had her ways of instructing me and I needed to listen. When I sat with the possibility that something might be seriously wrong, I turned away, didn't want to know. I saw how I had been giving my power away through disconnection. Should I have known better, taken better care of myself? I felt guilty and bad.

A few days later I was sharing my experiences with a friend. She commented that aging frightened her, and increased her avoidance of her body. I knew the feeling; ironically I'd discovered it as I struggled to become more present to myself. The challenge was to love wrinkles. The issue of weight was certainly part of the mix. I wanted to give up my need to maintain youthful beauty. The need for perfection was stressing. Soon our conversation moved to more positive ground. We agreed it was high time to appreciate who we were. That meant respecting and celebrating our bodies. We reminded each other of the dramatic performance *Vagina Monologue* which had played in our community. It was a relief to see younger women own their bodies and continue to grow in understanding.

How could I reconnect with my body? What remained unloved? The old fabric still shrouded me. Wasn't I weaving a new cloth? To help me see into the old story I choose to draw a picture of my womb. I wanted to talk to my body, make the insides visible.

Yes, my womb, my creative center! Using art helped me relax and keep me out of my head. Intuitive drawing with watercolor meant gathering paint, paper, and a brush. The difficulty of controlling the watercolor made it a useful tool. I sat feeling my body, breathing deeply into my womb. I started by using interesting colors to draw my ovaries; I then drew a cord that unfolded into a tree. Without thinking, I then drew a black, rock-like image in the womb space. When I stopped to examine the whole painting I realized that the black spot probably represented the fibroid. The weight needed lifting.

The process helped me touch my truth. If I truly considered the miracle of birth, the power and gift of a female body, I would certainly walk differently in the world.

Wanting more dialogue and conversation about our bodies and aging, I planned an afternoon tea with Ann and Dru. We had in earlier conversations being listening to each others' life process, acknowledging accomplishments and witnessing our cycles of change. We had often mentioned our struggles to accept our mature woman status. We discovered our resistance to looking too closely in the mirror, had difficulty accepting our added weight, diminishing eyesight and stiffness. A shared afternoon cup of tea revealed one thing and that was we wanted change. We agreed to become more aware of our negative self -talk and instead choose self respect. We tossed around words about aging, and settled on "wisdom." We had all lead rich lives, lives that wanted celebrating. Ann mentioned how many other cultures in the world considered their elders as teachers. As elders we could be offering the gifts of wisdom to the next generation. A dialogue ensued in which, with raised voices, we marked the fact that our own culture, in direct opposition, wants aging and death outlawed. We all agreed, "honor our age." I came home relieved to be talking and opening up with other women. I saw how sharing the truth provided new possibility.

Over the next weeks I deepened into the silence; the winter season protected the first awkward conversations with myself. I knew my soul had sounded a call.

Christmas

December brought the upcoming Christmas holiday buzz. Winter solstice was also approaching, and if I were to learn the gifts of seasonal cycles I wanted to engage them. Winter solstice is the shortest day of the year and a celebration of the return of the light. To celebrate the return of the light, I drove to the beautiful outdoor labyrinth on Spain Street to honor earth's cycles.

I stood in the receding afternoon light and stepped onto the path of the river rock spiral. The spiral walk reminded me to take small steps, which helped lightened my fear of change. This first winter without the ground of my work-centered life kept me surrendering to the new. Jumping in quickly only scared me. It was important to stay in the mode of exploration. I knew that I often retreated after taking new steps. But wasn't that ok? I couldn't walk backwards very well. I didn't even want to, for I stepped slowly, inhaling the scent of the redwoods, feeling embraced.

I resolved to stay connected to the messy, the fearful, the rageful, the wounded, the curious, the powerful, the fiery, and the doubtful. But would I do it? As I walked I felt the right and left turnings of the spiral walk calm me. When I stopped in the center circle I prayed for guidance and courage. I stood letting the air flow around me and prayed for friends, for family, and for peace in the world. As I began my walk outward to the beginning I felt grateful.

The last bits of the day faded and the dark engulfed me. The lights of the church went on at the other end of the path. While a part of me was drawn to the doors of the sanctuary, I choose to continue walking the path of the earthen spiral.

I headed home for a solstice dinner. Soup was winter joy in a pot, so I went directly to the freezer where I knew squash soup waited. One pot, soup inside and soon the beautiful orange liquid bubbled away. I loved the color of the soup, the beauty of the blue cast iron pot, and then the hearty smell. Finally I carried my bowl of hot soup to bed. Sula crawled in with me and we both sat enjoying the quiet evening. Before settling under the covers for sleep I turned over and looked out into the winter sky. The night felt expansive.

I rolled back over and took up a book before sleeping. I opened Dr. Christiane Northrup's book on menopause. She suggested a breath-stopping piece of information; fibroids usually indicate blocked energy in our creative centers!

Winter Recipe

Winter is a time to settle inside by the fire. There is nothing like a hearty bowl of steaming soup.

Winter Squash Soup
1 Acorn squash (cut in two)
1 yellow onion
3 cups of fresh apple juice
1 tablespoon of butter
Salt and pepper to taste

Bake squash in a 350-degree oven for 45 minutes, depending on the size of the squash. While the squash is cooking, slice the onion and sauté it in the butter. Cook the onions slowly and let caramelize. When the squash is done, scoop out the flesh place in a blender with the onions, two cups of apple juice and puree. Puree until desired consistency; add juice as needed. Serve with toasted pumpkin or squash seeds.

Spring

"Deep instinctual knowing is imprinted through our hands, returns us to the hands of our womanhood."

—Marion Woodman

Sprouting Wings

January dragged by in grey gloom. Winter had pulled me down to the edge of depression. February offered an upbeat hint of spring with the first sprouting of acacia. I looked forward to the light and budding of spring, but couldn't ignore the feelings of pervasive anxiety about my life. A new year lay ahead. What waited? I needed something to focus and calm me.

I knew walking the labyrinth would give me a fresh perspective so I set out on foot for town. Besides I hadn't walked our Sonoma treasure since winter solstice. The ring of redwoods circling my destination inspired me and pulled me in. As I set my feet on the clockwise spirals a light breeze tossed my hair. The winding path offered up fresh smells of air and dirt and tree. Presence replaced the fear of a chattering mind.

The twists and turns of the path's design reminded me that life was not linear. The spiral is a basic form of nature, and I wanted to be in unity with my own true nature. The labyrinth never let me down. I recalled that the Hopi used the labyrinth to symbolize Mother Earth. I needed her reminders to bring me back to the basics.

I focused on stretching the tightness in my pelvis, recognizing again how my life was changing. My critical hurrying voice had diminished, but my inner critic still wanted to rule the roost. Fear restricted my movements and kept me attached to old ways. I wound my way step-by-step around the curved path, once I reached the center my chest and shoulders relaxed. I stood quietly connecting with my breath and body. I sent a prayer of gratitude to my friend Alyssa for introducing me to the labyrinth. My mind had calmed, I sat down for my prayers. Soon the sun's rays found me, tickled my spirit and sent me back out the spiral with more presence. Only the bird sounds and a few passing cars pulled my attention from my measured steps.

When I returned home, I called my friend Kathleen to support the lift in mood. I did not want to fall backward into fear and collapse. Kathleen is a friend who keeps me out of my black holes with her innate aliveness. She also offers me a hand up when I become too trapped in old feelings. It was good to talk with her, and catch up on the happenings in her life.

She mentioned that the poet Maya Angelou would speak in San Francisco the following Sunday, at the Masonic Auditorium. Maya would get my blood flowing and my fire stoked. She always woke me up. After finishing our conversation, I reluctantly called to order a ticket for the event. I did it reluctantly, as my desire to stay tucked away in my hermit life tried to hold me back. I am naturally a "table for one" kind of person. I knew I should go, because I felt out of balance. While the dark inner labyrinths informed me of my need for healing, the outer spiral called. Hearing Maya's poetry would remind me of the juiciness of life, and perhaps open me to the sprouting energies of spring. Maya herself certainly represented the opposite of collapse and fear.

Sunday arrived warm and inviting for my trip to the city. As I prepared to leave, I struggled with prospect of the transition from the inner coziness of winter to the faster pace of city life. My simpler winter life had included little city stimulation, and I began to feel like a country bumpkin. Roaming the streets and hills of Sonoma, or what we used to call Slownoma, was different from the buzz of the freeway and the bustle of San Francisco. But by the time I'd dressed myself in city clothes and prepared a lunch to eat before the event, I felt excited.

My car easily found her way to Highway 101, the main route to San Francisco. Once I geared up into the flow of freeway traffic, I found joy in driving from back roads to main thoroughfares. I felt vulnerable entering the city, but I headed down Van Ness Avenue to catch California Street to the auditorium. On Nob Hill I walked out of the parking garage into a perfect San Francisco day. I found a seat on the steps; others sat around me enjoying the sun before Maya's event.

I gazed out over the city while I ate, recognizing Grace Cathedral across the street. I considered making time to walk the labyrinth at Grace, but realized the event would start soon. I didn't want to rush my experience. I thought again about my friend Alyssa, who had become a facilitator for the guided labyrinth events at Grace.

I closed my lunch bag and joined the crowds gathering for the program. To my delight, I found my seat very close to the stage. Maya arrived onstage in a dress of soulful oranges, the direct opposite of my despairing blues. Soon enough her rich voice and comfortable stage presence invited me in. Her words filled me from head to toe as her deep voice reminded me to open.

As Maya read poem after poem, her resonant voice carried the audience deep into her images. Her words were an elixir for my creativity and my mood. She was intensely herself, natural and full, a woman who lived deeply in her body. I felt her presence as hope. I sat entranced. Her poetry had power. She would continue to inspire me to be authentic and speak my truth. When the performance ended, I left the hall wishing I could have shared the experience with a friend.

I was still under Maya's spell as I drove out of the garage onto California Street, then back out to Van Ness. After several blocks I remembered my intention to visit the labyrinth before heading home. Too late, I thought. I crossed the Golden Gate Bridge and happily headed north to Sonoma, glad I had extended myself outward to explore and be inspired.

I loved turning into my dusty driveway on Seventh Street, a direct contrast to the streets of the city. The air smelled as delightful as the sight of my tabby cat playing in the field. I opened my front door and hurried to peel off my city clothes.

After dinner I called Alyssa to share my experience of the afternoon. We hadn't talked for months and it was fun catching up. Our conversation immediately turned to the labyrinth. I felt disappointed as I told her I'd almost gone to walk the labyrinth at Grace. I then asked if she planned to go with the Veriditas group to Chartres, France, in the spring. She said yes, and mentioned she would be one of the many facilitators for the large group.

I asked a few questions about the history of the labyrinth, and my curiosity grew. Alyssa mentioned Dr. Lauren Artress, who had founded Grace's labyrinth program in 1996, and was now its director. Alyssa told me that the original carpet spiral was designed and installed in the cathedral in 1997. As we talked, I learned that the weeklong teaching program in France included evening labyrinth walks. The thought of being in that ancient sanctuary at night excited me. I remembered the awe I felt the first time I visited Chartres as a young woman. At that time, I had been entranced by the beauty of the famous stained-glass Rose Window, and had not even known about the labyrinth. The more Alyssa talked, the more I wanted to go to Chartres. She suggested I decide quickly, for the tour had become popular and there were only a few spaces still open.

The next morning I excitedly spoke with the woman coordinating the trip. One place left, she told me. I had to think quickly. A spur of the moment trip to France had not been on my agenda, but I knew in my heart that I would go. It was time to stretch and jump outside the boundaries of my known world.

"Yes!" I finally gasped.

The coordinator asked me to mail a check to reserve my place. I had second thoughts after hanging up, but knew I was hooked. The labyrinth was calling.

Days later I received my paperwork along with a suggested reading list. The list included Dr. Lauren Artress' book *Walking a Sacred Path*. It was the first book I would read about the labyrinth. It provided me with a foundation. Artress wrote, "To walk a sacred path each of us must find our own touchstone that puts us in contact with the invisible thread." She described the invisible thread as "our soul hunger for the lost connection to our intuitive nature" as we long for a "creative, symbolic process that nurtures our spiritual nature, that feeds the soul."

I read on to learn that the labyrinth is one of the oldest contemplative tools known to humankind. It has been used for centuries for prayer, ritual, and initiation. The classical seven-circuit labyrinth turns seven times, the eleven-circuit labyrinth, turns eleven times. It was exciting to know that the ancient mystical tool was finding its way into modern life.

Its renaissance included installations in office buildings, churches, and hospitals the world over.

The more I read about the labyrinth and Chartres Cathedral, the more fascinated I became. For example, Chartres was one of the many twelfth-century cathedrals dedicated to Mother Mary. They were known as the Notre Dame Cathedrals. The twelfth century was a time when the feminine was revered. Since part of my search was to recover the sacred face of the feminine, I anticipated the inspiration this ancient sanctuary would offer.

During the following days I continued reading, but also set about organizing my travel. The first order of business was to make my plane reservation. I decided to travel on Friday, arrive early, and have one full day before the Sunday opening gathering. I loved the idea of giving myself a day to adjust to the time differences. In ongoing conversations with Alyssa I had also been been inspired by her stories of Glastonbury, England, so organized to visit the sacred sites there after Chartres. From Glastonbury I would take the train to London and fly home from there.

Once I had purchased my plane ticket I splurged and bought new luggage. I had fun shopping, and chose two suitcases, one small and one medium suitcase in a dark forest green. Other purchases included a journal and a small travel set of watercolors to sketch with. I wanted to bring along every tool of creativity I could carry. And yes, I would bring my camera.

Seeking Feminine Source

One afternoon I took *Walking a Sacred Path* out under the shade of the oak tree. I settled into my green chair and was inspired to read, "The labyrinth stands with a tradition that recaptures the feminine sense of the Source." My journey to soul meant recovering reverence for the feminine in all ways. I knew most of my life had been spent despising myself and other women. I had never really admitted that to myself. I wondered how many other women felt the same.

Reframing my life meant learning to love myself and know that self as the divine feminine. My personal religious history gave me no model. I had been raised a Protestant. While Mary had been part of my bible reading, she was not reverenced. Times have changed now, as the sacred feminine becomes more of a conversation in all churches. I thought back to a turning point in my life when I had met new faces of the divine feminine.

I had just arrived in Hawaii. I was recently divorced. I chose Hawaii because of a lifelong yearning to live in a tropical climate. A year before, I had traveled to the Big Island for retreat and loved it. After my divorce I felt a deep need for nurturance and change, and the island paradise seemed the answer. I ended up living on Oahu on the North Shore.

Beyond climate, I wasn't sure why I was there. I had many questions. My life on the islands proved a growing time, not easy but necessary.

Curiously enough, Hawaii gave me new insight into the sacred feminine traditions. Along with Pele, the fire goddess of the Hawaiian Islands, I was also introduced to Quan Yin, the Buddhist goddess of compassion. Meeting Quan Yin in the context of my earlier Vipassana meditation training made it easy to develop a relationship with her. While foreign to my Western and Christian backgrounds, both of these goddesses were of deep interest to me. I did not know why at the time, but later discovered where these experiences would lead me. I was recovering the threads needed to fill in the holes of my spiritual life.

Several months into my new life in Hawaii I joined a women's group. I needed support, especially since I was not only living in a new place but also beginning a new life outside of marriage.

Coming from my group meeting one sultry Monday, I passed a shop window and stopped when I noticed a statue of Mother Mary. I had never been drawn to her statue before. Synchronicity showed me the why of this new interest, for later that day I met a friend who invited me to an evening meditation dedicated to Mary. I accepted her invitation, and a few days later six of us gathered around a table to pray the rosary. The Catholic ritual was unfamiliar to me, and yet I felt peaceful as soon as we began. The prayer and group meditation nourished me.

During my time in Hawaii I developed an understanding of how much I was missing in my life. The guiding light of feminine awareness and power was one of those things. The dark side of that light was becoming more aware of my self-hatred, self-doubt and the wounds of my relationship with my mother. I had never connected the dots nor was I willing to feel the pain of my experiences.

I moved several times while I lived on the islands. Right before I returned to California I lived close to a Quan Yin temple. I felt excited the first time I walked toward the sanctuary. I'd seen small statues of Quan Yin in the homes of several women I knew. As I entered through the carved archway and walked the path to the temple, I felt at home in the gentle open room where soft warm air blew around me. Inside I found Quan Yin towering over me. Her statue sat on a large platform surrounded by offerings of tropical flowers, fruits, and food. Time dropped away as I took in the power of the sensuous, the earthy, and the spiritual. I felt nurtured in both body and soul.

I continued to go to the temple regularly, and found the fits of celebration around the sensual and the sacredness of my body. I began a long journey to heal my sexual wounds. Meeting the face of a goddess from another culture helped me open my heart, helped me put my feet on the ground. I was grateful to carry the soft, nurturing quality of Quan Yin's presence inside.

Living in Hawaii changed my life. In the years that followed I continued to explore other aspects of the feminine. I learned that she had many different faces, and that her teachings were a mystery. Years later I was picking up her hands of guidance.

My trip to Chartres would be an invitation to grow and deepen with the goddess. Closer to the time of my departure I called Alyssa to confirm the time of her arrival in France. She had plans to visit friends in England before Chartres, and said she would meet me on Sunday at our hotel.

We also talked more about her past experiences as a facilitator. She mentioned that Chartres Cathedral had two Black Madonnas, Our Lady of the Pillar and Our Lady of the Underground. Alyssa noted that the two had very different qualities. I had encountered the image of a Black Madonna after reading China Galland several years before. Her book *Longing for Darkness* awakened me to the potent beauty and symbol of these black-faced icons.

I was looking forward to my upcoming trip, but I was particularly excited about discovering more about the mystery of the Black Madonna. Visiting Chartres meant I would have an opportunity to develop a personal relationship to her. Reading about her in books was one step. Alyssa suggested I read Ean Begg's *The Cult of the Black Virgin*. I ordered it and briefly skimmed it, noting that the author listed many sites devoted to this icon of the sacred feminine. I decided to save the book to read during my travels. I looked forward to the journey as an opportunity to awaken to the magical, the mysteries. I wanted to recover the "unseen threads" that would guide me back to myself, and help me weave new relationships with my soul. The exploration of the feminine path was central to entering the mystery.

The golden fields of mustard, which began as sprinklings of yellow early in the season, soon became fields ablaze in yellow. Spring kept unfolding.

My favorite road for mustard awe here in Sonoma is Watmaugh Road. You turn off Broadway, the main road into town, onto Watmaugh. If you look up, the yellow fields pull you in immediately and keep your eyes glued in wonder all the way down the road. The yellow intensifies, then stops at Arnold Drive.

Spring walked herself slowly into the Sonoma valley. Tulip trees bloomed and invited me to sip their mauve fragrance. Pink cherry and white apple blossoms strutted their beauty. Winter had guided me inward, but spring drew me outward. I felt the sap rising. Where would an outward spiral take me?

As I looked for ways to honor my essential self, the unfolding springtime stimulated my own sprouting. I naturally began to think of seeds. The seeds I planted that season were needed to stimulate change. What did I need to initiate? What potential had I avoided? What had I loved and abandoned?

I had dabbled in painting for many years. In the late eighties I returned to school to finish the degree I had started years before, and my focus turned from psychology to art. I spent my last year of school in the art room and loved it. Since then I had left my paintbrushes stored in boxes. As much as I wanted to paint, I found myself resisting. Here I was, living in the middle of an artist community. All around me artists worked—painters, glass blowers, jewelers, and sculptors. Why was I blocked when it came to painting? What was I afraid of?

When I looked more closely, I saw several aspects to the struggle. A reluctance to give myself pleasure was one part of it. The other had to do with a fear of expressing myself. I knew how important cooking had been to me, and I realized I missed the creativity of its hands-on work. I wanted to express my creativity in new ways, and knew so much was possible. Still, I wasn't sure I could give myself more. I realized how much I felt like an urchin gazing in the window of the bakery. I needed to become the baker. But I couldn't do it in one step.

I began to understand that feeling free to express myself was part of my healing. It had been years since I had taken an art class. Perhaps it was time.

I examined the list of spring classes at the Sonoma Community Center, an old elementary school building converted for the community's benefit. I found a pottery class that sparked my interest, even though I had never tried pottery. The classes started around four weeks before my departure in May. It was time to jump off and try something new. Kneading clay, getting my hands dirty, felt risky but fun. What better way to get over a too precious idea of what my art should be? I felt pleased I could fit both the class and the trip to Chartres into my spring expansion.

Bowls

On the first day of class there were six of us sitting expectantly at our tables. My first slab of clay intimidated me with its moist coldness, the dirt of it. Our teacher suggested we begin by just playing with the clay. I patted and prodded it with my hands. The clay softened. I began to pinch small elfin beings out of the mud, soon after I decided they needed small mushrooms and logs to sit on. My imagination began to let go, but my critic tried to diminish my efforts. Around me, more accomplished potters were throwing large bowls and platters on the potter's wheel. But I was a beginner, and wanted to remain one. At the end of the class, we placed all our creations on the shelf to dry. I felt embarrassed by my simple, childlike images. But I also felt joy.

Each class that followed nurtured my confidence and inspired my imagination. About the third week in, we were all instructed to try our hand at the potter's wheel. I had expected to feel good about making an end product, but realized that exploration was more fun. I allowed myself to explore the wheel in my own way, in my own time, and finally brought home several bowls I'd glazed and fired in the kiln.

In the end, one of those bowls became a symbol of healing. I had started to bleed briefly during the time I took the class. The bleeding was a bit of a scare, but it only lasted a short time. I realized how the bleeding could become a new opportunity to honor my body, my female cycles. I thought of the previous winter, when the discovery of fibroids and the subsequent biopsy had led me through a spiral of negating my female organs and then finding my way back into a deeper relationship with my body.

With my blood flowing again, I wanted to take the opportunity to honor my cycle, my feminine wheel of life. I thought about using the blood in some ceremonial way that would remind me to honor my body. To modern minds, honoring our "moon cycle" or creating a ceremony around it is often considered strange, or associated with pagan ritual. But I knew from past experience that ritual, no matter how unusual, affirmed and grounded my life. It gave me experience to live life through the senses. I ultimately decided to take some of my blood and paint it on the insides of the bowl. The day the pottery was put in the kiln and fired was exciting to me. I couldn't help but feel the transformative metaphor of the process. I felt the gift of ritual.

When I saw the finished bowl with its earth-tone center where I'd placed that splash of blood, I felt happy. The bowl became precious, a container to remind me to honor my blood, the feminine in me, it bridges my inner and outer life. The vessel still sits on my altar holding symbols of the feminine. I change its contents seasonally; currently it holds a blue egg. The bowl has become a nest for the birthing of this writing.

One rainy morning I sat listening as the rain fell and sank deep into the dark soil. The drops of rain dripped off the upstairs railing. I noticed a few calla lilies growing along the border of the house. The graceful plants caught the rain in their broad-leafed arms.

It was a good day for writing. I could circle down into unmet parts of my self. I suppose rain invites the moistness of feelings, the soft as well as the torrential. My own spring rains wanted to fall heavily from deep inside, but I could feel the resistance, a rising desire to stem the emotional tide. Was I willing to wade in and experience my feelings, to meet myself?

I decided to stay in bed to meet the reservoir of my held-back tears. But first I went and put the kettle on to boil. As I lifted a cup from the shelf, I noticed the chocolate brownies left over from dinner with my neighbor Jim. Chocolate brownies, dark, rich, and gooey, lifted my spirits. I wanted to eat the entire pan, in which case I would be medicating myself. I knew how easy it was to use food to manage my feelings, or to try to fill all those empty places inside.

Still, hot tea and a brownie made a good rainy-day breakfast. I carried it on my favorite bamboo tray, stopped at my desk, and grabbed some writing paper. I returned to the warm covers of my bed, my favorite sanctuary for writing. Sula kept me company, as she perched on the edge of the bed and kept watch on a squirrel. She has an uncanny ability to just be in each moment.

I took a sip of tea and bit into the dense chocolate texture of the brownie. I was happy I was learning to give myself the luxury of a morning without work. Combining tea time with writing was a treasure. Writing was becoming more and more important in my life. But an inner voice challenged me: Selfish, selfish. I had met this voice before. Like most women I had been accustomed to caring for the needs of others, and I felt uncomfortable giving to myself. That selfish label just went with the territory, as did the guilt I had always felt when doing something just for me. My writing at first felt like a non-doing indulgence, a personal luxury. Then I saw how it grew me open.

But learning to honor those luxuries as a necessary part of becoming myself would take time. Getting in touch with what I wanted was one step; the second step was taking action on those longings. In time I identified the desires and saw they had remained unfulfilled because I believed them to be unacceptable. I still felt like that urchin looking in longingly with her nose pressed to the bakery window. I had left so much of myself out in the cold for so long. There was fear in letting down and receiving, my body responded with tight shoulders, cold feet and hands. Relaxing into life was something new for me. I was more comfortable with control and hiding out.

I fell back into memories of childhood in my New Jersey home. I saw myself practicing scales on the piano. Our piano sat along the wall opposite the tall cherry desk in our living room. Stiff, silk-covered chairs and heavy curtains further darkened an already stultifying room. Wooden shelves held photos and small paintings along with the appropriate books, leather bound, serious looking. We reserved the room for guests and rarely stepped foot into its formality. I usually held my breath and tiptoed around, even during my piano lessons.

The drop-front desk opposite the piano was the main curio, and a place of mystery. Small drawers above the desktop held miscellaneous items such as stamps and paperclips. It was my mother's desk, but she rarely used it, and always kept the top drawer locked. My sister Barbara and I often guessed about its contents. It seemed an official place, a hidden place. The desk was kept perfectly waxed, and shined like the exterior of our family, which covered the emotional abuse that prevailed behind closed doors.

It would be eight years ago that my mother was hospitalized permanently with Alzheimer's disease. My sister and I set about sorted her belongings one weekend. One of those days my sister took the small gold key and unlocked the mysterious top drawer. We waded through my mother's papers, and came upon letters tied in gold ribbon. We untied the bundle and began reading. The letters had been written by friends and family members. She had scrawled notes, the notes expressed unspoken words of anger and resentment. So many frustrations and bitter feelings had festered in her. She was not unlike many women around the world who were encouraged to stifle their voices, and who complied, silencing themselves. I was surprised by her words for my mother often complained. I had assumed she had said it all.

As I continued to drop into my past, I realized how important the process of life review had turned out to be. It gave me the opportunity to focus on parts of the past that held clues to the present. Without voice I remained buried in fear.

I thought about my mother, and how angry she had always seemed to be. I began to understand that she had used her anger to cover her fears and sadness. I, too, covered my truths, I felt a deep sadness, and a flood of fear flowed up from my belly. So much was hidden; I knew I was not alone with these feelings. I knew that giving up hiding would be risky, but longed to be fully human, open to all the messiness that lay buried deep inside. I wanted to feel compassion, that was the key to many locked rooms.

Spring Cleaning

My new awareness gave me a sense of hope. I stopped writing and went for a walk to clear my heart and body. When I returned home I felt inspired to do some spring cleaning. I had to clean the old out to give myself the new. I wanted to make space in drawers, to allow the possibilities of tucking the new inside. There were choices to make about what I really wanted to keep. Seasonal changes were, after all, chances for new beginnings.

My house, while creative, was often disordered. Living alone made it easy to slough off chores. I had moved into the house the previous summer, yet I had not quite made it home. It was time to stop thinking and do something.

The living room was less cluttered than some rooms so I began there. I felt less overwhelmed starting small. I began by sorting books, placing them back on the bookshelf. I ended up reorganizing them according to categories, not authors. I slowly moved around the room, taking the couch pillows out to air in the sun. I threw open the windows, vacuumed, and then turned to my lovely dark, weathered entry table.

It had been my habit for many years to create small still-life arrangements on it. The tabletop had been taken from an Irish bar in Philadelphia; I felt its indirect connection to my heritage. The beautiful wood represented fullness and beauty. A friend had noted long ago that my way of arranging objects felt like altars. I was happy to hear her feedback for, like many of us, I had taken the action for granted. I looked at the entry table and smiled, for it was truly an altar. Each season seemed to invite a change of elements. I cleared away last season's items, including pinecones and my winter touchstones of dried pods and berries. I opened my nature treasure box and pulled out a few eggs I used for Easter, and a nest I had found years before. I randomly opened an art book to a picture I liked, chose a picture of a woman grinding grain, and placed that on the altar. My altar then felt complete—except for flowers. I remembered a neighbor who'd invited me to cut quince blossoms whenever I wanted. The beautiful orange-toned flowers inspired me, so I slipped on shoes, cut across the driveway, and quickly returned with the blossoms. I placed the quince in a green vase, and felt fulfilled in creating beauty.

I vacuumed the carpet, retrieved the pillows from the front porch where they had been airing, and continued to clean throughout the house. When I reached the bathroom I set to scrubbing the tub. It was late afternoon by then, and I needed a spring-cleaning, too. I drew a bathtub of water. I chose bath salts with lavender, and floated some dried lavender flowers with rose petals, made the bath an unhurried affair. I soaked and soaked. My fingers were crinkled and my body waterlogged by the time I stepped onto the bath matt. I felt fresh, like a blank canvas. I also felt more lighthearted after having nurtured myself. The day was a letting go, a clearing and an experience of deep reverence, all at the same time.

Refreshed and at peace, I began to feel hungry. The morning had flown by. I needed to honor the change of season by cooking. Asparagus, artichokes, and strawberries are quintessential elements of a spring menu here in California. My favorite is asparagus. Asparagus is green and snappy and has a bright taste. I can't wait for it to appear in the market every year. I had bought several bunches of asparagus at the farmers' market the day before. I followed my hunger to the refrigerator.

My favorite way to cook asparagus is to simply steam a large bundle of the green stalks in a little water, making sure not to overcook them. I take them from the pan while still crisp, then plunge them into ice water to stop their cooking. I then add a little salt, pepper, and olive oil—delicious.

Making asparagus soup is equally simple. Cook the spears and then chop them. Put them in a blender with chicken broth and a sautéed leek, then add tarragon and about a quarter cup of half and half. The dairy adds a delicious texture and balance. At the same time there is more freshness to the soup without cream or milk.

I decided on the warm, creamy version. Soon I was nestled in the corner of my sofa savoring the rich, balanced flavors, and happy for my work. Sula purred quietly at my side.

Spring days called for frequent walks. Early one morning I decided to head toward Gerecke Road. I knew the stream that bordered the road would be full of winter waters. I loved the sound of the water rushing over the rocks, and anticipated the sight of a few wildflowers. I took a left on Lovall Valley Road and headed toward town, past the grapevines and a few peach trees. Soon I turned right onto Gerecke Rd.

I continued climbing enjoying the scent of fresh bay. The morning sunlight filtered through the trees. Soon I caught the sweet sounds of tumbling water. I was also rewarded by the sight of buttercups and delicate blue irises, all blooming in unexpected places. I walked higher up past the Collingwood vineyard with its vista of rock walls and rolling hills of grapevines. The vines were budding, beginning the cycle that would end with the grape harvest in fall.

I felt like a small bud myself.

A new excitement filled me, one I remembered as a girl. It reminded me of childhood summers when I set out for adventures. I'd take the canoe across the lake for a precious, carefree afternoon on my own. In that moment I wished for a peanut butter and jelly sandwich, proper cuisine for my budding self. I realized how, as a child, I had found sanctuary in nature. Making time for such wanderings on sun-dappled roads was allowing me to recover my love of nature. On the walk back home, I gathered a few gray-green weeds, cobalt-blue wild flowers, buttercups, and thick blades of green grasses. I felt happy.

I was consciously reclaiming and healing that child's soul. She was the one who wanted to bring the outside and the inside together, the one forbidden to get dirty or bring sticks and stones indoors. I felt sad to think how, as adults, we often lose the joy of connecting to the earth.

At home, I put the flowers in jelly jars and placed them next to the rocks and quince blossoms on my altar. It felt good to honor my childhood by bringing these treasures into my home. I was creating visible structures to remind myself of the sacred, the beautiful, and the joyful.

And I left my hands dirty.

Preparations

As the departure day for my trip to France neared, I enjoyed fantasies of French food and the French language I loved so much. I'd learned when living there before to begin the morning by dropping into the neighborhood boulangerie and buy croissants. I had learned to love bakeries there, and had come to see that they are the souls of communities, salt-of-the-earth places. There is magic in a bakery in the morning. It is soulful and sacred as the staff of life greets you. I have also felt forlorn going too late in the afternoon. The shelves have been picked clean, and you have to wait until the next morning for the crusty delights. I knew I would treat myself to a buttery, heavenly croissant as soon as I arrived in Chartres.

In anticipation of my trip, I decided to start my day with a visit to one of Sonoma's two great bakeries. Breads know my weakness, and each one calls to me in its own delicious way. So as I stood gazing at the racks of freshly baked loaves, it was difficult to choose which one would come home with me. In the end I choose a large French baguette, slid back into my car, and placed the warm loaf on the seat next to me. As I drove I mulled over all the possibilities for morning breakfast. I certainly wanted the bread toasted. I could slather the toast with butter, bury it in raspberry jam, spread creamy goat cheese on it, sprinkle on cinnamon and sugar, or cover it with fig chutney.

Arriving home, I did not waste a moment. Knife, bread, toaster. I finally decided on butter and blackberry jam, and paused reverently before taking the first crusty, joyous, bite.

Spring progressed, and I prepared for my travel. The dry ground of my burned-out work life began to green in the spring rain. I felt renewed just being outdoors. I reflected on my life as I pulled weeds. I felt frightened and yet more alive as I met those aspects of myself that had been trapped underground. I knew there were gifts in retrieving what had been hidden and abandoned. I wanted to provide a safe container for my own transformation and growth.

I realized that pilgrimage to sacred center was needed. I readied my hidden, inner self to step onto a pilgrim path.

Spring Recipe

Spring is a season to enjoy fresh greens. I like to choose greens like chard, spinach, or watercress for this recipe. It is easy and nutritious. Fresh watercress has a peppery taste.

Spring Watercress Soup

2 bunches of fresh watercress
1 shallot
1/2 tsp of chervil or chives
Salt and pepper to taste

Wash the watercress well, then cut the stems and leaves. Heat the chicken stock and chop the shallot. Place chopped shallot in the broth and let wilt. Next place the watercress in the broth and turn off the heat. Let the watercress wilt in the warm broth for a few moments. Let cool and then place the ingredients in a blender.

Add the spices and salt and pepper. Serve immediately in your favorite bowl. Garnish with a dollop of yogurt and a sprinkle of paprika. For a heartier soup add milk or cream.

Pilgrimage to the Chartres Labyrinth, France

As my time to leave for France approached, I paused to consider what becoming a pilgrim meant to me. I was reminded of a favorite passage from *The Art of Pilgrimage* by Phil Cousineau, which I'd discovered in a bookstore a few months earlier. He said, "Pilgrimage is the kind of journeying that marks just this move from mindless to mindful, soulless to soulful travel." So many things in my life were guiding me to become more mindful and soulful, and so this journey seemed meant to be.

My love of travel had begun in my childhood, with summer vacations. The first trip I recalled was to the White Mountains in New Hampshire. I treasured seeing new places and exploring different landscapes. Over the years, I'd found I required the adventure. I hadn't traveled in many years, and thought of travel as a lost love. I looked forward to recovering the lost joy and inspiration, and a deeper art of listening. I was headed to France, a country that already inspired my love of beauty. At this turn of my life I specifically sought sacred wisdom found in pilgrim travel. I hoped to renew my soul's life, to open new doors.

Finally, early in May, the day of departure arrived. As I carried my luggage to check-in at San Francisco Airport, I felt a strange combination of fear and eagerness. My age contributed to my feelings of vulnerability. The set of new green luggage and a journal for writing helped me feel some confidence. Nevertheless, my two small bags seemed unwieldy. I realized renewing my relationship with adventure meant I must regain my travel legs and honor my older body.

I'd hoped that leaving San Francisco at 4:00 p.m. would mean I could sleep en route and arrive more refreshed. However, I had trouble sleeping on the plane. While my fellow travelers slept, I sat writing and recalling the first time I boarded a plane to Paris, in 1969. I was twenty-one when I first stepped onto French soil, a naïve American girl who felt like a fledgling leaving the nest. I had left a good job in New York City to explore my childhood dream to live abroad. The company I'd worked for in New York had a division in Paris where I'd hoped to land a job. Instead, I ended up working for a French lawyer. I learned an appreciation for a different culture and fell in love with French art, especially the art of Matisse. After returning to my home in New Jersey a year later, I'd felt joyful and alive, inspired by my experience of French life. I'd carried those experiences with me, but I anticipated the new.

I filled my time on the plane by reading more about the Black Madonna in *The Cult of the Virgin*. Published in 1985, it was the first English book on the subject. Ean Begg, the author and a Jungian analyst, had done intensive research on the Black Madonnas.

I was especially interested in why the Madonna was black. Few art historians, theologians, or Church officials had ever truly explored or acknowledged her blackness. The Church's answer to her color was simply that candle smoke had blackened the Madonnas over time. Any deeper truth, if there were deeper truths about the Black Madonna's history, had thus remained sketchy and hidden. Most of the Black Madonnas were carved out of dark indigenous woods, such as oak or cedar. Folklore tells of Black Madonna carvings found in caves and trees that would miraculously reappear in their original locations after people tried to move them. The Black Madonna's many stories fascinated me. She was certainly a unique face of the sacred feminine.

I became more and more fascinated with the Black Madonnas and with Begg's premise that the Church was itself creating a smokescreen when it claimed the Madonnas were black because of candle smoke. While her origins are unknown, the fact remains that approximately 450 images of the Virgin in our world are black, and have survived centuries of war and revolution. It also intrigued me to learn that in France alone there were over three hundred Black Madonnas.

When I sat with the blackness, I considered the dark inner journeys I had taken into my psyche. I could relate to the way some female writers associated darkness with the womb, or the soil. And of course, many people have experienced dark nights of the soul. Black is also representative of mystery in many traditions. An inquiry into the lost wisdom traditions and what they meant to me was closest to the truth of my personal spiritual quest.

I was drawn to the mystery of the Black Madonna, in part because her secrets had eluded so many for so long. In a way, that was one of the gifts of her presence. Must we always have all the answers, I wondered. For me, it was enough just to be able to sit in her mystery.

I had recently discovered a book written by Caitlin Matthews called *Sophia: Goddess of Wisdom, Bride of God*. Matthews reminded me that the Madonna has roots in many traditions related to the goddess. Some believe she was related to Isis, who was worshipped all over Egypt and considered the mother of creation. Her symbol is the star Sirius, which rises in the sky close to summer solstice and the time of the Nile's flooding. Her considerable veneration spread outside Egypt as far north as the British Isles. Like other goddesses, she seemed to absorb the qualities of the goddesses who had been worshipped before her. It has been suggested that the Isis statues, which depicted Isis with her son Horus on her lap, were carried back during the time of the Crusades. Those statues may have been the precursors of the later statues of Mary and child.

I wanted to find my own truth of the Black Madonna. Caitlin writes that she was part of the "native spirituality of Europe," and that "these empowering statues call out to earthier instincts." Those words certainly spoke to me, and to my healing quest to live deeply in my body. Becoming deeply embodied, healing my fear of the body, and developing a connection to the earth were all necessary components to my evolving wholeness.

I was surprised to see how each exploration kept leading me back to myself. The whole process was asking that I integrate body and spirit. Why should I be surprised, though? My deepest wounds had created judgments and fears. I became aware of the subtle and not so subtle messages given me through my religious training. I had learned to praise the heavens and label my body as sinful, even without my early abuse. My recent Celtic studies were helpful reminders of times when spirit and matter were not separated. Little did I know that I would later find out that Chartres was once a Druid site of healing.

I knew that, like me, many people were seeking wholeness through the lost sacred principles of the feminine. Our world needed the balance of the feminine ideals. Western civilization has focused to a large extent on power and control, to counterbalance those qualities our culture needed the feminine principles of relationship, as embodied by the Madonna. It was interesting to watch the progress of feminine archetypes arise in the revival of the goddess. The Black Madonna in particular had not had so much attention since the twelfth century.

I was seeking her myself. What was out of balance in me?

I had written a few facts about some of the Black Madonna sites in my journal. One such site was the medieval French town of Le Puy, where a Black Madonna and child sat in the cathedral built on a holy hill. Legend tells us that five popes and fifteen kings came to visit her in the Middle Ages, and that Joan of Arc's mother walked the long distance from the west of France to pray.

I put down the book and looked around me at the dark cabin of the plane. Only a few other people had their overhead lights on for reading. I took up my journal again and began writing. I recalled a dream in which I was asked to turn toward the darkness. I was turning.

I'd copied a quote from Ean Begg into my journal, and it held my attention like no other. He wrote, "Underneath all our conditioning, hidden in the crypt of our being, near the waters of life, the Black Virgin is enthroned with her Child, the dark latency of our own essential nature, that which we were always meant to be." I was excited to read his insights, to open a new door in this search for my essential nature. I appreciated the psychological reference, because it made the process identifiable. No longer were the spirit's search and my body's need for healing separate processes. The Black Madonna became another face of ancient woman guiding me home.

I put down my journal and finally slept for a short period, waking just in time to buckle my seatbelt and prepare for our landing in Paris.

Twelve hours after I had boarded the plane, I arrived in Paris at Orly airport. I took my luggage, passed through customs, and went outside to hail a cab. In rusty French I asked to be taken to the Mont Parnassus train station. I struggled at first to figure out the schedule, but finally I boarded the train along with other rush-hour passengers. Light-headed from anxiety and a lack of sleep, I squeezed into a seat with my baggage beside me.

People smiled at my disheveled travel presence. Anticipation kept me awake as we sped out of Paris and headed southwest. Once outside the city, my eyes delighted in the fertile fields, some filled with golden yellow flowers. The landscape rushing by was reminiscent of the fields of mustard flowers in California. I was comforted. The color, the foliage, and the green hillsides all helped me feel centered in spring. Chartres Cathedral suddenly loomed out of the rolling landscape, sitting high on the hill. As the train slowed, I caught my breath at the magnificence of this cathedral.

Off the train, I hoped to hail a taxi. With none in sight, I waited for fifteen minutes and then began walking. How far could it be, I asked myself. I stopped a passerby to ask for directions to the Poste Hotel, and was told it was within walking distance. I started the climb uphill by first peeling off layers of clothes. The weather was much warmer than I had expected. After a slow and rather bedraggled walk I arrived, exhausted. I checked in at the front desk, and finally turned the key in the door of my room. I found it perfect, located on the top floor and, luckily, facing the square.

I tossed the suitcase on the twin bed and threw open the shutters. This simple action brought me joy, for it signaled my arrival. Before unpacking I went to turn on the shower, struggling a moment with the European plumbing fixtures. I felt delight as I stood under the spray of the shower, and the dust and anxiety of my travel rolled from my body. Afterward I pulled out clean clothes, dressed, and just sat by the window gazing out on the small plaza below. To the left I could see the tall spires of the cathedral, to the right a small square with a café. Destination dinner, I thought, and headed downstairs, straight toward the green awning of the café.

I stepped inside and sat at a table just off the street. My seat gave me the opportunity to watch the Chartres citizens on their way home from work. My ears delightedly took in the musical sounds of the French language—*bonsoir, un Perrier, merci.* No question, I was happy to be in France. I enjoyed a get-me-in-my-body dinner of steak and *pommes frites*; if potatoes and meat wouldn't help ground me I didn't know what would. I felt self-consciously alone, but I also felt the mystery of exploration.

After dinner I wandered the old cobblestone streets for a short walk. I felt infused with French life. But soon I began to feel the effects of jet

lag, and found my way back to my hotel room. It wasn't long before I
poured myself into bed and fell asleep.

The next thing I heard was the clanging of metal poles, and men
talking. It was Saturday morning. I lay in bed, smiling. Soon I became
curious about the noises coming from directly below my window. I finally
got out of bed and looked out on the square. It was the opening of the
Saturday flea market, and men and women were unloading tables and
boxes full of local treasures. The activity reminded me there would be a
marche, an open-air fruit and vegetable market. I recalled the joy I had
felt on market day in Paris long ago. I dressed quickly and headed for my
first *café au lait* in the hotel restaurant.

The small dining room looked out on a garden. I inhaled the rich
fragrance of coffee as I entered, and filled my cup with coffee and milk.
Café au lait is one of my favorites of all tastes of French cuisine, as are
croissants. I served myself several of the crusty delights with generous
portions of strawberry jam. I feel joy in my solitude but also ready to get
about my day, so I didn't linger. I walked out to the beautiful sunny day.

The fresh morning air and narrow cobblestone streets carried me
toward the Cathedral. Since it was Saturday I knew I could find the
market close by. Chartres was not a large place. As I approached the
cathedral I saw a young woman with a basket over her arm and her
young daughter in hand. When I questioned her, she pointed the way
down a small street. I breathed deeply as I saw market umbrellas and the
flash of colors of fresh produce in the distance. My steps quickened as I
anticipated oozing cheeses and beautiful fresh produce. I walked closer
and my soul lifted.

When I entered the vibrant market I immediately saw a table of
spring strawberries, rosy radishes, and fresh pea pods. Everything seemed
bursting with life. The experience, I noted, was part of seeing life anew,
one of the many benefits of traveling. While I loved the farmers market
at home, being in a French market was a peak experience. Perhaps it
was French soil, the French language, the romance of it. I finally chose a
box of rosy strawberries, and paid the tall, lanky man who stood behind
the table. When I struggled to find the right change, a French woman
standing next to me helped. Who says the French are unfriendly?

Onward, I was like a kid in a candy store. Finally I stopped at a
small table filled with fresh goat cheeses. I wanted to buy the whole table

of creamy logs, but ended up choosing two small rounds, one rolled in rose petals, another in herbs of Provence. I looked over tables of fresh radishes and peas, lettuces and more. I wanted to fill my basket with all sorts of goodies. But then I remembered that my only utensil was a small plastic knife. Best to keep life simple.

I headed for a corner of the market where I saw a *boulangarie*. Ah, fresh bread! I smiled. I then stepped inside the small shop happy to see shelves piled high with breads of all sizes. Again I stood back, inhaled the fresh yeasty smells, and purchased a fresh baguette, lingering to listen to French voices all the while. Well...bread, goat cheese, and strawberries sounded like a perfect lunch. As I stepped onto the street and felt the bustle of the morning, everything inspired my body and soul.

I wandered back though the colorful market streets. Along the way, red and yellow awnings fluttered in the morning breeze. A green storefront drew me in with its aroma of roasting coffee. Continuing on I walked into a small plaza where the flower stalls showed off their wares of feathery lilac, rosy sweet peas, and tulips of yellow and purple. Glorious morning, I thought. Realizing I wasn't sure where I was, I stopped to look around. I decided to turn right and head uphill. Soon I found myself back at the edge of the cathedral square. With packages in hand I stood looking up at the beauty and power of Chartres Cathedral.

I headed for the main entrance and stepped inside. Then I pushed open the doors and was welcomed into a cavernous dark space. It was disorienting, coming from the bright sun outdoors, but soon enough my eyes began to adjust. I looked up at the towering arches, the beautiful stained glass windows. The famous Chartres rose window overhead shed its mystical light on me. I slowly breathed in this ancient space, and felt the power and presence enfold me. Walking just a short distance into the sanctuary, I stopped at the first of several rows of chairs and looked down at the stones beneath my feet. There, laid into the floor, was the ancient labyrinth described in the book I had read. I remembered that Dr. Lauren Artress, with other members of her church, had first removed the chairs to get a better look. Her radical act then lead to the opportunity all of us would have to walk the labyrinth. I couldn't see much of it but as I gazed under the chairs the labyrinth felt vast.

I stood in awe, then walked down the center aisle. In her book, Artress had written that the labyrinth "was laid into the cathedral floor sometime between the great fire of 1194 and 1220." It would be several days before staff would remove the chairs and give us all our first opportunity to experience the mystery of this centuries old circuit.

My gaze then moved to the left toward the Virgin of the Pillar. She stood high on her base, her black face potent, her robes gold and white. I walked to the open space and lit a candle in honor of my pilgrimage. My first prayer was for the health of friends and family. I then went into the chapel and sat in front of Mary, allowing myself to open to the quiet and presence of the moment.

And so my journey had begun.

In time, I started to feel tired and hungry, so I left the sacred space and walked back out into the bright sun and chatter of the day. It was a strange contrast as I made my way through the streets carrying the peace of the cathedral with me.

I climbed the stairs to my room, glad to have my lunch in hand, and curled up on the bed. The warm air blew soft folds in the curtains. I rested for a while, grateful I could follow my own rhythms as I adjusted to the time change. Hunger stirred me to spread my French picnic on the white knobby bedspread.

After eating every morsel, I fell asleep and awoke in darkness after an amazing dream. Mother Mary was standing beside a large stone. She rolled it back to reveal an opening into darkness. Women were walking out of the dark space, and Mary was telling them it was time for them to come out of the underground. I felt curious.

I sat up reading for several hours after, then drifted off to sleep knowing my friend Alyssa would arrive the next afternoon to share my room. We had much to catch up on since that telephone call many Saturday's ago in February. There I was in France, only a few months later. I could not help but reflect on the power and mystery of synchronicity, and how a telephone call can change our lives.

I awoke early on Sunday, adjusting to the time change and feeling more grounded in France. I took the morning to wander the streets. For me, wandering was part of the joy of travel.

I came upon two interesting shops. One was a coffee and tea shop. I peered into its window and caught sight of a beautifully aged and yellowing photo of Chartres. The image was stunning and simple. The other shop sold antique linens. Loving fabric as I do, I walked in and browsed with delight. I would have loved to bring the whole shop with me, but settled on a small linen handkerchief. On my wanderings the day before, I had chosen a few small treasures to carry back with me. I had recently begun to consider the joy and possibility of grandchildren, and loved the thought of gathering treasures from Chartres to share with another generation. I laughed to myself, for my son wasn't even married at the time. But someday, maybe soon, he would be. I felt happy as I carried that handkerchief in its small package along the medieval cobblestone streets, knowing the joy could be passed on. Soon I headed back to the hotel.

Alyssa arrived later that afternoon. We had a chance to catch up, then headed to an opening reception for our pilgrimage. It was fun to meet other people over a glass of wine. Most of us had traveled from the United States. I felt the collective excitement as we set out to make time for soul walking.

Alyssa and I woke early the next morning. I was excited about our first day of class. We were to meet in the ancient monastery nestled below the cathedral. Several of us left the hotel together. As we walked across the large cathedral plaza and down the winding path along the cobblestone streets, we became reacquainted and shared our excitement. We gathered in the large upstairs room whose windows looked out on a garden. Our class began with prayer accompanied by the haunting music of a flute which set a spacious tone The quality of the day was inspiring I was moved to pick up my watercolors. I had brought along a small travel paint set and small pad of paper.

It was easy to be a pilgrim that day, moving into the ancient ceremonies. I felt grateful to be a modern woman weaving together the labyrinth and the tradition of the Black Madonna. Lauren opened the day, and spoke about walking our prayers. I resonated with her words, much as I had at the labyrinth in Sonoma. But Chartres encouraged me on another level. Lauren reminded us that for many centuries Chartres had been a center of pilgrimage that focused on the Virgin and the feminine. As she spoke, I listened and drew the beautiful windows and French landscape framed in their panes.

Dr. Artress reminded us to become aware of the many birthing symbols in the cathedral. Her words inspired me to look more deeply into the stained glass windows in the sanctuary that reproduced the image of Mary and child. Dr. Artress suggested with similar focus for the sacred feminine that we take note of the importance of the two beautiful Black Madonnas in the cathedral. I had visited the first, Our Lady of the Pillar, the day I arrived in Chartres. The other was Our Lady of the Underground, whom we would meet when we walked the crypt. Lauren also spoke of one of the cathedral's treasures, an ancient relic called the Tunic of Mary, a large linen wrap believed to have been worn by the mother of Jesus. I had known nothing of these treasures in Chartres.

I saw the importance of the cathedral in a new light. It truly offered symbols to remind us of the divine creative principles. It felt healing to image birthing rather than the suffering of Christ on the cross. The multiplicity of the birthing imagery was inspiring to me. I was happy we were there in the spring, for the season mirrored the joy of blooming and birthing. As the morning class ended, I felt happy to be journeying toward the birth of awareness in myself.

After class I joined a woman named Susan and her friend for lunch at our hotel. As we ate, we all talked about the surprising gifts of our pilgrimage to Chartres.

At dusk we gathered for our first labyrinth walk. Anxiously, we lined up waiting outside the West Portal. It was amazing to anticipate being in the cathedral after closing hours. We had no idea what to expect. Finally we were invited to walk inside, and told to remain in silence for the entire evening.

One by one we entered through massive wood doors. Once inside, my eyes adjusted to the dark as the last purple rays of the day filtered through the large rose window. A staff member greeted each of us with a rose and pointed us toward the labyrinth. As I turned to the right I saw its full diameter graced with the subtle light of votive candles. It was a stunning sight. I was struck by the power and size of the cathedral, and by its silence. The only sound was the gentle shuffling of our footsteps as we gathered at the edge of the spiral, ready to begin.

One at a time we were invited to enter the labyrinth and walk, each person allowing space so we were not walking on top of one another. Tears fell from my eyes as I walked quietly toward the first loop of the spiral. As I stepped I realized that my arrival here at Chartres was a perfect synchronicity, a spiral walk that had started months ago when I chose to change my life. I prayed for a teaching or an opening that would move me closer to my life.

It didn't take long before I received my first invitation. I was walking behind a woman who started skipping and dancing—right left...right, left. How strange I thought, then looked at the pious, serious, spiritual self who was walking. I started to skip with her, entering the experience with a lighter heart. Lightness filled me as I met others in the center. I felt a bit disoriented as I took the outward turns back toward the entrance. There was wonder and enormity for I could be counted as one of thousands of pilgrims who had walked that very labyrinth.

Prior to beginning our walk we were invited to walk in silence and then after finishing take time to sit and write. I wanted to sit and watch others as they completed their walk. A I jotted a few notes I was aware that the experience was being written in my body. As I left the mystery of the evening I stopped briefly at the Mary chapel to light another candle. Her presence was a light in the darkness of the cathedral. I felt her protection as she stood over me, her head crowned with small red lights, a beacon in the night.

As I walked back to the hotel I felt deep gratitude for being able and willing to make such a pilgrimage. Not far from the cathedral I met a woman named Kay, and we walked together. We shared briefly some of our experience of the labyrinth, the mystery and awe. I learned she was an American married to an Englishman, and currently living in northern England.

Kay said, "This is my third time at Chartres. I come regularly. Each year I feel the same mystery, and it enriches my understanding. I never tire of coming."

A camaraderie quickly developed between us, and we planned to meet for breakfast the next day.

After leaving her, I pondered the message of lightening up. Was I trying too hard? It was certainly true, both in life and in my spiritual practice, that I was putting forth a great deal of effort. What would a joyful and fulfilling path of my own look like? I recalled skipping along the path of the labyrinth. Joy seemed to be a shadow part of my life. Was I afraid of it? The labyrinth, I hoped, would become a tool to help me let go.

The following day we continued our studies which included tours of the cathedral with Père Legaux. All of our experience was inspiring, but for me the treasure of the day was visiting the Tunic of Mary. Tradition holds that Charlemagne brought the tunic to Europe from the East in the eighth century. In modern day the large piece of linen was carefully protected in an airtight reliquarium. Historical sources say Mary wore the tunic at Christ's birth. There is no proof, of course, although the linen wrap and its fragments have been dated to her lifetime. We also learned that the tunic was considered the artifact that repeatedly saved the city of Chartres from invasion and destruction. One noted example occurred in the tenth century during a Norman invasion. The Bishop of Chartres waved the tunic from the top of the hill; after a short period of time the Normans fled.

Seeing the fabric brought the sacred into a different dimension for me. I felt connected to the sacred fiber, to its earthly symbol and the great mystery of birth. It was of little consequence whether or not Mary had actually worn the tunic, for I appreciated the spiritual metaphor. Being in the presence of the sacred, ancient fabric inspired my personal love of fabric. It became a beautiful symbol of women's lives, how we are connected through time with the threads of our lives, our hands, and our fabrics. Mary became present for me in her humanness as I thought of her wrapped in that linen. The fabric was a bridge.

We gathered again later that afternoon to hear Richard Feather Anderson, a teacher of sacred geometry. He invited us to consider the subject of sacred space. He spoke a new language of the harmonics of space and pointed us toward nature as a teacher of sacred proportions. He helped us understand the proportions of space within the cathedral. The stonemasons and architects who built the sanctuary had applied this understanding in their work. Richard reminded us to look not only in the cathedral but also in nature to see the principles of organic growth.

I recalled my walks in Sonoma, where I often picked up pinecones. I knew I would look on them in new ways. It is through these sacred proportions that we appreciate the miracle of creation.

Richard asked us to draw a variety of forms. We started with circles, and then we drew two intersecting circles. The form in the intersection of the circles is called a "vesica piscis." He called it the mother of all forms. I was entranced by the many mysteries of creation. Learning through experience, we saw how the intersection of two circles created a new form. We understood how the *vesica* became the form out of which all other forms were born. I listened in wonder. That exercise was the beginning of more exploration, for ultimately sacred geometry became a part of my journey.

Richard Feather then took the class to the cathedral. He pointed again to the birthing symbols in the stained glass, and reminded us to look between the forms to the sacred proportions that made the cathedral a masterpiece in design. The lesson also invited me to look at my own body, and the sacred proportions of her design.

The mystery of the sacredness of the feminine became real that day. Learning by experience in the cathedral, then our lecture on geometry gave me pause. I began to feel the womb, the darkness of that creation space as a gift. There was a power and presence of depth, one I had never experienced. I hadn't honored the power of birthing for as a woman I had been trained in shame. Power had been eclipsed by shame and core despair. My Christian roots had never honored my femaleness. As a girl I had been taught that God was a male, that he had the power, and that his word was law. I felt disregarded. There was no Mother aspect to spirit, no feminine to mirror me. Was I then a lesser species, not divine, not part of the Oneness? How in Western culture did the divine feminine get lost?

I knew I was sourcing underground parts of myself. Then I remembered the dream. Mary had invited me to come up from the underground. What wanted to be birthed in me?

I knew the gifts of the mystery would unfold later that evening when our group would visit the crypt where Our Lady of the Underground presides. I was fascinated, for I had not heard of her before. Somehow I had missed her in my reading, but I could not help but recall Ean Begg's comment about the "crypt of our being."

It was dusk again when we gathered outside the lower level of the cathedral. Our group entered the crypt below the main sanctuary through a small door, and walked single file down the narrow stone stairs. The entrance and subterranean space felt unique. The atmosphere was of finding oneself in a great womb. It was there we would find the mysterious statue later in our visit. We were asked to sit for prayer and meditation in the small chapel where medieval pilgrims are said to have come to honor the Tunic of Mary. I felt gratitude to be walking as a modern pilgrim, to be part of that past.

As we sat for prayers, a deep musky smell permeated our meditation time. Afterward we had the opportunity to view more fragments of the tunic, which hung on the walls. I reveled in being up close.

I felt a palpable wisdom in the space, an ancient power different from the cathedral above ground. The Mother Goddess, her earthen sanctuary all around us, sat looking out. The carved wooden statue called The Lady of the Underground was beautiful. The original statue had been burned and then re-carved. What was its original black form? No matter her age, she did in fact feel ancient and powerful. I was drawn to the dark, warm wood. The mother and child sat with simplicity. I noticed a crown of oak leaves, some say connected to the times of the Druids. Behind her hung a colorful woven tapestry; the colors were vibrant and suggested a flame. She seemed to speak to me of times past, of reverence for Her.

I took time to sit with the Mary of the Underground and experience the connection I felt with her. Her true nature felt revealed to me through the rich wood. I enjoyed the earthy quality of her presence. Once again I found myself focusing on how my life had been split from my body, disconnected from the earth—disconnected from the Divine Mother. For the last several thousand years in western culture the Mother had been lost. Or had she gone underground? I wanted to be part of the history that revered the Mother, and participate in the narrative that recovers her.

Following our time with Our Lady of the Underground, we moved into ceremony. We had been instructed to bring a piece of paper on which we had written something we wanted to let go of. Each of us would walk the long hallway of the crypt, place a piece of paper in a large caldron, and then proceed to the end of the hall. There a stairway would lead us up to the main sanctuary.

I waited my turn and then began my walk, breathing into each step. The low ceilings simulated the dark tunnel of birth. Time and the footsteps of other pilgrims walked in the unseen with me. Red-toned lamps that hung from the ceiling lit our way, and invited a quiet contemplation. The mystery and the invisible sounds of ancient ceremonies resounded down the pathway. I carried my slip of paper with words inspired by my labyrinth walk the night before. It said, "I release the concerned and serious spiritual self." My paper dropped in the cauldron, knowing it would soon be burned. As I walked away I left behind a part of myself to be transformed by fire.

But then, as I walked toward the stairs to return to the sanctuary, I remembered the holy well situated close by. Our tour had included a visit to the well days before. I recalled we had been told it was used in Celtic times for healing. Were those the days when the first statue of Our Lady of the Underground was placed on this sacred ground? I imagined drinking of its water and feeling renewed. I felt the mystery and knew the wisdom of Our Lady lived on there. She guided me to remember. I was happy to be her pilgrim.

At the end of the ritual I, like the others, walked back up the stairs to the magic of a candlelit labyrinth. I felt blessed to have the opportunity be there. Staff invited each of us to walk the labyrinth once again. I felt a sense of rebirth as I did, and contemplated the importance of ritual.

My time at Chartres had been enriched with our ceremonies. The deep quiet in the cathedral mirrored my own soul sanctuary, a place of presence. I was reminded that my life was always in a process of transformation, and saw how easily I had let my days become consumed by a busy schedule. I made a commitment to bring more ritual into my life when I returned home. My journey into aging would remind me, for each day would become more precious. It would take me a long time to integrate the experiences I had at Chartres, but I would never forget them.

I felt excited as I walked back to the hotel. Even so, I fell asleep easily.

Saturday was our last day in that extraordinary time out of time. A beautiful breakfast was followed by a communion service guided by Lauren. The service offered us an opportunity to reflect.

Afterward we got to say our goodbyes to one another. While my journey had been a solitary, inner process, I had appreciated our shared time. We had been strangers when we began, but we ended as fellow pilgrims.

I asked Richard Feather Anderson to jot down a brief summary of his lessons about the Chartres Cathedral. Here are his words:

Chartres Cathedral is a temple that functions as a three-dimensional cosmological mandala, telling a creation story through its windows, sculptures and, on the most essential and primary level, its proportions. The length and width of the cruciform floor plan fit within a lens shape, called the vesica piscis or "mother of form" by the Greeks because it contains all the ratios and shapes needed to create all the vibrations and forms of our universe. Remembering that the cross is a multi-cultural symbol representing the law of manifestation, the basic underlying symbolism of the cathedral's geometry communicates that one is entering the Womb of Creation (womb of Mary, vesica piscis) in which one may experience the Mystery of Incarnation/Reincarnation (Christ, the Cross).

That afternoon, after Alyssa and I had packed, we decided to go to the Mary chapel for the last time. We placed yellow roses at the base of the Madonna's statue as we silently spoke our prayers of gratitude. We passed though the massive arches of the cathedral for the last time that day.

The power of the symbols in Chartres would find its way into the crypt of my own being. All the symbols led to the mystery, perhaps a message from the divine feminine within. Learning to walk my prayer brought me into my body and brought me closer to healing the separation of body and spirit. I was glad to open new windows for my soul to speak. I saw how important Chartres would become in offering me a new model of joy and love to replace the old model of suffering. The more conscious I became of the sacredness of life, the more I renewed my soul. Chartres became an overarching container, a womb of transformation. The cathedral itself, the sacred geometry in the vaulted spaces, revisiting history in the cloth of the sacred tunic, the Black Madonnas, the labyrinth, the ancient healing well, the rose window, all collaborated in informing me of the divinity of the Mother. Such a place lives deep in each of us.

It was foggy as Alyssa and I walked downhill from the hotel to board our train. Other friends, Judith and Thomas, shared our journey. We all settled into our seats, carrying with us the fullness and treasure that would continue to deepen our lives.

I learned before saying my good-byes that Judith lead sacred tours, Glastonbury was one destination of her pilgrimage trips. We said our good-byes in Paris, and I boarded the train to Glastonbury. As the train left the city and the soft green hillsides and scattered wildflowers slid past the window, I wondered what mystery lay ahead, and what unfolding it would inspire.

Glastonbury Quest, England

When I stepped from the train at Castle Carey, the sky was overcast and rain seemed imminent. I was happy to see that the taxi I had arranged for was there to greet me. I climbed in and gave the driver the address of the cottage I would stay at in Glastonbury. As we drove along English roads flanked by hedges and Queen Anne's lace, I envisioned English afternoon tea as much as the mystery of this place of pilgrimage. Snatches of legends about King Arthur, Avalon, and Joseph of Arimathea floated through my mind. Some say Glastonbury was also the home of the goddess Brigid. I had heard her name celebrated in Ireland.

I had been drawn into the ancient Mother's arms before Chartres, but visiting the cathedral and physically experiencing Her presence had brought me closer. I knew that there were many faces and aspects to feminine divinity. There was no question that I was drawn to the more earthy aspects of the sacred. I had been entranced by Our Lady of the Underground. I knew that St. Brigid was in essence the same presence as the Black Madonnas I had met in France. What part of my search would unfold in Glastonbury?

As we rode along the winding roads I felt the beauty of the land. Glastonbury, like Chartres, had been a place of pilgrimage since before the Druids' times. Ancient ceremonies were celebrated on the land near wells, in sacred groves of trees, and on hilltops. I felt the sensual beauty of green rolling hills that invited feelings of softness and aliveness.

As we drove through the countryside the beautiful Isle of Avalon soon came into view. Her shape was that of a woman lying on her side. There was no question in my mind that the goddess lived in the land. The tower of Saint Michael, part of a ruin of a fourteenth-century church, stood visible on the top of the hill. The earth's mysteries stood waiting to be revealed, another sacred landscape inviting the soul into remembering. I enjoyed wondering about the possibilities of having lived or traveled here in other lifetimes.

The taxi turned down several small tree-lined streets, then slowed and pulled into a driveway. We drove down a cobbled drive and stopped at the front of an English cottage. The owner must have heard the taxi making its way up the drive, for he opened the front door of the cottage just as I closed the door to the taxi. John, the owner of the bed and breakfast, showed me to my room. It was small but warm, and looked out on a small garden. A small chair in an English print graced one side of the room. I felt tired, but set about my ritual of showering and changing my clothes.

John had suggested I eat at a small cafe downtown, so I set out for the ten-minute walk from the inn. It felt good to stretch my legs and feel the ground under me. I turned the corner onto the main street and walked a block or two. A light rain began to fall as I approached the restaurant, where a warm light glowed from the tavern-like windows. When I stepped inside I felt at home in the wood-paneled room. I chose a small table close to a front window and ordered a potato and leek soup. Along with some hearty bread and a cup of tea, it warmed me thoroughly. Potato and leek soup is a comfort food, and this one was delicious, sprinkled with fresh chives. I felt nourished. I was anxious to get on with my evening, so I didn't tarry. I asked for my bill and left.

It was dark when I stepped back outside, and I headed home the way I'd come. The rain had stopped and a full moon shone through the clouds. I had thought about visiting the Tor that evening. Considered a holy hill for millennia, its name originates from the Celtic words for "conical hill." Now rising out of the plain, it was once surrounded by water. Although I had been looking forward to seeing it as soon as I arrived in England, I worried a bit about the dark and the chance that the clouds might thicken and the rain return.

When I arrived back at my room I decided to go to the Tor after all. The clouds were clearing, and perhaps it would be fun to walk in the dark, especially with the full moon to guide me. I pulled on my hiking boots, borrowed a flashlight from John, and then, encouraged by good directions I started my trek.

The full moon rose and shadows formed. As I crossed the lawn and a small creek, I could see the tall, grassy mound stand tall through the trees. I was glad I had practiced walking in the dark before. My shoes sank into the damp earth, and as I began my climb through a fragrant apple orchard I felt happy and adventuresome. The orchard was full of sweet white blossoms. My only surprise came when I heard a rustle, and a cow appeared out of the shadows. She reminded me she and her kind were traditionally associated with St. Brigid, the feminine goddess connected to land and animals.

As I walked though the apple orchard I also recalled that the apple was considered sacred to the dark goddess. Apple orchards were considered to be sacred groves. The five-pointed star at the apple's core is an Egyptian hieroglyph for the underworld womb of transformation. Legend counts the Isle of Avalon as a place of transformation. I considered what I had read about the legends, which spoke of this land as the sacred Western Isle of the Dead.

I sauntered on, enjoying the fresh spring air and the full moon. At the end of the orchard I turned left to begin the climb. The steepness began to feel daunting, but the softness of the evening and the scent of the apple blossoms permeated my body and helped me press forward.

I began walking the uphill spiral. I stopped several times and sat down for a moment to ease the spinning sensation I felt as I walked. The bright moon helped me see on the unknown uphill path.

As I approached the top of the hill, soft guitar music floated down to greet me. I had not passed a living soul on my walk up, so I was delighted to turn the corner and see several young people sitting inside the tower, gathered there to sing and enjoy the full moon. Their music invited me to sit down, and while I didn't know their song I hummed along. I drifted out of time into the ancient weave of moonlight, the tower, and the song. After listening and sitting for some time, taking in the view of Glastonbury below, I started the walk back to my lodging.

Lights from the town sparkled as the moon shone down on the western hills. I felt the timeless walk back and forth between present and past, imagining King Arthur, the Druids, and St Brigid. Did she come here often as legend reports? Did she walk this land as I had done? On the first turn of the path I stopped to feel the rich dark night and the mystery of the hill. So many others had come to the Tor before me to drink of the sacred presence. I let myself sink deeper into my body and descended slowly down the path with the moon lighting my way.

I soon felt myself touch flat ground at the bottom of the Tor. The gentle earth supported me, and I felt more confident as I found my way back to the path through the orchard. I felt invigorated by the moonlit walk. The spring blossoms of the orchard also lit my way. I listened for the rustle to see if my bovine friend would come again to greet me, but she had slipped away into another part of her homeland. I soon found the low spot at the base of the hill where the stream wound its way, crossed it, and reentered the yard of the bed and breakfast.

I had left a light on in my room. As I opened the door and stepped inside, I felt like a young girl, returning from one of my canoeing adventures.

I was unusually energized by my outing, and realized that walking in the dark at home in Sonoma over the years had prepared me, as had my camping trip on Mount Shasta. I saw the gifts that lay in challenging my fears. Through those experiences I had developed trust and courage. I was glad I had risked the full-moon journey. Pilgrimage gave me such unexpected gifts.

I fell asleep still feeling the invitations of the mystery of place; it felt as though the Tor had led me to this place, and guided me along its spiral pathways.

The next morning brought sun, with a few clouds dotting the sky. After an unlikely breakfast of yogurt, tea, and toast, I set out for Glastonbury Abbey.

According to myth, Glastonbury Abbey was originally inspired by a vision given to Joseph of Aramathea. He built a small wattle church that he dedicated to Mother Mary in 630 A.D. The church is said to be the first Christian church built in England. At the time, the people of those lands worshipped the Celtic Goddess Brigid. Even earlier legend speaks of the area called Glastonbury, including the hill called the Tor, as a religious center for the Druids.

I walked to the abbey ruins in the center of town. As I entered the abbey grounds, a green grass park stretched in front of me. All around me stone walls and arches created a beautiful landscape. They were reminiscent of the past, and the intangible spiritual energy remained.

I imagined Druid and Christian each walking this land with sacred attention.

When I walked through the north entrance of the ruins as the ancient monks had done, the sun was shining between the patches of stones casting shadows. I just wandered for a while. Then, with a map in hand, I found my way to the remains of the Mary Chapel, consisting largely of a subterranean section that included a stone altar at the center. I stepped carefully down the rock stairs to the crypt area below ground. The first thing I saw was an old well lit by the morning sun. I was drawn to walk over to it. I noted how many cathedrals and churches like Chartres Cathedral included healing wells. I then walked to the altar. Although it was darkened by shadows, it held a loving essence. I could feel a quality of reverence there; the heart of Mary lived in the stones.

I then walked to the Abbot's kitchen, a small stone building that contained a fireplace. I felt as though I was standing in an ancient kitchen. Herbs and grains had been placed there to set the tone, and helped me imagine the early monks cooking. As a cook myself, I put myself back in their times, and could almost see them cooking over the fire, gathering herbs in nearby woods, preparing food for their community.

Next I walked back outside to the rear of the building to visit the egg stone, or *omphalos*, that represents the goddess as the Egg of Life. I also remembered St. Brigid's role as goddess of childbirth. The rough-cut, dark egg stone had a small indentation on the top, and was once considered a place of blessing surrounding birthing and menstruation. It was customary to sit on the stone, and so I did. It was cold at first, but suddenly a powerful current of energy seemed to draw me downward. There was no question in my mind that the ancient traditions were living in the stone. How many women had come before me? To this day I cannot explain why two days after sitting on the egg stone I started my period; I had not menstruated since the winter of the previous year, when I fell. My body definitively responded to the sacred turn of life force there on the abbey grounds.

After my visit to the sacred stone I offered a prayer to the abbey and its ancestors. I then headed back out to High Street to take a short lunch break. It was easy to return to the café where I'd eaten the night before. I ordered and savored a fresh green salad and English black tea—the real thing. While eating lunch I considered the history of Glastonbury.

I was interested in the legends that placed St. Brigid there several times during her lifetime. It is said that she came just before she built her abbey in Kildare in 648 AD. I wondered if she had come here to pray, perhaps receive guidance about her large endeavor. It is also written that she lodged on the west side of Glastonbury. While I didn't have time to visit Bride's Mound, I knew it dated back to the time of the Druids. One legend speaks of a wooden shrine dedicated to Mary Magdalene. Learning about the overlays of various spiritual traditions contributed to the puzzle. It was enriching to add to my relationship with the ancient feminine, giving me threads to weave my own tapestry to help me source the missing pieces of the sacred feminine tradition.

After my short lunch, I set out to visit the famous Chalice Well. I left the bustle of the main street to travel along narrower, less busy roadways. The houses were wreathed in climbing roses or dotted with spring flowers of all varieties. I loved the beauty of the English landscape.

As I approached the Chalice Well gardens I could feel the serenity of the place. An iron gate with the *vesica piscis* symbol rested open as I entered through an oak pagoda graced with roses and other shrubs. I was excited to see the symbol, and recalled learning about its origins during our study at Chartres. I remembered drawing two same-sized circles to create the overlap, and that the beautiful orb formed by the overlap is called "the mother of all form." The name "vesica piscis" is roughly translated as "bladder of a fish." The fish shape is well known as a symbol of Christianity. The vesica is one of the many shapes that make up creation. Of course it would be used in sacred sanctuaries.

I was interested in the vesica's prominent position at the gate. It felt like a clue in a timeless puzzle. "Enter here," it said to me. What was more natural and inspiring than this sacred image inviting me into the garden? I stepped onto the cobblestone path, admiring the many shrubs and flowers and feeling welcomed.

I decided to begin my walk at the top of the gardens, where the wellhead was located. I couldn't see the wellhead, but felt the joy of walking in the spring air. The smell of roses lingered and a few birds sounded in the distance.

When I looked up further down the path, I realized I could see the Tor. My distant view felt quite different from the previous evening's adventure. Its phallic symbol was definitely the masculine aspect of the landscape and it related to the beauty of the rolling hills which were invitingly feminine. Certainly the garden, walked in the daylight, felt soft and receptive.

Finally I could see the wellhead cover resting against a rock wall in a circle ringed by a low stone bench. I stepped down into the quiet of the place and sat down. I was surprised to find that the well cover was rather ornate. It was made of wood and iron, and had been designed in the nineteenth century. The design was none other than a vesica piscis. The spring was capped to keep the water clean, but I felt grateful to be sitting at the wellhead. It reminded me to be grateful to water, giver of life. I was one of many who had come to the spring over thousands of years. The water at the well was a gift for healing, the spring considered sacred.

The garden offers two springs, one white and one red. The Blood Spring with its iron-rich water flowed red beside me; the white spring was located elsewhere on the land. I was a modern pilgrim, but the history of Glastonbury flowed with the water, and included the suggestion that in Druid times chambers below ground were used for initiations or ceremony. The ancient rituals included ceremonies in earthen mounds and caves where blessings, teachings, and transformation were enacted. I felt close to that world and those times, sitting there at the well, and reminded myself to spend more time in sacred respect for life.

I got up slowly from the bench and started to walk down from the top of the garden. The water ran stream-like alongside the path in controlled flow forms. The flow forms were designed specifically for the garden to enhance the life force of the water. Each form, with a narrow entrance and exit, created the resistance necessary to move the water in a figure eight. The tiered forms kept the water charged with healing energy.

Bluebells and daffodils bloomed along the path. I passed a very large yew tree said to be 18,000 years old. I stood in awe of this great elder. I had read that the yew is indigenous to the British Isles, and that the earliest fossil record of one species dates back to 140 millions years ago. Later in my travels I learned that the tree is legendary for its connection with the goddess and with death and rebirth, and was also sacred to the Druids. It was often planted at the entrances of sacred places. The yew was reverenced as a protector and a symbol of longevity, rebirth, and transformation.

I continued to follow the flow of the iron rich water. My adventure ended at a pool at the bottom of the garden, whose shape mirrored the vesica. As I gazed at the shape I felt it becoming integrated in my body. I had walked with it throughout the day. The garden became another cathedral to me, a sanctuary beyond time.

The day had turned warm by the time I reached the pool. The pool had small benches surrounding it. Low green shrubs, cascading blue clematis, and more bluebells all invited me to sit. I noticed a fountain with water bubbling out of a lion's head. I cupped my hands and drank of the cool, healing water. An elderly couple and a young woman in an orange skirt had placed their feet in the water in the vesica pool, so I did the same. I felt joy as I removed my shoes and splashed my feet and hands in the cool, red, iron-laced water. I sat on the bench awhile, appreciating the deep quiet. I noticed several purple irises blooming near me, while the scent of small pink roses reminded me to breathe deeply. I would recall that experience of the garden again and again as a place where my soul sang.

I left the garden reluctantly, but I wanted to include the ritual of afternoon tea in my day. I headed to a small English shop filled with young and old enjoying their traditional afternoon tea. I sat at a table toward the back of the shop and ordered my favorite English breakfast tea. I chose a few tiny sandwiches of cucumber and watercress and an orange scone. My Scottish grandmother would have been pleased to see me enjoying myself that afternoon. It was she who had sparked my love of this wonderful ritual, so I raised my cup to her.

I finally wandered back to my lodging, tired and filled with the experiences of the well, the abbey, and the Tor. As I settled into my bed I felt gratitude for the sacred pilgrimage.

The next day I returned to London to board a plane home to California. I was ready to be home. I felt the gifts I'd received, and looked forward to the fruits of the summer. I knew the experiences of pilgrimage would continue to grow me.

$Summer$

Returning

Summer in the Sonoma valley begins in May. I was glad to be headed home from my travels. As the airport shuttle exited the highway and meandered up the two-lane roads toward my rural town, I smelled the familiar tartness of drying grasses. The heat of the day lingered over the hillsides. It was hard to believe that I was in California. Already, Chartres and Glastonbury seemed a lifetime away.

I was delighted to step onto the threshold of my home on Seventh Street, both exhausted and invigorated. I dropped my suitcase at the front door and listened to the warm air for news of the day. Sula bounced across the grass from her field exploits to greet me. She looked less herself, for her winter tabby fur coat had thinned. I gathered her up and walked around the living room, circling like a dog to find my place. I finally settled on my yellow sofa to hear her story. I asked her if my friend Billie had taken good care of her. Sula made sure I knew of her suffering, with a look that said, "How could you?" Cats know how to get to you simply by turning their backs.

As we sat communing, I took in my known world, my home. The altar table held my rocks and shells. The sun's rays fell on the faded carpet in the west. Sula's food bowl empty. Yes, I was home.

As she jumped from my lap I realized it was her dinner time, and way past my own. The sound of an opening can meant dinner for Sula

79

and a return to life as usual. The ordinary tasks of life became nurturing ground to walk on. My next task was simple: Throw off travel clothes and draw water for a bath.

A bath would comfort both of us. Once the tub was full I climbed in and relished my favorite lavender salts. Sula sat perched on the edge of the tub while I sank deeper in the water, feeling the pleasure of soaking. The joys of anticipation and difference of travel were replaced by the rituals of returning. Once I felt rendered limp and puckered, I stepped out of the tub and gave Sula the deluxe towel rub. I dried myself and slipped into my robe and made tea. I crawled into bed with tea and toast, my second favorite ritual. It felt delicious to be home with Sula curled on my feet.

I felt disoriented when I woke at the first signs of light. My first thought was, "Where am I?" Reminding myself that I was finally home, I climbed from bed and threw open the front door. I put the tea water on to boil, opened more windows, and life as I knew it came to me in its gentle details. After tea I pulled on summer pants and slipped on a shirt. Sunglasses and sandals were the only additions I needed to claim the day.

Familiar sights were refreshing as I turned the corner and headed up Lovall Valley Road. Soon I met up with the delicate icons of wine country, the grapes themselves. Endless rows of green grape vines spread out ahead of me. As I wandered I felt grateful to be living in Sonoma. Further down the road I followed my nose to a California buckeye in bloom. I am always surprised by the sweet fragrance of their blossoms; it seems in stark contrast to the sturdy heartiness of the tree.

Scent surrounded me as I stopped at the end of the road and inhaled the lavender plants bordering the path. Soon it would be the peak of the season. Around the middle of June the local lavender farms open their gates. Lavender harvest means festival time in Sonoma and Napa counties. The festivals include lavender sachets, creams, and wreaths or grazing at tables of lavender smoked chicken, lavender crème brulée or brownies or…or…the choices would be endless. I felt grateful for the gift of living in California wine country.

My pilgrimage venture faded as I stepped back into everyday life. But the reminder of my quest travel was to bring the sacred home. I recalled that Phil Cousineau suggests, "bringing home the boon," which means sharing the treasures we gather. I noted how quickly we put pictures and experiences away in drawers. Chartres needed to be shared. I looked forward to talking about the Black Madonna, the labyrinth, and the experience of pilgrimage. Many of my women friends shared my quest for the "deep feminine ground" in themselves. Some participated in a monthly dream group. Others shared the joy of walking the labyrinth in Sonoma. I felt lucky to be able to travel and then give back. The following weekend I organized a small gathering.

Sunday late afternoon arrived, a balmy summer day. I threw open the French doors and we sat in a circle. I had gathered my photos and notes, made iced tea and a plum tart. Six of us sat drinking our tea as I shared Dr. Lauren Artress' teaching morsels and my photos. After my travel stories I enjoyed catching up on my friends' lives, which included their experiences with the dream group. Our informal sharing was filled with enthusiasm. We talked about our spiritual lives and heard about the birth of one woman's new grandchild, the illness of a mutual friend, and the celebration of a successful art show. I wished we had more opportunities to share like this.

At the end of the afternoon my friend Barbara reminded me to look again at Sue Monk Kidd's book *The Dance of the Dissident Daughter*. Kidd writes, "We've lost the idea of God having a womb." I had forgotten her wise words. The image of God with a womb was a strong symbol which reclaimed the feminine. I recalled our lectures in Chartres when Dr. Artress pointed to the birthing and creativity images in the Cathedral. The only religious icon I carried from childhood was a crucifix. Being in Chartres Cathedral had offered healing for body and spirit. New foundations were inspired.

Before too much time elapsed I planned a thank you meal with my friend Billie. The lunch would inaugurate summer. Summer was the season for picnics, outdoor dinners, and get-togethers with friends. As I searched for inspiration on my cookbook shelf, I discovered a lost treasure. A small cookbook, *Mud Pies and Other Recipes*, is a delight. Its author, Marjorie Winslow, put together a backyard cookbook for dolls. Examples of recipe names include *Marigold Madness*, *Tossed Leaves*, and *Putty Fours*. I laughed while I considered a new business of similar summer luncheon menus served on rocks, in walnut shells, and on leaf beds. I knew I would invite my friend Judy to come to such a luncheon. Recovering childhood delight and magic lightened my heart.

The day of my lunch for Billy was warm but not too hot. I set up the folding table on the lawn under the oak. For me, summer rituals included bringing out summer tablecloths, changing plates, and pulling out the new ice cream maker. I chose my favorite red and tan striped tablecloth with red napkins, and gathered jelly jars to hold roses from the struggling bush on the fence. Then I made an easy pasta salad with cucumbers, cherry tomatoes, and feta cheese. Fresh mint growing along the far side of the house made a perfect tea to accompany the salad.

I was carrying the last plate outside to our table when Billie arrived. Glad to see each other, we settled into our chairs on the lawn. After catching up for a few minutes she looked around and said how much she loved the wide-open land and the cool shade of the oak. We both sat in silence for a while as the sun dappled through the trees. I served the salad and poured tea. As we ate she shared that she had completed a large paint project in her home. Besides sharing our love of beauty, Billie and I amazingly share the same birth date and birth time. We both love our solitude. Few people understand this need, so we talk about it often. That afternoon was no different than others. We give each other a mirror that nurtures. She also shared the title of a new book called *Table for One*, a must-read for every loner.

After clearing our lunch plates I carried out my surprise dessert—homemade ice cream made with coconut milk, lime juice, and lime zest, topped off with fresh raspberries. I find it fun to throw caution to the wind with food experiments. The experiment with the ice cream had gone well. Sharing food is always a deep joy and a source of great contentment for me.

Billie left soon after dessert. We knew each other well, and had agreed long ago that savoring life and friendship in short visits works well for us. It's a rhythm that's well suited to people who love their space.

Later in the day, when the light crept under the shade in my art room, I leaned back in my chair, feeling contented and full. I was actually experiencing a quality of life I wanted, something I had not felt in a long time. I knew the joy came from taking time and honoring what I needed. I had discovered first-hand how exploring my needs, addressing issues of self-care, and acting on them made a big difference in my emotional and spiritual well-being. I appreciated having the luxury of time to take care of my emotional and spiritual needs while for most people it's very difficult to cut out even a few minutes a day to nurture themselves.

The day after my lunch with Billie, I awoke feeling content. Had I actually created a new standard where well-being replaces anxiety? I felt the bright stillness of the summer morning. The joy was like that of a child who wakes up on a summer morning. The clue for me was a once "early childhood." The joys of just meandering or musing or sitting in a sandbox letting sand flow fingers.

What would I love to do to inspire summer childhood? The weather report predicted ninety-eight degrees which meant catching the cool of Bartholomew Park. I arrived exactly when the gates opened. I headed uphill through the tall grasses, and caught site of a few spider webs illuminated in the morning light. The webs were strung between the dense grasses, the strong yet delicate filaments turning silver as I stopped to inspect them. Nature knows how to stop me in my tracks. She reminds me to make time for small cameos of beauty.

As I walked further along I dropped more deeply into my body. Reaching the tree-lined portion of the path I appreciated the dabbled light, the dark shadows. Both light and dark danced with the wave of the wind, each necessary to reveal the other. I turned in several directions taking imaginary snapshots of still life images, one more beautiful than the other.

I rounded a curve and saw a small bundle of dry grasses lying in the middle of the path. When I bent down to pick it up I realized it was an abandoned nest. Since nests are treasures to me, I gently carried it with me as I continued on my way. It was a lovely metaphor to reflect on.

Soon I made my way down the rough wooden stairs and reached the creek, where I stopped to perch on a rock to wash my face and neck in the cool water. Delightful water spiders scampered and skitter across the surface of the water. Feeling nurtured I turned back home.

Several weeks later I woke suddenly in the night to the patter of rain falling. Since our rains typically stop in April or May, this late rain was a curiosity. I got out of bed and opened the front door to let in the smell of the fresh moist air. I stepped out into the light rain and felt joy. I use to thrive in heat, but menopause has changed all that.

Solstice Food

Summer solstice arrived on a Friday. I prepared morning tea and mused into the mist of the boiling teakettle. Out of the mist came memories of my childhood summers, which included warm humid days, succulent Jersey tomatoes, and corn grown in our backyard. Add to this the sparkle of fireflies, the smell of cut grass, and the click, click, click of sprinklers—that was summer in southern New Jersey.

Corn, tomatoes, and summer sprinklers, even in my imagination, sounded delicious. Since it was a Friday morning I stopped imagining and headed out to farmers market. The inspiration of fresh vegetables from the garden was instilled in me as child. We lived on five acres and always had a family plot full of peppers, green beans, corn, and of course Jersey tomatoes. While my sister and I hated weeding, we both celebrated the succulent tomatoes and sweet corn.

As I approached the farmers market I saw the flurry of the vendors' tents and the crowds who came to enjoy the bounty and share cooking tips. I perused the tables, and gathered fresh salad greens and a few early tomatoes. At another vendor's table I gathered onions and beets and the last bouquet of coreopsis. Happy with my treasures, I returned home and set to weeding and tending my own small garden.

Later in the day I headed for my favorite green chair, aware of the circle of the day. It felt good to just sit. Soon I caught the chirp of crickets, first one, then another, then a full chorus. I realized that solstice had come and gone and I had not taken my usual labyrinth walk to celebrate. It seemed I had preferred to stay close to home to mark the longest day of the year, but I wanted some sort of celebration. An outdoor dinner seemed to offer an alternative commemoration.

What to make? Since I seemed to have instant recall of childhood, I thought about fried tomato dinners. It would have been a similar evening in New Jersey when my sister went to the garden. My mother waited in the kitchen and heated the cast iron skillet until the oil sizzled. Beside the skillet sat a plate of flour, seasoned with salt and pepper. Tomatoes still warm from the garden were thickly sliced, then dipped into the flour one by one and set to brown in the pan.

I held these memories in my body, so I deftly began the process. Iron skillet, tomatoes, flour, oil…begin! The tomatoes sizzled as I dropped them into the pan. The smell of the cooking tomatoes, past and present, were similar, filling my house with their dense sharp smell. The sound of frying intertwined with the cat's meow. Sula hoped a fat chicken sat cooling on the stove just for her. The lazy summer memories floated through the house as I cleaning the corn and waiting for the water to boil. Soon corn and tomatoes were ready.

I balanced my large yellow plate of tomatoes and corn in one hand and a cup of mint tea in the other, and headed outside. I sat savoring both past and present. The first bite into the crisp outer crust of the fried tomato tasted warm, and as delicious as I remembered it. When I had consumed the last morsels I realized my own tomatoes would not ripen until the end of summer, but I looked forward to watching them grow.

Later that evening I took up my journal, along with a bowl of vanilla ice cream, and curled up on the sofa. As I dug into the creamy mound I drifted back in time again to my childhood. My father had owned a dairy business; so milk, butter, and ice cream were abundant in our house. But we were often monitored, with locks and controls put on pleasure. There was tension at mealtime tension about what we eat and how much. My mother meant well in her position as the headmistress of all food police. My mother's voice mirrored our culture's obsession with slimness. I struggled to relax, savor, and enjoy food, still wavered as I gained weight.

Mother's stiff concern was the opposite of summer relaxation and joy. Summers for my mother included girdles and fashionable attire. No season came with days off except when we were away at camp. Camp meant nature, swimming and fun. I wanted to reclaim sensual summer delight. I wanted to savor life and spark more aliveness.

Solo Camp

One warm summer evening, as I sat on the back step enjoying the night sky; I longed to sleep outside, spend a night under the stars. Why not go camping, swimming or canoeing? As I sat looking up at the night sky I asked myself if I could challenge the fear of camping alone? But I immediately imagined the pleasure of sleeping under the stars. It would be a new experience for me.

While I wasn't as young or as limber as I once had been I could risk a night or two somewhere. But where was that somewhere? The last time I had been camping was in the nineties. I remembered going to Mt. Shasta, a beautiful sacred landscape just north about four hours. Could I remember where I put the camping gear? Back and forth, I considered the pros and cons. Was I fooling myself? My aging body, already stiff and complaining in the morning…would it enjoy rolling out of a sleeping bag spread out on hard ground? "No risk, no joy in outgrowing my limitations. Take a risk, dare to claim freedom," I said to myself. I could return home to my soft bed soon enough.

I recalled camping at Lake Siskiyou with friends years before. I also knew there were campgrounds on the mountain. My online search showed me I could find space at Panther Meadow. When I woke the next morning I knew it was to stretch and explore by adventuring. Out of bed and in my robe I headed to the garage to search for my camping gear. It was tucked in the corner covered with dust. My camping gear included my old blue tent, a faded green sleeping bag, and a cook stove. It was all I needed. I wiped it off and sat it out in the sun to air and headed back inside for breakfast. I knew that I would need to just go.

After breakfast I gathered some food, my ice chest, and a sketchpad. To make it easy I planned to stay for only a day. That gave me time to stretch beyond my fear without pinning myself down. If I wanted to stay longer I could. I spent the morning doing laundry, packing a few cloths. Since I wouldn't be gone long I poured a large helping of cat kibble and filled her water bowl. What next I thought. I didn't want her to remain indoors so I knocked on my neighbor Liz's door and asked her if she would put Sula in at night. I told her where I was headed, packed the car and set off in the afternoon.

As I turned the car east I had second thoughts. What am I doing? Hadn't I just gotten home? Guilt came quickly again as I reminded myself of my trip to France. Whose voice was that? Mine or one from the past?

When I reached my destination, Mount Shasta, I had no idea what to expect. The long ride had been hot and boring, and with each passing mile my anxiety had grown. But as I drew closer, the mountain loomed pristine and white against the sky. Awe replaced anxiety, yet a touch of fear lingered. The closer I got to the great mountain, the more insignificant I felt. I promised myself that I would not turn back.

As I entered the higher elevations I caught the cool scent of pine trees, and opened the car windows to take in the fresh clean air and open vistas. Exactly four hours after leaving Sonoma I turned off the highway into the small town of Mount Shasta. I found a market right away and stopped briefly to buy peaches and a flashlight, an essential I had forgotten. No, I wasn't a camper.

Driving through town, my anxiety intensified again. Soon I turned off the main street and began the steep drive up the mountain. Its peak reaches 14,000 feet. My campground was just over halfway to the top, but still at an exhilarating 7,500 feet.

Arriving at the campground I took my purse, locked the car, and wandered through the campsites, hoping to find one at the edge of the campground. I checked in with the ranger, and then found a site close to the west boundary. My insecurity increased. Was I crazy to be doing this? It had been years since I had put up my old blue tent. Placing my feet deeper into the dry earth encouraged me. Breathing in the fresh mountain air, I felt more solid. Even though the air and earth were dry, I heard the sound of water running in the distance.

It took two trips to unload the car. As I set up my tent and cooking area I began to feel more connected. I realized I could enjoy the feeling of setting up a rough and ready home, an outdoor hearth place. Hearth had grown its meaning in me, and it now helped me to feel safe, drawing a circle around me.

As I finished pounding in the last tent stake, I noticed a woman in a nearby campsite. She sat wrapping bundles of sage. As I watched her lay out the sage, I felt I was witnessing some ancient ritual. I, too, loved herbs. I turned toward her and smiled.

She beckoned to me. I walked over to her site and I sat on a log. We introduced ourselves and she began telling me her story, how she had come to be in Mount Shasta.

"I come every year at the same time to gather sage and wrap it," she told me. "It's a vacation for me." She went on to say she had driven from Colorado alone. Besides hiking and gathering sage, she said she liked to spend time at Stewart hot springs, which I had not heard of. I considered visiting the springs just as she had done.

I was amazed at her courage to camp alone, and respected the beautiful ritual she gave herself each summer. I wanted to grow more connected in the way she seemed to be. A part of me wanted to talk with her about my fear of camping alone, but I felt too awkward, and eventually walked back to my tent. I wished I were not so shy, but that was another conversation to have with myself another time.

I have always remembered Susan as one of the ancient ones, sitting wrapping her sage, traveling a distance to restore herself and gather sacred herbs on the slopes of the sacred mountain. In my mind she joined a long tradition of women's ancestry, and became a reminder of women who lived their lives well and on their own terms.

Alone again in my campsite, I was astonished to discover how quickly I could become afraid. Even in broad daylight it was easy to begin to project fear into the night ahead. I imagined that night slashers might lurk in the brush outside my tent. That was old thinking I knew. I also told myself that the world was in fact not as safe; women do need to be more careful than ever. I knew there were plenty of campers around me, and invoked the goddess to protect me. Besides, I had the rest of the afternoon ahead of me.

Once I felt that my site was completely set up, I wandered down the path to find the stream. The coolness of the water on my hands and neck and the smell of the pines calmed my fears. Nature helped me reconnect to my center, to that quiet place inside. Mother Earth reminded me to settle deeper into myself and let go of the mind chatter. She reminded me to be restored, to find a steadiness inside.

I remembered a trip I had taken with friends many years before. Five of us had made the four-hour drive from Sonoma to a campground near the town of Mount Shasta, at the base of the mountain. We hiked, cooked dinners over our camp stove, and swam in the cool waters of Lake Siskiyou. I recalled sitting on the edge of the lake with my friends, awed by the wonder of a mountain night sky.

I suddenly longed to return to that spot. A swim in a mountain lake would help me claim joys I had forgotten. I had always loved swimming in fresh water but had rarely made time to actually do it. A mountain lake it had to be. Lake Siskiyou was waiting.

The cool fresh waters of the mountain stream felt good. I realized they had helped me find balance, as well. Was it a good time to go over to the lake, which meant driving back down the mountain? Maybe I would wait until tomorrow.

I took in a deep breath, smelling the fir and pine all around me. As I walked back up the path I tried to remain as present as possible, and felt the spiritual quality of the mountain. I hoped I would be able to sustain that awareness. I continued on past my campsite, taking the path to the meadow. It was July, and the wet, sub-alpine meadow was spectacular. I marveled at the tiny wildflowers and bubbling springs that ran through the meadow. Rivulets of rushing water tumbled over small stones. Around the water was a barrenness that seemed strange, though I knew it was common at this elevation. Unsure of myself, I stopped before I reached the end of the meadow, and turned back the way I'd come.

Once back in my campsite I took up my journal. A nervous fear crept over me, a fear I finally labeled as fear of openness and vulnerability; with no walls about me I felt exposed to the vagaries of nature and to the unknown. As I wrote I felt a strange juxtaposition between awe, beauty, and fear. Perhaps it was normal. Did others around me feel the same and not speak of it?

After several pages I turned to my sketchbook, which always helped me focus. I sat and sketched several varieties of pine, names of which I would learn later. I collected several of their cones, which I found fascinating. I remembered Richard Feather's talk on sacred geometry at Chartres, and promised myself I'd learn more about the geometry of nature. Relaxing, finally, I sat with my back to a tree for protection. The day was still warm, the unknown still present. I sat with the sun on my face and began to find protection and safety in nature.

Finally it was time for cooking, so I set up the camp stove. I had brought a few vegetables to sauté, and a few fresh tomatoes and cucumbers to slice. The smell of food sizzling and the dimming of the sun reassured me. I actually enjoyed cooking on the Coleman stove; it reminded me of the time I prepared a wedding dinner on such a stove on Whidbey Island in Washington. Our lives are funny and interesting, and each of our memories is unique.

After dinner I heated water, and sat enjoying my herb tea as the dark closed in. Later I stretched out in my sleeping bag next to the tent, taking in the magnificence of the night sky. On the mountain I felt close to heaven, as the stars peppered every inch of the sky. I wasn't use to being able to see the multitude of stars in the night sky, all of them bright enough to touch. I soon slept, for it had been a tiring day. I was glad to have pushed the edges of my comfort, giving myself more of life.

I woke only once during the night, to the sound of people singing.

I awoke with the sun early in the morning, which reminded me to be grateful for the sun's life-giving rays. I heard the call of a few birds, smelled the pines and the dusty earth. The grace of the day could reach me when I was more silent. I felt more of a desire to pray, to feel grateful, and to offer gratitude to all creatures, to sun, to wind, to water. I rolled from my sleeping bag and immediately felt stiff. Even though I had brought a pad to cushion me, my back was sore. My stiff legs also complained, but I set out for a short hike to stretch my muscles and enjoy the beauty of the mountain. I walked to the meadow again, enjoying its trickling water sounds and wildflowers, its funny stunted trees. It was a sight out of time, magical and invigorating. I hoped the native tribes were continuing to keep the land sacred.

I soon forgot my stiff body. Walking outside my known world had allowed me to grow beyond my wounding and my fear.

I returned to my campsite and decided to spend the rest of the day at the lake, and perhaps return home late in the day. Part of me wanted to stay on camping for another night, but I wanted to honor the simplicity of this one step.

I packed up the tent and cooking gear, and headed back to my car as my neighbor headed out for the hot springs. I gathered a few pinecones to take home and place on my altar as a remembrance of that day at Mount Shasta.

Once down the mountain, I headed west across the freeway and followed the signs down Barr Road to the Lake Siskiyou. The ranger at the campground had suggested I travel the back side of the lake to avoid the hoards of summer vacationers on the campground beach. I found the road easily, but felt unsure as I faced the unknown. I kept driving until I saw an obvious access to the lake.

The parking area was cool and shaded. It was a small beach with only a few people stretched out at the edge of the lake. I was happy, for this place felt perfect. I noticed a wide trail to the left of me that seemed to curve around the lake. If I wanted to walk, I would. Bathing suit on, towel in hand, hat on my head and a book under my arm, I headed for the beach. I wondered exactly how cold the water would be. I felt free.

Once at the lake, I opened my towel and sat down, enjoying the warmth of the sun on my skin, the air not too hot, everything perfect for a swim. It was barely noon.

I could resist no longer. I put my feet into the ice-cold water. It was fun to take it slow, wading in until the water reached my ankles, my calves, thighs, waist, and chest—underwater. I came up gasping. It was freezing, but delicious. I swam to keep warm, moving toward the center of the lake, then swam back to shore. A paddleboat passed me as I continued to swim. By then my body was used to the temperature, and I relaxed. I didn't stay in the water long, but I loved every minute.

Out of the water I warmed in the sun, put on my shorts, and headed for a walk. As I walked I could feel the beauty and pleasure of recovering a joy lost in the past. I felt the sacredness of the place, and even saw a canoe, which set my heart to remembering. No question—I had recaptured the goodness of my childhood summers.

On my return home to Sonoma that evening, I felt renewed courage and power. My fragile feminine self had definitely gained strength and a sense of self worth. Was it my travel and the Black Madonna who inspired me to grow beyond my fears? A wobbling and unsure self found more ground. I did not want to limit my life because of my fears.

Bringing home the memory of Lake Siskiyou swimming encouraged my next step. There were no lakes to swim in the town of Sonoma, but there certainly were pools. I phoned a friend who had a swimming pool in the complex where she lived, and asked if she would consider the idea of a group swim, perhaps one other woman friend and the two of us. She laughed, for she had wanted to get out and swim herself.

Our summer swims settled into a weekly get-together that included iced tea and gelato. By the end of the summer I felt more balanced, having given myself permission to relax and enjoy the simple pleasures of life. I posted pictures of water lilies, lakes, and canoes around my home. I was glad to feel the renewal of my love for lakes, and wanted to explore further what they meant to me.

It was in the middle of August when my friend Judy and I began planning a summer picnic. It was to be a belated celebration of our birthdays, and a chance to share our love of food and beauty. I suggested Bartholomew Park as the cite of our moveable feast. We divided the work, planned the menu, and chose a date.

Planning our menu was half the pleasure, since we both love cooking. Our final choices included a large salad, a mushroom frittata, French bread, goat cheese, olives, and a lemon tart. Judy is the mistress of lemon tart, mine not half bad, but I left this one to her. Tarts always sound complicated, but a lemon tart asks for a good crust and curd. Lemon curd takes a bit of watching when it cooks, but its ingredients includes lemon juice, sugar, eggs, and lemon zest.

I made a generous salad for the meal, and bought bread, drinks, and cheese. Judy made the frittata. For the salad I cooked small yellow-fin potatoes, drained them, then showered them with fresh dill and sea salt. I blanched green beans, which simply means placing them in boiling water for a few minutes then taking them out and plunging them in an ice bath. I placed the beans on a towel to drain, and then started dicing the other vegetables. Halved yellow cherry tomatoes, slivered red onion, red peppers cut in chunky wedges, and radishes sliced paper- thin fell into the bowl. I washed watercress and chopped basil, which I would toss in to brighten the flavor at the last minute. I ended the preparations by combining Dijon mustard, olive oil, and lemon juice for my dressing.

I always enjoy serving food that is produced locally, and feel lucky to live in an area where local artisan producers provide an abundance of good food. Judy and I share a love of cheese made from goat's milk, so I chose a local variety made by Laura Chenel. Her love of goats had inspired her to launch her company more than thirty years before, after studying the art of making cheese in France. When she returned home she became the mistress of the United States cheese industry.

I pulled together the other ingredients: bread, olives, and a few ripe cherry tomatoes. I finished the preparations just as Judy arrived. She was happy to see the sun. She lives in Mill Valley, a town just across the bridge from San Francisco, so her summers often include fog and cooler temperatures.

We loaded everything into my car. I had packed a large tablecloth and a blanket, and Judy had brought her recently found china plates and glasses. She loves to shop garage sales, find treasures, and bring them home to what she calls her Martha Stewart play station. We laughed each time she reported a new find, and joked that soon the station would take over the house.

Bartholomew Park was our destination for our picnic. We were happy to find a parking place close to the gazebo area, for carting all our wears was going to take time. When everything was finally unloaded, we found a perfect spot at the edge of the formal lawn area. We unpacked napkins, plates, silverware, fresh olives, the salad, goat cheese and a baguette of French bread, frittata, sparkling water and pomegranate juice to spike the water, the lemon tart, and blueberries onto the yellow tablecloth and sank delightedly into the fragrant wild grasses.

As soon as we settled in, we raised our glasses to toast our picnic heaven, and then dug in to all the goodies. After the last bite of lemon tart we stretched out and rested, letting the warmth of sun and earth fill us. Before finishing our day, we lifted our glasses in honor of another year of sharing.

Gathering Joy

Days later I took my walk just past noon. I bent down to rattle the rattlesnake grass that grew close to the ground. I appreciated the soft breeze that brushed my skin. Yes, I was slowly coming into my body, treating it with more respect.

Rather than denying myself the joy of food, I indulged myself that day. Rigid systems and rules were not nourishing or inspiring. Summer was the perfect time to connect with this growing of myself. And as the grapes were coming into their fullness and the summer season into its abundance, I, too, connected with nature's mirror. The tomatoes had reddened, the morning glories had bloomed, the blackberries were plump and waiting to be plucked; the sunflowers were bursting with their yellowness, melon called to be cut, and the tang of mint and basil reminded me to take my time and linger. I lingered outside to catch the first star, as an August moon beckoned.

Summer Recipe

Summer is a time to go to farmers markets or your own garden to gather fresh tomatoes. Nothing says summer better than the smell of a fresh juicy tomato. Perhaps you have a Sunday childhood food favorite.

Fried Tomatoes

1 cup Panko flakes (Japanese breadcrumbs)
Pinch of cayenne
2 eggs beaten
Salt and black pepper
2 large unripe tomatoes, cut into 1/2-inch thick slices, ends removed
1/4-cup vegetable oil
1 tablespoon unsalted butter

In a large bowl combine the Panko flakes and cayenne. In a separate bowl beat the eggs and add cayenne and salt and pepper. Dip the tomatoes in the eggs and then dredge them in the Panko mixture, coating both sides well. Place a large cast iron skillet over medium heat and coat with the oil. When the oil is hot, pan-fry the tomatoes until golden brown and crispy on both sides, about 3 to 4 minutes on each side. Carefully remove the tomatoes and drain on paper towels. I like to top with a dollop of cold creamy yogurt.

$\mathcal{F}all$

"Blossom and leaf fall, the ebb and flow of the circling year."

—Mara Freeman

Harvest Rituals

Fall announces itself in the beginning of August in Sonoma. One day the light changes ever so subtly, the temperature drops a notch cooler.

That year the gentle nudge reminded me to give in to the ebb and flow of the seasons. No sooner had the harbinger sung his quick fall note than summer returned with soaring temperatures.

Everywhere in Sonoma County, fall is harvest time. Celebrations abound in many towns. It is the time of the year when the plaza in downtown Sonoma overflows with people who come to be outdoors. Salute to the Arts, an event in the beginning of August, is dedicated to the abundance of fine art, food, wine, and music. As the fiery rays of the summer sun shone down, they reminded me to enjoy, for the rainy season would come soon.

Harvest means gathering the bounty of fresh fruits and vegetables. Farmers market tables are a feast for both eye and palate. I always revel in the bright red and yellow peppers, variegated eggplant, fresh basil, nectarines, every succulent variety of tomatoes, and fresh flowers delicate, robust, and fragrant. The sun, earth, water, and the tender care of the growers make these treasures possible.

Harvest time also means turning our attention to the valley's grapes. News of predictions of tonnages and sugar content are common conversation. There is excitement and anticipation in the air. Most years

I listen to figures with a ho-hum attitude, but on those blazing August days when I looked for Sonoma Country tonnages I found a surprising number of 330,910 tons harvested that year—not so ho-hum.

One Friday toward the end of August I made my usual trip to the farmers market. This trip was a harvest celebration, which meant gathering seasonal peppers for roasting and ripe tomatoes for sauce. I reveled at the quantity and variety of tomatoes that included Early Girls, Green Zebras, Gold Girls, and Rainbows. Even my own crop of tomatoes was ready for picking. Tomato sauce seemed to call.

I carried my treasures home and stacked them on the kitchen counter. The light filtering through the kitchen window fell on the beautiful harvest. My body became aware of the seasonal difference, ever so subtle but inspiring. I looked forward to softer tones of fall light, which would ultimately include the winter grays and between-the-world colors of misty mornings. I have always loved the seasons when shadows become longer, when the days become readable. Sharp forms don't focus the eye as a result it becomes easier to read between the lines. While I feel the pull inward, others tell me they have more energy in the fall. Whatever our truth, it is a season of letting go while turning toward the dark season of earth's cycle in the northern hemisphere.

I headed for the garden to bring in my own tomato harvest. I also gathered basil from a pot on the step and headed back to the kitchen. The tomato sauce I had in mind was simple. It involved sautéing onion with red pepper flakes. I chopped the tomatoes and added them to the pan with salt and pepper, and waited. Since my aging stomach does not take to garlic, I did not include it. I let the rosy brew cook on low heat for about twenty minutes. As soon as I turned off the heat I added the chopped basil. After the sauce cooled I pored it into containers. Freshness and simplicity were important to me when I cooked. I liked tasting the uniqueness of each vegetable.

The end of September offered the rattling sounds of the grape gondolas carrying their cargo to Sebastiani Vineyard just down Lovall Valley Road. Living in vineyard country offers me the joy of agricultural cycles. Sun, water, and the vineyard workers' care produced bountiful harvests. The crop yielded the fruits of many who had labored. Being a part of the harvest meant enjoying the pungent smells of the grape crush and imagining the delicious varietals wines that would appear on the shelves when it was their time. Harvest brought gratitude, and I turned to my writing to include this appreciation daily.

As I sat writing I realized it had been just a year since my Aunt Annie had died. I recalled her love of humor and medium-rare roast beef, and I smiled. I also reminded myself of the quality of my life just a year before. My overworked body, mind, and spirit had been unaware. Much had changed over the year, and again I felt gratitude.

One part of my learning had been to make time to listen to my body and follow the seasonal signal to stock the pantry. Discovering the body's need for seasonal food changes was one part of the listening. Fall rituals helped me transition, and break my old pattern of resisting change. When I checked the pantry I found that the shelves were bare. Over the summer I had used up my stocks of beans, maple syrup, coconut milk, almonds, and pastas.

I also checked my supply of batteries, and wooden matches to light winter fires. Only one box of matches remained on the shelf. Diamond matches were one of those household items I could take for granted. They signaled a comfort I never thought about. The blue, gold, and red colored boxes are reminiscent of childhood. When I thought about it I realized they had been in my life for some fifty years. For fun I checked their origins. The Diamond Company had been in business in the United States since 1881. It seemed that the original match was created in 3500B.C. in Egypt. At that time matches came in the form of sticks of pinewood, which were impregnated with sulfur. I added the boxes of matches to my supply list with appreciation. The fall tasks helped me return to the sensibilities of hearth. It was a time for me to cozy-in and dream new dreams for the year to come. Placing cans, bags and boxes on my shelves was comforting.

The end of October brought the rich colors of fall leaves. Burnt orange and harvest yellow began dotting the landscape of the Sonoma valley. The grape leaves contributed their unique beauty as they turned from crisp dark greens to gold, yellow, and burnished reds.

I saw how stocking my cupboard was also a need of my spiritual life. I would need nourishment for both body and soul over the fall and winter. Spending more time indoors invited me to gather books, maps, and music to nurture my journey. My natural turn was to follow my path in Celtic spirituality which gave me a model to integrate not separate.

My summer experiences had shown me that I had trouble letting go of control, letting life flow through me. I knew the need to control was the opposite of my desire to be more open. I truly wanted a soul life, not a life driven by a wounded past. My Celtic heritage was helping me to rekindle such a life; its history was already written in my bones.

I woke one morning from a dream. In the dream I was walking in a New England landscape. I felt happy, kicking the scattered leaves. As a child I had loved autumn, and New England was the place to see the season in full dress. The tree-lined streets of maples in New Jersey where I had grown up were as beautiful.

The dream invited me to take a walk down a country road. The hills in the distance were aflame in color while to my right was a large grove of birch. I stood listening to the rattle of the leaves as the wind blew through the branches. They seemed to be speaking an invitation.

Forests had been places of sanctuary in my childhood; they were physical and emotional world healers. I picked up Mara Freeman's book *Kindling the Celtic Spirit* and read about the importance of trees. Many trees are sacred among the Celtics. Mara reminded me of their gifts of dyes, fuel, medicine, and materials for houses. The Celts lived with reverence for those gifts. Modern peoples see trees as timber. I knew the dream was calling me to move deeper into my connection to the natural world. Trees were an important part of my community, and I wanted to reinvent the quality of reverence. I recalled David Abram's reference to the "more than human" world. Trees were always living community to me and offered me sanctuary and wisdom. As a child I loved birch and noted in Freeman's writing that the first Ogham inscripton was written on a birch switch. The Ogham is an alphabet used for inscriptions in the Irish language as an alternative to the Roman alphabet. I began to understand that birch was an ancestor, and felt the timeless wisdom of my explorations. Since fall was just unfolding I looked forward to listening more to the indwelling wisdom of trees.

By late September summer had faded, but temperatures soared without a drop of rain in site. My body longed for rain as did the plant and animal kingdoms about me. The grasses were so dry they had grayed; there was brittleness to the landscape. Rain, when it came, would bring everything back to greenness and vibrancy. I looked forward to that first storm when life would be renewed.

Body, mind spirit needed moisture. Creativity needed the waters of source to inspire. Writing had become my daily ritual, but I still would doubt and question myself. I felt that the deeper I went into my true self, the more aware I became of fear, and the fear was based in the need to "get it right." I was afraid to share from deep inside, afraid to open, afraid to break the rules, afraid of being judged. While I became more adventuresome in painting, I was still unable to write without hiding.

It took me awhile to honor the truth that I truly wanted to write a book. Taking my writing more and more seriously were big steps toward challenging the old order of things. I had begun writing in a journal format, but making the work interesting to readers was another step. To know myself I had to take risks, to speak my truth I had to water the dried streams.

It was late one day in October when I heard the first rains arrive. I felt delight and relief. They seemed overdue, but in fact they were on time. I felt happy. It was in the wee hours of the morning that I woke to hear the patter of raindrops. It sounded like a steady downpour. I rolled over and fell asleep, anticipating the fresh smells of morning. I woke early and crawled from beneath my comforter, happy to see it was still raining. A walk in the rain sounded like fun, but my body argued to stay warm and snug indoors. Celebration won out.

I dressed and headed for my favorite sanctuary, Bartholomew Park. The park had indeed become a haven for me over the previous year. A deeper relationship with my essential self had come from deepening my relationship with nature. I recalled Mary Oliver, the poet, who speaks of her woodland sanctuary. Since childhood I had found safety roaming the woods and spending time with parsley shoots in the winter greenhouse. It is sad to think how our world has changed; it is not safe for most children to roam the byways of streams and woods. But then parents can walk with them. For me the world in the woods was, as Mary Oliver has said, an "antidote to confusion."

I felt grateful as I drove to the park and considered the gift of time I had. Just taking off for a morning walk was a luxury, I knew. The park was empty. I headed immediately for the hiking trail, buttoning my coat around me and pulling on my beige knit cap. I began to have second thoughts, for the rain was blowing in thin sheets from the north. However, the wild weather felt refreshing. My eyes drank in the subtle yellows and golds of the grape leaves. A frog or two croaked their delight.

As I reached the top of the path, I breathed in the delicious smell of damp leaves and grasses. The rain had knocked leaves from the California oaks, scattering a tossed blanket of rust under the bare branches. I walked farther up the path to see that the dry streambeds had already absorbed the rain, but here and there water gathered in pockets and puddles. I felt relief in my body and the delight in the change. As I turned around I caught site of the bright green mosses on the rotted stumps and sides of oaks. One cameo of beauty after another turned my head.

On my way back I gathered a few leaves and acorns. Before closing the gate behind me I gathered a few leaves and acorns to take home to my altar.

Once home I gathered firewood. I carried my nature treasures to the altar table and dropped the wood on the hearth. I crumpled paper and stacked some kindling on top. A strike of the match and a few pinecones left from last year served as an instant fire. Once the fire was going I added the larger logs. At last it was roaring, and I sat musing.

I picked up my nature journal. I used colored pencils to draw the mosses and oaks. My sketches included a branch with oak leaves, a rough looking acorn and the glorious green yellow of the mosses. It felt good to see the world through my drawing. I had to quiet the critic who jumped to judge my rough sketches. I decided I would work again tomorrow on my drawing, and set my attention to warming myself by the fire.

On such a rainy day, soup was a necessity. My love of soup is well known. It is comforting and nurturing. Soups can be made in a short time or a long time. Pre-made stocks help to create the short versions. The long versions include homemade stocks. The stock will carry the flavor of whatever you put in it, whether vegetable, fish, beef, or chicken. My habit is to prepare a vegetable stock while I cook other things. Put water to boil, cut vegetables of your choice—except for broccoli—add herbs of the moment and salt and pepper. This is my version. It takes about an hour for the stock to be ready. It is easy to freeze.

Hunger caught up with me, so I took stock from the freezer, put it to heat while I cut carrots and parsnips, then added parsley and thyme.

The ingredients were simple, but they satisfied my longings for root vegetables. I cut everything in a small dice so it would cook quickly. I sautéed leeks, added everything to the stock to cook, and before long lunch was ready.

Celtic Remembering

After lunch I sat musing on Halloween, which was only a week away. Since the Day of the Dead is a celebration in many cultures, I wanted to make an altar. It was natural for me to think of ancestors as I wove the mystery of those who went before me into my present life. The fall was an anniversary of my aunt's and my father's passing. My Scotch grandmother also came to mind. She was a good storyteller, and I was happy to find in Mara's book the term "ceilidh," which meant "visit" in Gaelic.

In the tradition of my Scottish ancestors the "ceilidh" house was a place where people would gather to share stories and music. This relationship with their neighbors and with the sacred in their everyday lives ran parallel to the sacred cycle of nature. They celebrated and prayed at these gatherings, as well as in nature at springs, wells, and meadows, and at bonfires. Such rituals wove my ancestors to the stories written in earth's resources. A deep part of my being missed a structure and container for such sharing, for a life that had a sacred center holds meaning.

So how did I want to celebrate the season? I wanted to set up an altar with photographs, candles, and nature treasures. To connect to the season I turned to Mara Freeman's writing for inspiration. The Celtic word for the season of Halloween is "Samhain," which signals the dark half of the year. The word comes from two words meaning "summer's end." In the seventh century the word was Christianized and called All Saints' Day, which honored the souls of the holy dead. Samhain, it is said, was a feast held at Tara, a hill and gathering place in County Mead, the celebration of the Celtic new year. It was also the time of the year when the four provincial kings came to sit with the high king. Lighting fires at this time of the year was part of the feasting and celebration.

As I read about these ancient traditions, what I resonated with most were the bonfires built to mark the festivals. I felt the appeal of islands of light for the upcoming winter darkness. The idea of a bonfire was appealing, but impractical where I lived. So instead I planned a gathering at my home to include a dinner by the fire. I also asked everyone to bring a story about an ancestor. My Celtic past became a mentor and, I looked to it to show me new ways to be present to the great spiral of life.

My Halloween gathering was a success. I made a large pot of Carrot Ginger Soup, baked corn bread, and roasted some almonds and cashews. Susan brought persimmon cake to finish our meal. We shared stories and ate as we sat around the fire. The experience fulfilled my longing for a ceilidh house, a place to gather and tell stories.

I felt happy to create celebration in my life and reflected on the process of owning my truths. Each step brought me closer to a hearth life, a life I could call my own. Seeking home in myself asked me to honor self. I began to respect my love of silence.

As a woman I had played many roles. I felt the pressure of the modern-day expectation to become a successful everything—mother, partner, worker, creator, communicator, cook, designer, friend. I had tried very hard to be many things, and "tried" is the key word here. *Not-good-enough* drove me. Listening to our deepest promptings grows us closer to our soul path. I knew I could give up the old pleasing ways to claim wholeness.

I looked forward as usual to Friday's farmers market for inspiration and fall bounty. I put on my blue parka and wrapped my warm grey scarf around my neck. The wind had picked up that morning.

When I arrived at the market I felt warmed. My eyes landed on a table piled high with pomegranates and persimmons. I choose a few bright-skinned pomegranates and a rosy yellow squash, and headed home.

As I walked, I mused on the pomegranates, so mysterious to me. I loved the beauty of their crimson skin, cracked open to reveal white flesh and dark crimson seeds. I recalled the connection between pomegranate seeds and Persephone. In a nutshell, the Persephone myth tells of her imprisonment in the underworld after Hades tricked her into eating pomegranate seeds. Who could refuse the juicy red seeds? Persephone finally returned home from the underworld to her grieving mother, Demeter, but was required to remain part of the year in the underworld. The myths of the descent of Persephone mirrored our seasonal cycles.

As the dark underworld of winter approached, there was always the promise of her return in the spring.

Many of us feel like Persephone, abducted from our known life by similar circumstances. Fear had been a large of part of my life. It can be easy to be drawn in and down to the victim's narrative, and lose the bigger picture. When I arrived home I took out the pomegranates. When I cut one open its tough outer skin released the juices, I felt the aliveness of the startling redness. The seeds initiated me into the dark. How could I carry these seeds from the dark into the light?

Fall Recipe

Fall is the time of the year that I enjoy making stews with fresh vegetables and beans. This stew is adapted from my favorite cookbook *Field of Greens* by Annie Somerville.

Variation on North African Vegetable Stew

1-can organic chickpeas, drained
1 16-ounce can of tomatoes with juice, chopped
1 quart of vegetable or chicken stock
1 medium onion cut into pieces
2 tablespoons grated fresh ginger
3 large yellow Finn potatoes cut into chunks
1 large carrot cut into large chunks
1 red bell pepper cut into thin strips
1 small head of cauliflower, broken into florets
1 teaspoon turmeric
1 tablespoon chopped fresh mint
1 tablespoon chopped cilantro
1/8 teaspoon of cayenne pepper
Salt and pepper to taste

Heat the olive oil in a skillet and add the onion and a pinch of salt. Sauté the onion until it is translucent, then add the ginger, cayenne and turmeric. Stir and cook for a minute. Add ½ cup of vegetable stock, potatoes and the carrots. Cover and simmer for 10 minutes, then add peppers, cover and cook for 5 minutes. Next add the cauliflower florets and cook uncovered until heated through. Then add the canned tomatoes and chickpeas and a cup of vegetable broth. Cook for 20 minutes. Add salt and pepper. Right before serving, stir in the fresh herbs. Annie suggests you serve it over a bed of couscous. (See her recipe.)

Year Two

Winter

"I cannot live without my life."

—Emily Brontë

Thanksgivings

November turned cold and the last warm days of fall faded. The dark spiral pulled me inside. I felt happy as the cold and dark kept me under the covers. The year before, I had moved into the dark of the winter season in fear. I felt the breath of possibilities, and there was less resistance to turning inward. Looking forward to the winter's rest, I felt a knowing. Annie Dillard gave me a beautiful metaphor: "I bloom indoors like a forced forsythia; I come in to go out."

Each season became my guide; I listened for the resonant tone of its offerings. I felt contented knowing my shelves were stocked, the wood piled high.

One morning at 5 a.m., I crawled out from under the covers to pull on my warm socks and old flannel robe. A few coals remained in the woodstove from the night before. I stirred them into flame with the fireplace poker, glad I had carried the wood indoors the evening before. A few pieces of kindling and a log produced a good fire, and the crackling heat soon comforted me.

I still felt a looming conflict about the upcoming Thanksgiving and Christmas holidays. Would I face the holidays alone, without family again? Turning sixty the previous March had put my life in a new perspective. I was no longer midlife. That phrase, "turning sixty," had a certain ring to it, and the challenges of change lay ahead. The vulnerabilities of being single and older seemed overwhelming. I continued to feel the weight of my culture's aging myths, and a responsibility to write a new mythology.

I put the kettle on to boil, rinsed the teapot, put out honey, and chose a cup. My hand reached for my white mug with two smiling cats. It was no accident I had chosen that cup. It was a gift from my son Matt, and I felt the emptiness of distance as I held it in my hand. The coming holidays were already stirring feelings otherwise buried in my fast-paced life. Matt had left California just over a year before. He went to join his cousin in a business on the east coast and made his home in a loft apartment in the center of Philadelphia.

I returned to the fire with my black tea. Memories of a visit we'd had the previous year floated around like the steam rising from my cup.

It was a cool Sunday morning when Matt and I made the half-hour drive from Philadelphia to my hometown in southern New Jersey, and the streets of my childhood. Haddonfield, a small Quaker town with cobblestone sidewalks, remained a place that time had forgotten. It had been more than eight years since the last time I'd driven into town, the day my sister and I had sadly taken my mom to a nursing home. Memories of my mother's failing health and Alzheimer's disease hit me hard as Matt and I drove past my old house.

Its sandstone façade stood as staunch as I remembered. The spacious lawn and mature trees framing it were its saving grace; nature softened the formality. I was surprised to see the house for sale again. My family had sold it many years before, and I had always wondered who had moved in. Part of me was tempted to go up to the porch and ring the doorbell. Who made it their home now? We drove to the end of the lane and then turned the car back toward town.

Although it was Sunday, with most of the shops in Haddonfield closed, I'd hoped my favorite bakery would be open. McClintock's made the best cinnamon buns, a treat well known to me as a child. My son and I stopped and, yes, it was open. We bought several buns and walked along enjoying their sticky cinnamonness, a taste of childhood Sunday breakfasts. Small memories bring unexpected joy.

As we wandered up the street, I saw how little the town had changed. The colonial brick and wood buildings, the town clock, all kept a similar cadence. The old Camden Trust Bank and the Presbyterian Church held court on the same block; a flower shop had replaced the dry cleaners I'd known as a child. As we headed toward the train station, I noticed a new store. We crossed the street and found a cooking store, and went inside. Matt and I share the joy of cooking and an interest in skillets and whisks. We roamed the aisles while he told me about his new restaurant discoveries in Philadelphia.

As we were leaving the store, Matt stopped and grabbed a mug with smiling cats. He knew I loved cats. "Here, Mom, take this back as a memento," he said.

The cup, the memories, and a candle brightened the gray of my solitary winter morning. I promised myself I would call Matt the next day. I included Dawn, his partner, in my thoughts. They had met at work and were living together. A new cat named Tiger shared their loft. I had met Dawn during my last visit, and seen their growing commitment. No news yet of their future plans. Marriage? Perhaps children?

I took another sip of tea and smiled down at the cats on my mug. My sadness loosened while the ritual of tea and fire nurtured me. I still had the holidays to consider, but I turned to the seeds of my dreams and creativity. A hearth moment.

What did I long for in the cycle of winter and the year to come?

Winter invited dreaming, that was sure. It was a time for mystery and magic. I reminded myself to buy a new dream notebook. I loved recording and then reviewing my dreams. As I made the mental note, I remembered that the women's dream circle would meet that week. Judy had organized our group based on Connie Kaplan's work on dreams. I had initially resisted the structure, but felt differently after reading Kaplan's book *The Woman's Book of Dreams*. I had read other books about dreaming, but this one gave me new perspective. She wrote, "The womb is the dreaming organ."

I appreciated Kaplan's thoughts on menopause, which included the suggestion that "menopausal women disconnect from the moon and reconnect to the sun (hot flashes)," which means their "relationship with fire becomes stronger." Her suggestion resonated with my own experience. I needed fire to warm me, fire to grow me, and fire to transform my life. I was grateful to women like Connie Kaplan who became guides when the unknown was the only known. Honoring the gifts of the feminine arts—like intuition and the dream life—became more important than ever.

I also felt a new appreciation for women's groups where I could share, validate, and appreciate dreaming. I looked forward to the dream group's monthly meeting. It could provide an outer hearth for my journey of solitude.

I carried my thoughts into the shower, and then dressed in warm clothes for a walk up Castle Road to the park.

The ritual of walking was a precious resource, a harmonizing reminder. Castle Road, which led to Bartholomew Park, still held the essence of the Sonoma I'd known in the late sixties. The homes I passed—an adobe, another with a white picket fence, Villa Rosa—were like old friends. At the end of Castle Road I stopped briefly to admire the old stone posts and the dark, heavy wrought-iron gates that towered above me. I walked through the gates into the park, past rows of grape vines and crabapple trees, then uphill to the walking path.

I felt the gifts of wildness embrace me when I reached the redwood stairs. As I wandered down the path, I spied the smooth, silvery heads of mushrooms. For nearly a month I had watched the mushrooms' progress as they pushed out of the earth, shook off the dirt, and bloomed into the moist air. Their unseen root system, called mycelium, began as a single thread. Thousands of mushrooms related by one root system could cover a hundred miles or more. The mushrooms I saw on the surface were only part of the story.

I also belonged to an unseen web that, like the world of the mushrooms, was much greater than it appeared on the surface. I would have passed by these beauties the year before. I would have been in too much of a hurry, too busy thinking, not aware of my feet, let alone the earth below my feet. Hurrying had become disrespectful. I did not want to be disrespectful of myself or of the world. I stopped and breathed deeply, happy I had chosen to slow down and deepen my life. Mother Nature reminded me to root myself in her soil.

At the bottom of the stairs, where the stream and redwoods met, I remembered my fall the year before. That fall had given me a wake-up call to be present to my body, to my womb of knowing, to my body's knowing the deep feminine. I smiled as I recalled Kaplan's quote about the "womb as a dreaming organ." The womb was unseen like the mycelium. The human body could root itself in many kinds of wombs. The womb of nature was my favorite. Glad for the fresh air and the walking, I recognized how they helped to move the sadness that lingered inside. Walking moved my breath as well as my stagnant feelings.

A loamy dampness pervaded the woods and drew me down, down into the ground of life. I felt deep satisfaction as I dropped into the hilly terrain at the end of my walk and headed back down Castle Road toward home. It was a workday, so I showered and prepared myself for cooking.

Before beginning work, I picked up Kaplan's book again. She referred to something she called the "dream weave," an invisible field. "It is the invisible pattern of connection that links human thought to form, and possibility to awareness. Physicist Fritjof Capra calls it the web of life consisting of networks within networks of increasing possibility."

My mind wandered back to the mushrooms and the presence of the web that joined them. The thought of these invisible connecting webs was mind-boggling.

But work called, so I tied my apron around my waist and set to cooking.

I'd felt moments of conflict since I had returned to cooking part-time. However, I was grateful for the craft and joy of creating for others. I would deliver eight dinners that night, each a three-course meal of an entrée, a salad, and a dessert.

As I turned recipe cards and foraged in cookbooks, I landed on a stew. The recipe for African Bean Stew came from Annie Somerville's cookbook *Fields of Greens*, one of my favorite sources of vegetarian recipes. This stew always offered an exploration in creativity. I often used her recipe as a base, then expanded or deleted, varying it with seasonal vegetables as Annie suggested. I called it "Variations on the Theme of North African Vegetable Stew."

I had not planned ahead enough to soak and cook the chickpeas the recipe called for, so I pulled several cans from the cupboard. I always chose brands that use only organic ingredients, which assured me no mystery ingredients were hidden within. I began chopping vegetables into large chunks, then mixed the fragrant aromas of turmeric and cinnamon, with sweet peppers, onions, cauliflower, zucchini, and tomatoes. I sautéed the vegetables.

As I returned to the familiar tasks of my cooking business, I felt old habits creeping in. My habit of hurrying to get to the end product created anxiety. I remedied this by stopping for a moment, walking away from the stove, and reconnecting to my joy—another chance to slow down, savor, and learn presence. I finished cooking the vegetables, making sure they remained crisp, not overcooked. Soon the squash began to fill the kitchen with its rich, dense fragrance, reminding me it was time to take it from the oven.

Over years of cooking, my whole body had learned to sense the absolutely right moment to add the thyme, or take the pumpkin bread from the oven. There were a thousand and one other acquired bits of kitchen wisdom written in my body. It was easy to take this knowing for granted, so easy to overlook this everyday life-wisdom. But it was indeed a source and network of body wisdom. That simple awareness reclaimed the sacredness of the day.

Once the squash cooled, I cut it into chunks and added it to the stew. I tasted the mixture and corrected the spices, adding a hint of my curry spice mélange. The ingredients bubbled and simmered a few more minutes. I switched off the heat and let the pot cool on the stove. The fragrance of the stew enticed me, so I took a bowl from the shelf and filled it for myself.

I seldom ate after cooking, for I usually felt full. After so much tasting, chopping, and sensing, I actually felt as if I had eaten. But there was more to it than that. I often forgot to give myself a serving. Was it guilt? Was it, "Hey, that's for the guests," or, "There won't be enough for the others"? Or was it even, "I don't count"? The subject of women and food, especially single women and food, could fill volumes. Over the years, I've tried again and again to make peace with my passion and my struggle.

Serving and preparing meals for others was familiar and comfortable for me. However preparing food with care for myself was another matter. Yes, the learning to care for and nourish myself was a process. But on that winter morning, after my year of learning to be present with myself, I consciously served myself a generous portion of delicious stew.

When I finished my lunch, I set back to work washing fresh greens and cutting apples and fennel for a salad. I prepared a dressing of shallots, orange juice, rice vinegar, and olive oil, bottled it, and set it on the table. Dessert consisted of pears poached in pomegranate juice with cloves and a cinnamon stick. I packaged the meals and put them in the refrigerator for delivery later that afternoon.

Thanksgiving came upon me unexpectedly. I had made no plans, and somehow felt okay about it. As the frantic pace of the holiday season grew around me, I wanted to slow and deepen. It could be exhausting to buy into the fracas. The joys of holiday decorating, buying gifts, baking, and sharing meals could also turn into back pain, headaches, and anxiety. I wondered how I could stop overdoing and retain what was best about the season. I wanted to keep the joy and celebration and reject the false standard that more was better.

What would this year's holidays bring?

A couple of days later, I ran into the pothole of my food issues when I sat enjoying a bowl of rice pudding made from leftover basmati rice. It must have been more than thirty years since I had tasted the comforting creaminess and sweetness of rice pudding. I popped a raisin into my mouth and slowly finished the bowl. It felt good to nourish myself with small pleasures. But as I swallowed the last morsel the food police rang her siren, stop you are eating fat-rich food. The intensity of the finger-pointing over this modest pleasure shocked me. I just wanted to enjoy food. Why such a battle?

Women's food and body issues still hounded me; they seemed like guardians at the gate of enjoyment. I knew other women shared my struggle. With sadness, I examined the old patterns of restricting and withholding pleasure from myself. My inner food police had less of a hold on me than they'd had a year earlier. But I had put on several inches around my waist, and I wavered in my acceptance of my new shape.

The holidays provided a perfect opportunity to challenge the old myths and laws about restriction and guilt. The answer lay in finding a balance, but to reach it meant giving myself a second helping instead of saying no.

I felt happier and more nourished in celebrating the bounty of my life. I had become more willing to receive and nourish imagination, body, and mind. Receiving life instead of controlling it was another quest.

Winter's rain and colder weather kept me indoors for a few more days. Still, I wanted to take flight, rather than stay present. Meeting myself in darker eddies was always a push-pull experience. The sun dropped below the hills early in the evening; morning ground fog followed. I remembered the Celtic suggestion that the fire of summer could be brought indoors for comfort. I loved this metaphor of bringing the fire of the sun inside and using it to light fires in home's hearth. I was slowly learning to do this in more ways than one. Bringing fire to my life meant tending to the inner fires. The season of winter was a perfect time of the year to stoke the fires of my heart and creativity. Tending these fires in the dark time helped new creations to gestate.

Thanksgiving week arrived and I began to feel the aloneness of being single. I planned a last minute get-together with a few other single women I knew. We put together a simple menu and planned it for early in the afternoon.

Thanksgiving week also included celebrating Matt's birthday; he would turn thirty-two. As mothers everywhere do, I stood back with amazement to watch the turn of child to adult, boy to man.

Matt was born on a crisp November day. I laughed remembering my pre-labor activities. Around six that cold evening, I craved a hot fudge sundae. In 1973, Sonoma didn't have an ice cream store open past five. So my husband and my mother-in-law, Jenny, and I made the twenty-minute drive from Sonoma to Baskin-Robbins in Napa. The short trip fulfilled a classic pregnant woman's desire. We entered the ice cream shop and ordered our desserts. Just moments after our ice cream arrived, I bent over the table with a fierce labor pain. A flurry of activity followed, including scooping our sundaes into to-go containers and speeding home.

Five hours later, Matthew Hayden's perfect fresh face, lively and awake—and perhaps lured by the promise of ice cream—came into the world. He was ready to live fully, and continued to teach me about the joy of life.

These and other memories of him reminded me to celebrate, to light candles and fires, to bring light into my life. I felt the dampened and darkened hearth of winter warmed again with emotion. Making time to feel my aloneness, to feel the missing embers, took presence. The gray winter days provided a special challenge to my feminine sensitivities and my fears of the dark holes of depression.

Thanksgiving Day arrived bright and sunny. It turned warm, so my friend Rose and several others set our table outside. The day began with Rose leading us in a song called "Bountiful." For me the song was the highlight of the day. We parted later with full hearts. As I returned home I recalled the previous Thanksgiving and the impact of my emotional opening. I was grateful for life's flow.

Birch and Pine

The day after Thanksgiving, the sun's rays beamed through the living room window and settled on the pinecones and acorns resting on my nature table. I longed for a Christmas tree, but it was too early in the season for the tree lot to be open.

What to do? What beauty and inspiration could I bring into my home for winter?

I recalled a magazine photo of a birch branch standing in a living room and accenting an antique table; my eye had recorded the beauty. Why not bring a birch branch into the house? I loved the unique whiteness of birch bark. The tree's name originated from the Old High German word "birch," which meant "shining white." I also loved its black diamond-shaped markings and feathery branches. The birches so common in my New Jersey childhood felt like my ancestors.

I remembered my favorite florist in town, Ann Appleman. Perhaps she could find what I wanted in San Francisco's flower market. I called the shop and Ann picked up the phone. "Yes," she said, "I will look next Tuesday after the holidays." I looked forward to picking the branch up and wondered where I would put it. I didn't know what size branch she might find.

I considered how else to create a hearthful home during the winter season. It was raining as I set some fresh leeks to sautéing. Rain streaked the windowpanes, and the crackling fire harmonized with the sound of water dripping from the porch roof. I loved the hearth feeling of being indoors during rains. Last year had been very dry, and I hoped enough storms would bless California that winter. Water tables always caused great concern in our state, since we grew more than half of the nation's fruits, vegetables, and nuts.

Thanksgiving had reminded me to continue to give thanks. Here was something I felt gratitude for—the element of water. Earlier in the week I had read an article on the questionable sources of bottled water. Water was easy to take for granted, but since I was learning to give gratitude more regularly, I acknowledged the gift of its presence. Water makes up seventy five percent of our planet; water is life. We've learned it's healthy to drink eight glasses of water a day, and after long summers without rain, the Sonoma valley welcomes every drop as winter deepens.

I pondered the gifts of water in my life. Both bathing and swimming were important to my body, because those acts kept me balanced. Yes, I felt grateful for water.

I returned to the stove to finish the potato and leek soup I had started. Making soup in winter was a comfort, as was caring for the quality of my life. I wanted to bring this caring to the world I lived in. Honoring the elements of my planet would be another step. How could I bring this awareness into my daily life?

I always enjoyed seeing bowls filled with water and floating flowers. It would be no stretch to simply have a bowl of water on my altar to remind me to give gratitude each day. I searched the kitchen for a bowl and found a glass one on the bottom shelf. I remembered a small bag of shells stuffed in the hall cabinet where I kept fabric scraps, odd buttons, and handmade papers. I took the bowl, put the shells in the bottom, and filled it with water.

My water came from a well on the property. The Sonoma valley had abundant water resources, and in fact had many hot springs. But water concerns continued to grow as new homes and vineyards were built, and many solutions were considered. It was up to me to take steps to conserve. I would not take water for granted.

As I placed the bowl on the altar I realized the table didn't display the bowl to its best effect. I looked around for a better spot. I took the bowl, walked around the room, and placed the bowl near the hearth. The firelight caught the glass, and the shells sparkled. I felt pleasure in this small change and the action of giving thanks, and said another prayer of gratitude. Moments later Sula uncurled herself from the couch, came to the bowl, and drank. I laughed. Sula had confirmed her pleasure in water on the hearth.

The following Wednesday I headed to the flower shop to pick up the birch branch. It would feel good to bring my love of nature into my home. Ann had found a graceful nine-foot branch. As long as it was, we had to arrange for a truck to deliver it. I felt like a kid anticipating a new bike.

The branch was clearly too tall for my low-ceilinged abode. I remembered feeling cramped when I first moved into the house, but somehow the cave-like space had become a natural setting for my inner quest. After all, caves had been the first cathedrals, natural settings for spiritual retreat and places of worship. My own cave had beautiful rough-cut redwood beams. I considered hanging the branch horizontally. By the time it arrived later that day, I had made a plan.

A beam did seem the likely place to carry the size and weight of the branch. A spot over the dining room table looked like the perfect location. I removed the cloth I had draped there months ago, then spaced and hammered four small nails into the rough redwood. I picked up the branch and hung it across the nails. The branch fit perfectly. I stood back and admired it with great pleasure, for it looked exactly as I had imagined it. The white bark stood out against the dark redwood beam, with the feathery branches creating a canopy above the table. It would bring light into the dark solitude of winter. Having the tree in my home made it a more inspiring sanctuary. This limb had been severed from the mother tree, and I gave respect to the spirit of Birch.

I walked the neighborhood with new eyes after that, as I turned to trees with more awareness. I was building a relationship with my world and with the wisdom of trees. I wanted to experience trees as living members of our planetary community. This was a step toward evolving my consciousness and helping to turn around the disconnection of my human family. That disconnection had put us where we were, in a great global crisis. I hoped small steps would help.

Once the branch was in place, I began to anticipate the joy of hunting for a Christmas tree. I was in the holiday decorating spirit, and looked forward to the pine scent, to trimming the branches, and to wrapping the tree with white lights.

Over the years, most of my Christmas ornaments had been broken or lost. I decided that year I would decorate my tree, using elements of nature. I smiled, considering the possibilities.

Although it was a sunny day, I wrapped a red scarf around my neck and imagined it was snowing. Snowfalls had been regular events at Christmastime when I was a child. But it had been years since I had seen a white Christmas anywhere but in my imagination.

I drove to the tree lot close to the square on Spain Street. I crunched across the pine-needled field, inhaling the sharp, delicious smells. It took several turns down aisles of trees before I chose mine. It was less than perfect, but interesting. It was about five feet high with a quirky top. The man in charge of the lot smiled as he helped me wiggle the tree into my Honda trunk. I tied the trunk down and headed home. I placed the tree in water and left it outside intent on waiting for the perfect moment to bring it indoors.

A cold snap finally inspired me to bring the tree indoors. It felt like Christmas. Once the tree was secure in its holder I set about weaving the small white lights. Next I added a nest, a cranberry swag, pinecones, and dried apples on threads. The tree needed something sparkly. I remembered some gold brocade ribbon I had found in my Aunt Annie's sewing box. It felt good to weave her into my holiday.

As the days grew shorter, I felt the darkness covering me like a blanket. My body felt the womb quality of the darkness, and I reminded myself that the dark held potential. I revisited my fears of depression in winter. I began turning on the lights of the Christmas tree around dusk.

While the dark descended one evening in December, I sat with the sparkle of the tree lights. My lamps were off, and I just sat enjoying the magic of the lights and the dark. I picked up my journal and decided to head to bed. I walked to my bedroom in the dark; it was fun to feel my way along the hallway. As I settled into my bed, I recalled walking in the dark as a young mother.

It was the winter of 1973, and Matt was two months old. I stayed at home to care for our baby while Stephen ran the business we owned in Sonoma. Our shop closed at five; he returned home shortly thereafter. I'd prepare dinners, but we had agreed that I would have an hour to take a daily run. Our home was nestled in the quiet Lovall Valley, and the road curved in a large loop, a perfect place to walk. As the winter days grew short, and the sun dipped behind the hills before Stephen arrived home, I considered giving up my evening outing. I loved running, but I had never run in the dark. The experience would be a new adventure.

The first few nights I found myself running in darkness, I felt afraid, so I carried a flashlight. Mostly I feared tripping and falling. While I knew the road well, I still had to breathe deeply and challenge myself. At first I walked and then ran slowly. Soon I learned to feel for the uphill grades, the bumps in the pavement. I gained confidence.

I began listening for the sounds of the night, including the goats, sheep, and turkeys who shared the valley with us. I especially loved the goats. I could hear the rustle of their movements as they made their way through the grasses. After running the first part of the loop, I'd start around the curve to the next half. I'd smell the eucalyptus tree where the road climbed slightly uphill. In time, I learned to smell my place on the road. It became a fascinating exercise, and eventually I gave up my flashlight. My progress felt exhilarating.

Once I became accustomed to the feeling of the dark, I sometimes lost all sense of my body except for my legs and the sound of my shoes on the pavement. Learning to run in the dark was an experience of trust and surrender.

As I looked back on those dark-time walks from the comfort of my bed, I realized they had given me a way to confront my fears of the mystery, the unknown. I felt inspired to walk in the dark again.

And so I began—but not without reservations. I knew it was less safe to walk alone in the dark than it had been in 1973. The world had changed. I needed to factor in the reality, or at least the potential, of violence. It felt significant, though, that as a young woman I'd run the end of Lovall Valley Road. Now, years later, I walked the road at its beginning, in town. I wouldn't let my fears stop me.

I stepped outside with my flashlight and headed up the road. Once on Lovall Valley I walked on the soft earth of the vineyard. A car approached, its lights shining in my eyes. The same headlights illuminated two young bucks on the left side of the road ahead. They waited to cross the road. When the car passed, I could hear them dance across the asphalt. The young deer seemed to invite surprise and mystery. I walked on, remembering the small rack of horns I'd found in Bartholomew Park last January. Each year the buck sheds his antlers, and then regenerates them. I had considered the rack a gift at the time.

On my return home, I searched for the image of an antlered figure I had seen in Celtic mythology books. Cernunnos was a god of fertility and regeneration. His figure appeared on the silver cauldron called the Gunstrap Cauldron. I found him mentioned in *Rekindling the Celtic*

Spirit, where Mara Freeman wrote, "He embodies the wisdom of deep communion with the wildness of the world."

Would I be able to give up my old fears and receive the gifts of the dark? I felt a need for the wildness to disengage me from the tethers of intellect, control, and fear. Besides, I loved the beauty I found when I ventured outward.

I picked up the book again after tea and ginger cookies and continued to read. I had become increasingly interested in the equinox and solstice. Winter solstice was drawing near. I saw an interesting picture as I turned a page. It was a small drawing of Ireland's Newgrange, a large earthen structure located just north of Dublin. Built around 3200 B.C., it was called a "passage tomb." The photo revealed a large, dome-like structure covered on the lower sides with quartz. It had been built to receive the rays of the sun's rays on winter solstice, to light the passage and inner chamber. According to legend, the kings of Ireland had been buried at the ancient site. Another myth holds that the mound was the home of a race of Irish supernatural beings called the "Tuathe de Danann."

I imagined the dark entrance of my own womb, an inner chamber being inspired and regenerated by the light of source. In that moment I knew that Ireland would someday become a pilgrimage destination for me. Yes, the seeds of winter were resting in wait.

Even though I was working during the holiday season, I wanted to enjoy the quality of each day. The winter rains continued to invite rich stews, meat loaves, savory soups, and casseroles. I felt the pull to join the frantic Christmas whirl, but I kept my feet on the ground and set limits. I had agreed to cater two open houses for around thirty people each. The parties were a week apart, so there was minimal pressure. I kept the menus simple with fresh foods of the season, pears, cabbages, and a wild rice salad with nuts and cranberries. Rich cheeses and smoked salmon on cucumber complemented the fruits and vegetables, as did the roasted candied nuts and a red pepper salsa with breads and crackers. I varied the food a bit for each event, but I always made sure to add touches of greens, berries, and fresh herbs to create beauty. Food was my favorite gift of love.

At winter solstice I prepared an impromptu event for a few friends at the labyrinth to celebrate the dark and the return of light. I set small votive candles about the edge of the labyrinth to light our way. At the end of the gathering we drank cider together, having walked in the dark and embraced the season. Afterward I sat for a moment under the trees to enjoy the beauty of the candles, the smell of the redwoods, and the velvet darkness surrounding me.

Several days after the solstice event, I felt a torrent of anger and despair. I walked the edge of rage that day, shouting, my emotions triggered by a conversation with a friend about food. Rage was uncomfortable. While food was the trigger for my feelings, the dark of the year had also brought up strong emotions. I felt out of control. I knew it was important to let go of my "nice girl" inhibitions and honor my feelings. Old comfort zones kept me trapped.

I let myself rant and rave, not even knowing the origin of my anger. I knew much of it came from being treated as though I was invisible, from not being seen for who I was. I needed to feel and see myself. After I climbed into the shower to let go even more. Finally I felt more peaceful and aware. There was a way out of the tangle of emotions, and that was to meet them. I needed to stay out of self-judgment. My need to control could be replaced by setting my boundaries. Through this dark passage I would spiral into the light.

The holidays raised so many different feelings, and as a single woman I felt particularly vulnerable to them. It was natural to feel alone and have bouts of loneliness, especially with Matt living far away. However, the more I ran past the truth of myself, the more unseen I felt. Just bringing up those emotions raised my feelings of guilt, as if it were somehow unacceptable to speak emotional truths during the holidays. Wasn't I supposed to be singing tra-la-la?

It became obvious that my ground of self was still forming. For several days I sat listening to my inner voices and challenging the lies. I still doubted myself. Was I antisocial? No, I was just who I was. Giving myself respect was what I needed. Difference was to be celebrated; I wanted to include all my quirks and uniqueness. I was like my Christmas tree with its quirky top.

Like so many women I had made a habit of exhausting myself during the holidays, trying to do it all. It was an important time of the year to find balance. I was in the process of understanding what balance was for me. One thing was clear, I loved giving to others. I'd always felt that a gift of time spent for another was an important gift. I decided to make biscotti as Christmas presents for friends.

My holiday open houses went smoothly, except for the tray of cucumbers which dropped on the way to the car. I was happy when the last food was delivered and I could put up my feet. I learned to listen to my body and her needs more closely, including the frequent resting and rubbing of sore feet.

With my events over, I relaxed and looked forward to Christmas. Friends had invited me to join them for dinner at Piatti's, a restaurant on Sonoma's square.

Christmas day arrived misty and cold. I opened presents sent by family and friends, giving myself the gift of enjoying the day. My walk just before sunset set a tone. The vineyards felt stark and bare. The dried vines faded into a misty fog. The pink cast of a setting sun bathed the vineyard in a rosy blush. The rough sturdy grapes climbed rusted metal supports. The colors of the metal, the last rays of light, and the vines blended into a different quality of beauty. The bare vines would be pruned soon, to wait dormant until the spring. Feeling peaceful and inspired by the sunset, I looked west to a fog bank that covered the hills just as the sun dropped below the clouds. I turned toward home to get dressed for Christmas dinner.

The evening had grown colder, so we all arrived at the restaurant bundled up and rosy-cheeked. Ten of us gathered for a mellow and warming holiday meal.

New Year's Eve had always felt to me like a forced holiday. I rarely went out. When friends called to ask what I was doing for New Year's Eve, I'd always tell them I was a "stay-at-home." That year was no exception. With each call I gave a similar response.

As New Year's Eve came and went, I looked ahead with anticipation.

Winter Recipe

Winter is a wonderful time for brisk walks. When we return home and the early dark cocoons the world, soup is the best thing to come home to.

Curried Sweet Potato Black Bean Soup

1 baked sweet potato
1 cup cooked black beans
2 teaspoons curry powder (or chili powder)
1/2 medium red pepper
1/2 baking potato sliced thin
2 tablespoons chopped parsley (Italian)
1/2 cup chopped fresh spinach
1 1/2 cups apple juice

Bake sweet potato until soft. Scoop out of skin and put into blender with apple juice. Blend until smooth and creamy. Add a bit of olive oil to pan and sauté chopped red pepper. (Add onion or green pepper if you like.) Add thinly sliced potatoes and apple juice to cover the bottom of pan so potatoes don't burn. Cook until potatoes are soft. Add sweet potato broth, curry powder and beans to pan. Cook till flavors marry. Chop spinach and parsley and add at last minute so that the greens stay fresh and do not overcook. Add salt, more spice and more juice as needed. Sit in you favorite chair and enjoy the evening or afternoon.

Spring

"The light of nature tells us that life is pilgrimage, a journey to the stars along the Milky Way, her hero-path, a voyage across the great water in which she is a ship, rudder and guiding star."

—Ian Beggs

Spring sat in the wings waiting to go on stage while January continued to weave its traditional grayness around me. I felt a germinating change and found rest in the darkened days. Winter gave me shelter, and the darkness helped me let go of the known, as the gray misty mornings and slanting rains softened and veiled the external world. But the more I let go of false strengths and masks, the more I needed the transformative fires of the hearth, a feminine place to birth my essential self. Growing deeper into my life meant listening and invoking the nurturing Mother. The fire offered its light and warmth and the oak at the west window provided a shelter.

Winter in its restful state lies quiet, but the unseen spirit of form remains. I have had hints of that unseen world, but never made time to explore it. Natural to my thinking was fear and doubt of the unseen. Still, winter and spring interwove in the Sonoma valley.

The rich green grasses and bright yellows of bursting mustard reminded me to open while winter suggested quiet..

I felt a resistance to letting go of winter for I loved the sheltered inwardness with the rains and misty afternoons. Perhaps it was the draw of my Irish genes beckoning me to the love of the mists. I'd never liked transitions, their challenges, the standing in the in-between, the space between knowing and not knowing. But then if the mystery of life was to unfold me I needed to let go.

As I opened toward spring I found I needed tools for bridging the inner and outer life. I was slowly learning how to honor the transitions, not to hurry myself along to the next thing. One needs a cocoon to molt unconscious habits and choose new life.

So this Irish heritage of mine…what in fact was important about it? How could I bring the inner quest and aging into a circle of growth and inspiration? My past had driven me underground into hiding. But as I choose to explore my inner life I saw that as many I hide my true selves out of fear. In my youth I had been taught to be silent, to never challenge or speak out. So hiding also invited silence.

The pattern of feeling safe in non-confrontation had grown out of fear of humiliation. I watched how I retreated, making myself smaller and smaller. My throat tightened; I felt safe in the quiet. My words, my creative flow were easily stifled. At times I became invisible even to myself, or at best seen and not heard. I behaved as I'd been trained in those early years—I covered my truth, put on a good face, showed no emotion. As a child, a freshly pressed dress and shiny patent leather shoes helped carry off the charade. It is common to catch myself buying a new sweater or pair of shoes to dress up the feelings of inadequacy, fear, or vulnerability. But I was growing…steadily growing. Patience was key.

I put on a pot of tea, and stopped to appreciate the sounds of a roving band of raucous crows and a chorus of happy frogs, all contented with the grayness of the day. While I could not translate their cries or croaking, it was somehow clear to me that they were not protesting the mists. I took my glass mug off the shelf. I liked the clear view it gave me. Lemongrass tea would brighten my spirit. My musings over the winter months had offered both sweetness and treasures. Cinnamon toast was one of those precious memories, so I gathered a crunchy piece of whole grain bread, a generous slathering of butter, and a quick mix of cinnamon and sugar. Sweetness was somehow something I rarely gave myself. High time. Sweet, sour, salty, and spicy—I needed it all.

Dark/Light

I sat with my tea and listened to the rain as it hit the porch, then dropped off into a trough running to the ground below. The water sat in puddles, slowly absorbed into the earth. I turned to my writing, wanting to grow more present to the black, white, and grey of winter life. I was also curious about my relationship with darkness.

I recalled a woman I had met the summer before. Maryanna Bock had taught a class on color one weekend. Initially I was drawn to the class because of my interest in watercolor painting. But the class was so much more. Maryanna spoke of the spirit of color, and the bridge between light and dark. I was fascinated. I went to my files and took out her writings. "Darkness needs to be known by the soul," she said. I paused to feel her words resonate through my body. She continued, "One must feel its impulse to fill, to hold, to contain. It gathers all things within itself, secreting all that it holds. Darkness warms and nurtures all that she enfolds in her intimate embrace. The mother darkness, the womb of all of Life is the container that holds the inner and outer universe as it comes into being gathering all things within itself." Her words sunk deep into my body. Yes, Mother Darkness holds the universe as it gathers "all things within itself." I felt the Mother in that and recalled my dream of turning toward the vast dark night, the dream handed to me by my female ancestors. This recognition of the need for a womb, for the resting and receiving was absent in the culture of my modern world. My own longing for darkness became more palpable. I began to understand the processes I had drawn to myself over the year.

It was several days later when I noticed the bright splash of early mustard announcing the arrival of spring, I returned to Maryanna Bock's words about light: "Light delineates, focuses and individuates the diversity found within the Darkness. As the Light radiates it encounters the infinite potential held with the darkness. It illuminates a singular creation, birthing it in the present moment." The light illuminated my potential, but the potential darkness was where I gestated. I felt darkness hold me and urge me to continue my quest to essence.

The gentle movements of wind chimes from a neighbor's porch brought me back from my reading. I listened attentively to the gentle clapping of metal. The sun peeked though the clouds and a hawk announced his hunt. I felt grateful to Maryanna for giving me the bridge of words. I was seeking inclusiveness, and her words helped me see how deepening my relationship with the seasons connected me to the earth's cycles. Wasn't I, as John O'Donohue suggested in his book *Anam Cara* "a daughter of both light and dark?" I went back to Maryanna's words inviting me to feel "the light which had retained its kinship with darkness." Hold both the light and the dark!

St. Bridgid's Crepes

As the end of January drew near I began to think about creating a ritual to honor the turning of the season which begins in Sonoma early. The mustard heralds the shift and though we still had winter rain ahead there is an air of spring about. I was happy to discover the Celtic calendar celebrates cross-quarter days, which are the midpoints between the solstices and equinoxes. February 1, called St. Bridgid's Day or Imbolc is celebrated as the beginning of spring. In Christian tradition the holiday is called Candlemas. Here in the U.S. it is Groundhog Day.

I was excited to reencounter St. Brigid, for her tradition was part of my heritage. Her holiday and reverence is considered to be a bridge between the old and the new. As it is celebrated in modern times, Imbolc honors both the pagan goddess Brigid and the Christian abbess St. Bridgid who was born in 453 BC. The goddess Brigid is said to be the goddess of a fire, of inspiration. She became another aspect of the divine feminine to reverence. Her connection to fire and inspiration were natural to my love of hearth. As was her association with the wisdom of sacred waters. Many wells in Ireland were dedicated to her, and I hoped to visit them someday. There were many weavings of traditions about the Abbess St. Brigid who founded an abbey in Kildare, Ireland. I was fascinated by the fact that her church, constructed in the sixth century, included a fire temple; her nuns tended its sacred flame. She felt like kin, and I hoped that this ancient woman would help me rekindle a deeper soul life.

What did she mean to me, a woman of the twenty-first century? I looked for ties and found information online about a modern day order of Brigidine nuns who had established Solas Bridhe a Celtic Christain community center. The members of the community continue to teach through ritual, prayer, and their commitment to social justice How would I bring the traditions of Imbolc into my modern life?

Since St. Brigid's holiday was celebrated at the beginning of February, I felt the gift of ritual as a way to bridge winter and spring. It was customary on her holiday to make offerings, which might include making barley cakes or placing cloth out on a bush for her to bless. Another option and tradition was to gather rushes to weave a cross, and hang it high in the house to win her protection.

Food celebration was the most natural place for me to turn to create a ceremony. First I lit a candle. Then I set about planning a meal, but I felt thirsty and warmed milk milk with honey. I made an offering of milk to St, Brigid. After all Imbolc also called Oimelc means "ewes milk." Spring was the time of the year when lambs were born, and lactating time for the mother sheep. Milk, nurturance, and new life were all woven into the holiday. I gave Sula equal opportunity to celebrate with her own bowl of milk.

Refreshed and satisfied, I began to consider the Irish tradition of barley cakes as food offerings. I didn't have barley flour, but I could compromise with amaranth flour. What could I make with it? Crepes were a favorite of mine, so I made batter in the blender with milk, eggs, flour, and butter. When the batter set up for a few minutes I heated the skillet and poured in a cupful. I swirled, waited for the crepe to cook a minute, and then flipped it over. I made two plates of crepes, and while they sizzled in the pan I set a beautiful table. When all was done I sat down for my ritual. I added a dollop of orange marmalade on top of each crepe and offered them up to St. Brigid. The crepes were delicious. I prayed to St. Brigid for her guidance.

In a striking note of synchronicity, I later learned that crepes were traditionally served in France during Candlemas, which honored Mother Mary. I was glad I had chosen a food close to the heart of the feminine. I also found it intriguing that I had unknowingly incorporated a tradition from France, a place I dearly loved, in my celebration of my Irish ancestress. I realized that all faces of the feminine were interrelated. After I enjoyed the ritual meal dedicated to St. Bridgid I longed for a walk.

I packed up my watercolors and paper and then made the short drive to Bartholomew Park. I reversed my usual path and began my walk where I usually ended it. Turning right out of the parking lot I crossed the blacktop and headed for the gazebo area, which was lush with green grass. I walked the narrow path and crossed the small bridge where the stream was still rushing with winter rains. Leaving the formal garden area, I headed past the wild and graceful stand of bamboo. Moments later I clicked open the gate to a landscape filled with heavy overgrowth and tall trees.

The path narrowed as I skirted the overgrown blackberries and inhaled the scent of bay. I settled myself at a wooden bench tucked away at the end of the path. The air was fresh, and warmer than I had expected. A steep hill rose in front of me just on the other side of a creek. It was covered with bay and manzanita, and my favorite redwoods towered directly in front of me above the meandering stream. The cold bubbling waters enchanted me, while the sun filtered through from above. I sat taking in the earthy scents, feeling connected to the sprouting of new life.

I filled my cup with water from the stream, picked up my brush, and stroked a swath of color across the paper. I hesitated in that first stroke—the voices of "getting it right" wanted to interfere. But I did not heed what the voices said. I began with green, a color I didn't usually use, then stroked a yellow, floated a gold wash on top, and then played with other colors, just doing whatever I wanted to do, following no rules, making no plan. It wasn't easy to allow myself to just play. But wasn't this a time for exploring? I wanted to bring more color into my life. Why should I be afraid of color?

As I sat immersing myself in the colors on my paper and in the cool green of the grotto, and listening to the gentle rush of water over rock and pebbles, I felt received. I realized that this was a new experience for me, to feel received just for being, for sitting and dabbing a bit of color on the page —no product, no list, no achievement.

Black Madonnas

Weeks later I sat with thoughts of a spring pilgrimage. For years I had wanted to travel to Ireland and yet the timing didn't feel right. I considered France and my desire to deepen my relationship with the Black Madonnas. Chartres had only given me a taste of the power and presence of these important feminine icons. I knew that pilgrimage enhanced my body wisdom and empowered spiritual growth.

I picked up Ian Beggs' book again, *The Cult of the Black Madonna*. I turned to the map of the locations of the Black Madonna sites to visit, and was immediately drawn to them. I recalled a summer trip I had taken several years before to attend a painting workshop in a small village close to Toulouse. A French woman who was part of our group told me there was a Black Madonna in a cathedral in Toulouse. I couldn't take the time to see her then, but I knew I would return sometime. Was that time drawing near? I knew that my own healing and growth would be inspired by such a journey, and my relationship with the feminine would be deepened.

Perhaps that was exactly what I needed. Something inside felt out of balance. In truth, the world in general felt out of balance. The United States was involved in a war again and I felt anxious about travel and sad for our planet. When were we going to resolve our problems without violence? And yet, my past visits to France had laid some groundwork for travel, so that I felt more at ease there than most any other foreign country. I decided to at least explore the possibilities.

The next day I called my travel guru, Scott. I was surprised when he told me that if I left before April 10 I could travel roundtrip for five hundred dollars. The itinerary could be left open regarding destinations while I was there, and I could even change return dates for a small fee. I trusted Scott to find the right hotel accommodations, so I only needed to buy the plane ticket and a rail pass. In the end I decided to visit three Black Madonna's and leave open the possibility for two more if I chose.

Finally a rough sketch was in place. I asked Carol to care for Sula, and made a mental note to pack lightly, a lesson I'd learned from my trip the year before. I realized how vulnerable I felt to travel alone when the world was in a state of unrest. But I knew I wanted to go. I also knew that the mystery would guide me, and that the seeds of sacred travel would sprout as spring unfolded.

Spring Recipe

This Spring recipe mirrors the fresh new life bursting about in nature. The light meal is delicious and fresh tasting.

Spring Rice and Vegetables

1 cup of Basmati white or brown rice
1-pound medium asparagus

1 cup shelled English peas
2 tablespoons lemon juice
½ cup extra-virgin olive oil
½ cup thinly sliced basil leaves
½ cup lentils
1 tablespoon grated lemon zest
2 tablespoons of chopped parsley
Salt and pepper to taste

Bring a large pot of salted water to a boil. Add rice, stir, and lower heat to simmer. Cook for about 20 minutes, stirring occasionally Do the same for the lentils, they will only take 15 minutes. Break off the tough ends of the asparagus and place in a sauté pan with enough water to just cover the stalks. Remove the asparagus while still crunchy and transfer to a bowl of ice water to stop the cooking process. Remove from water and cool on platter. Put the lemon juice in a small bowl with salt and pepper. Gradually whisk in the olive oil. In a large bowl, combine the cooled rice, asparagus, peas, basil, and parsley and lemon zest. Toss with your hands to blend. Adjust seasonings as needed. To add more punch to the salad add olives of any variety.

Pilgrimage II: The Black Madonnas

Aboard my flight to Paris I felt challenged, for I was no longer a beginner on this path of pilgrimage. Here I was on my way to France, one of my favorite places on earth. And yet I felt afraid as I clipped myself into my seat. The trip would ask me to go to a new edge of myself—no dancing the light fantastic among sunflower fields. At the same time I was not walking barefoot up steep slopes to do penance. The journey I anticipated would be something in between. My soul invited me to grow down to meet her.

So all I could do in my seat aboard Flight 297 was to expect the best. I had an open itinerary, a rail pass, and hotel rooms reserved. I'd put a rough sketch in place, to arrive and leave from Toulouse. The rest would be revealed as I made my pilgrimage. If it unfolded as I hoped, I would travel to four Black Madonna sites.

I fell asleep for a short time, then woke and took the book *Descent to the Goddess*, by Sylvia Perera, from my travel bag. I wanted to revisit her interpretation of the ancient Sumerian myth of the journey of Inanna, the queen of heaven who descends to her dark sister in the underground. I had first read the book just after I'd left my marriage in the late 'eighties. A friend in Sonoma had taught a class on the myth, and it was particularly meaningful for me at that time in my life. Divorce was a life passage, a descent into some very dark places, and the class been a source of support. I appreciated Perera's Jungian skill in developing the psychological symbolism, and in bringing a modern woman's perspective to the ancient texts.

I didn't have to read far to find treasure, or in Perrera's words "renewal in a feminine source-ground." The ground she spoke of was recovered by descending into the inner worlds. I was embarking on an outward journey, it was true, but I knew that pilgrimage meant turning to my own inner world to face the unknown. Inanna's journey reminded me that I had to give up the old clothing and heavenly ideals to become whole. While I wasn't giving up jewels and clothing, I was removing old story garments that weighed me down and ruled my life.

Who was the goddess Inanna? Perrera suggested that some aspects of her represent "the liminal intermediate regions, and energies that cannot be contained or made certain and secure." She explained that Innana symbolizes "consciousness of transitions and borders, places of intersections and crossings over that which implies creativity and change." I found comfort in her language, for it is often in crisis and crossings that we change.

Perrera's book helped me remember to turn to the compassion of Innana to help me on this journey. I felt wrapped in the dark, the airplane a cocoon speeding through space. I stood up to stretch for a moment, noting a few lights sparking the darkness. I turned to my journal to explore further, to examine the facts of my human journey to heal relationships, specifically reconciliation with the feminine. It was clear that my healing process was following a spiral.

Like so many woman of my generation I felt un-mothered. I had begun this journey out of that complexity of longing. Over the previous year I had needed to speak and feel that longing, to look again at the patterns. Through the course of my life I had compounded those un-mothered aspects of myself by disassociating from the feminine self. For a long time I simply had not liked women. Out of a desire for approval from my father I had taken on his values, which overshadowed my feminine psyche. I became acceptable and efficient and goal oriented, always striving to be better. I sought to please and identify with men. But at last I had recognized the need to leave that way of coping behind. I was in search of my own truth, my own life and inspiration.

When I landed in Paris I felt exhausted, but a coffee helped me negotiate Charles de Gaulle Airport for my connecting flight to Toulouse. Once at my gate I sat with unwanted heavy inner baggage. I was acutely aware of a shroud of fear hovering over my happy anticipation of my journey. I felt confused, because normally a trip to France held nothing but joy for me. I couldn't quite pinpoint the source of my fear. Aging contributed to my feeling vulnerable and uncomfortable traveling alone, something I had noted the previous year. I also felt uneasy because since the United States had attacked Iraq just months before, and still occupied it.

Anxious or not, I was in France, and there was no going back—at least not yet. I felt better knowing I was closer to my destination in Toulouse, just an hour away.

Once in Toulouse I made my way through Blagnac airport and walked out into the warm evening air to hail a taxi. I had lost track of time, but once settled in the taxi I located myself as a passenger in rush-hour traffic. My legs felt like wooden pegs from sitting so long on the planes. I felt a bit dislocated as the driver negotiated several streets and large boulevards, but I was also happy to be there. I hadn't remembered Toulouse being so large, but it is a modern city noted for its aerospace industry and for the pink of its brick buildings.

The driver finally turned left onto a quay running alongside a canal. He stopped at a corner where a small hotel stood looking over the water. It seemed charming. I happily paid the driver, swung my bag from the cab, and walked inside.

A vase of lilies at the main desk cheered me as I checked in. The intimate quality of the hotel felt nurturing. I took the elevator to the fourth floor, pleased to find that my room was tucked away on the top floor. Blues and yellows decorated the room with a very French accent. I felt exhausted but happy, jumped into the shower, and threw on lighter clothes, ready to go downstairs and enjoy French food. I rummaged through my suitcase for my hairbrush, and realized I had forgotten it. I changed my plans, deciding I had better search for a pharmacy so that I could buy a brush before dinner. Wild, wet hair or not, I took the stairs quickly to the ground floor and felt better as soon as I stepped out into the fresh air. So many hours cooped up in airplanes and airports had unnerved me.

The concierge had told me I could find shops and a bakery close by. I walked two short blocks, took a left turn, and saw a line of shops of all sorts. I found a hair salon, a bakery, an antique store, and a hardware shop.

People rushed past me, all of them seemingly headed to the same place. I looked in the direction of the flow and saw a large train station across the canal. Scott, my travel agent, had done his homework. I remembered he told me he had found a hotel close to the station. I'd only be staying in Toulouse for two days, so I was glad to have transport close by. I began to unwind as I walked, feeling a part of the wave of humanity.

I looked for a pharmacy to buy the brush I needed, so I wouldn't sit down for dinner looking like a crazy American with flyaway hair. French women were always so impeccably dressed and coifed; I would have felt horribly embarrassed if I weren't so tired. Several blocks along I found *le pharmacie*, I identified it by the green cross on the sign. Perhaps because French pharmacies don't carry the world of merchandise American drug stores often do, their efficiency comforts me. I felt calm and collected in the store's cool order. While I had trouble remembering the French word for "brush," I finally saw what I wanted on a shelf. I paid the clerk and left the shop.

I had not seen a restaurant and felt too tired for any more searching that night, so I stopped in the *boulangerie* on the way back to my hotel. I saw sandwiches stacked under glass and ended up buying brie and ham on baguette. What could be more French? Food and brush in hand, I headed back to the hotel.

Back in my room, I took a warm Perrier from the mini bar next to the bed, flung open the windows, and looked out. The scent of the sycamore trees blooming greeted me. I settled into a blue upholstered chair and looked around my room. Beside the chair sat a small dark wood desk. Old wallpaper printed with yellow flowers and violets covered the walls.

The bedspread's heavy blue fabric matched the chair. I admired a small yellow pillow that I hadn't noticed before. A dresser with an antique mirror above it sat across from the bed, and an elaborate wall sconce marginally lit the room. The bathroom had an enormous tub with a showerhead. As I bit into my crunchy French baguette and brie, I felt joy. France is the ultimate palette-pleaser for me.

The chatter of people running along the sidewalk below my window subsided and quiet descended. I could hear the wail of police sirens, the closing of a door nearby. As dusk fell, I leaned out the window to see streetlights reflecting on the canal, and a barge painted violet. As stars began to appear in the sky, I listened to the soothing sound of water lapping at the edges of the canal. I returned to my chair and realized my eyes refused to remain open any longer. Eight o'clock, time to sleep.

I awoke at two. All was quiet except for the sounds of the canal and someone playing an accordion in the distance. So uniquely French, I thought. Well, I had traveled for change to inspire and renew me.

I picked up my journal to record a dream. My memory of it was sketchy, but I remembered three women. One of them was saying, "This is the place for women to receive gold." An interesting dream! What did gold mean here? Was it a reference to a psychological property? Perhaps my journey would reveal more. I knew an alchemist's hand took lead and turned it into gold. I hoped my fears would be transformed.

I felt like a foreigner, while normally France felt like home. I had to face my truth. I had felt the fear of leaving home, the fear of the unknown. But in the past I had not allowed myself the emotion. If I looked clearly at my life I had felt fear for many years before I began my quest. Travel amplified that feeling. Learning to feel safe in the world continued to be part of a lifelong healing process. I also knew that it had taken a long time to allow those feelings to rise to the surface. The specifics of my journey asked me to feel the fear and do it anyway. I was in France to visit the Black Madonnas, and to listen to the dark in me.

As I wrote about my sense of feeling like a stranger, of feeling alone and touching some of the old patterns I had ignored in the past. I saw that travel was shining a light for me into my darkness. I needed to leave home to learn more; I needed to bear the tension of the emotions of fear. I said a prayer to the angels who accompanied me. While traveling felt groundless to me, I knew that true groundedness meant being at home in myself. I knew that with each step I took to recover trust in myself, I would come closer to gaining that ground of self. Fear stopped me from opening to love, from being present from truth. But fear didn't have to run the show.

I finally fell back to sleep having brought light into the darkness of fear.

I awoke at 8:30 to a brisk April morning. My time-warped body longed to continue sleeping, but my curiosity wouldn't let me linger under the covers. I hurried to dress and walk downstairs for breakfast.

Sun filtered through the hotel's front windows into the small dining room on the first floor. A laden buffet table against the back wall awaited the guests, with inviting little tables scattered around the room. Only a few businessmen lingered over their coffee. As I headed for the buffet I spied the small pots of yogurt and accompanying bowl of rough brown sugar typical of a French breakfast. My stomach felt uneasy and I knew I'd best abstain from French coffee that morning, so I served myself tea and added a crunchy roll with some strawberry jam on the side. I felt an immediate sense of renewal, and wondered what the day would hold.

The weather had shifted; a wind had begun blowing. I gathered my raincoat and map and headed outside. A lighthearted *bonjour* from the desk clerk, Monique, followed me out the door. I turned to wave my reply.

Over breakfast, I had decided to just wander through Toulouse and save my visit to the Black Madonna for the next day. I knew I never felt settled in a foreign country until the second day. Sometimes it took longer. Walking the streets and getting to know Toulouse would help.

I walked toward the center of town, stopping once to ask for directions. I was surprised to notice I didn't like asking for help. I realized that it made me more vulnerable. I pointed a finger on my map, and a *s'il vous plaît* got me what I needed.

I wandered past modern business high-rises on my way to the older part of town. In fifteen minutes I came to beautiful cobblestone alleys that inspired my sense of adventure, and connected me once again to the France I loved. As people bustled past me I began to enjoy the mixture of architectures, much of it Romanesque. I looked up and noticed the double street signs, one giving the French name and the other written in Occitan, the traditional language of the Languedoc region, which mixes Spanish and French. I wandered into various squares and reached Place Wilson, with its cafés and brasseries that reminded me of Paris. I stopped to peer into patisseries, those wonderful bakeries that specialize in pastries and sweets.

Soon I came upon a large stone church with a nondescript exterior. I entered the high-ceilinged sanctuary through a side door. While well lit, the building, with its marble and stone floors, felt cold. Unlike the warmth of the stained glass and inspiring architecture of Chartres, I didn't find beauty in its walls. I looked around briefly for a statue of Mary. When I spotted her I halted, surprised. The statue seemed metallic in its whiteness, as cold and distancing as the plain and uninviting building. I turned and left right away, returning to the outdoors where the wind had grown cold. I gathered my raincoat around me and shivered in a kind of shock. A Mary icon had rarely turned me away before, but this Madonna somehow mirrored the cold winds that blew inside me and through the city.

I suddenly felt like a stranger in France. But those feelings were not just about being far from home. I had felt like a stranger in my own family, even a stranger in my own life because I had become estranged from myself. I stood there on the Toulouse sidewalk feeling overwhelmed. I decided to go and sit down in a small park across the street.

As I sat watching the leaves blowing across the bright green grass, I saw that being a stranger had been a theme throughout my life. It was frightening to face it. I knew my travel would help me turn the lead to gold.

I pulled my coat around me against the wind as I walked back across the street Somehow I felt less vulnerable, and walking helped reinvigorate me. I was hungry and it was lunchtime. I came upon an indoor market with fresh produce, local cheeses, jams, nuts, and fish. Smells of sharp cheeses and fresh leeks sparked my inner cook, as the everyday task of food shopping helped me feel more in my body. I bought some of my favorites, fresh goat cheese and strawberries, a natural in spring but also a reminder of my trip to Chartres two years earlier. I also purchased a French string bags I loved so much. Putting my purchases in my new bag, I wandered outside and found a great addition to my lunch. A crepe maker was busy at work in front of the store, and reminded me of the joy I'd felt making crepes for Imbolc in February. I bought a wonderfully gooey chocolate creation.

I wanted to sit down to enjoy my lunch, and remembered another park closer to the hotel. I found my way back to it and sat down on a bench near a lovely fountain. Water arched off the rounded flower-shaped stone and fell down into a shallow basin. The water wriggled and splashed, pooled and settled. It felt grounding to sit and enjoy my cheese and berries. The water calmed me, and I began to relax and enjoy Toulouse.

After lunch I walked back to the hotel and settled in for a long soak in the tub. I reflected on the feeling of never being at home in myself, of the anxiety that had run my life. Claiming my authentic self gave me balance, but the more difficult task was to honor that self. I was learning what gave my life balance.

How could I feel safe anywhere in the world when I couldn't honor who I was?

At last France began to feel like home again. After my bath, I stayed in for the rest of the day. I took a long nap, read, and wrote. I felt guilty not going out and seeing the sights, but wasn't this part of just being myself?

The next morning I awoke to an overcast sky. I parted the shutters to see a play of clouds and dark sky as the trees lining the canal tossed their leaves about. My plan for the day was to visit the Black Madonna. It was important I visit her, since the next morning I would head to Carcassonne and Limoux by train. I dressed in warm pants with a heavy sweater and carried my new backpack. It looked as though rain was imminent, so I took my umbrella. An undercurrent of anxiety still clouded my travel. But the sacred called.

I took the stairs down to the first floor and pushed the edge of my confidence. I used my rough French to ask Monique for directions to L'Eglise de la Daurade, the church that housed the Black Madonna. I showed her the map and she pointed out the way.

Once on my way I found it was easier to follow her directions than I'd feared, and I began to feel more confident as I walked across the larger boulevards and small streets. When I reached the sidewalk that paralleled Garonne River, I turned right. I knew I was getting close to the Daurade. I had read that the church was on the famous pilgrimage road called Santiago de Compostela, which traverses France and ends in western Spain at what legend says is the tomb of the Apostle James. Realizing I was traveling part of the Compostela road excited me, and I felt the strength and pleasure of being part of a long line of pilgrims. It pleased me to be a twenty-first century American woman walking in the steps of thousands of other seekers, in a different time and world but still the same in the ways that mattered.

I felt goose bumps as I approached L' Eglise de la Daurade. Like Chartres, this church had old roots. It was originally the site of an oracle, and had many incarnations over the centuries. It held a special fascination for me because the name was derived from "*deaurata,*" which means "covered in gold." Historians say the mosaics that once adorned the church were backed in gold leaf. I recalled my dream about finding gold in Toulouse. The metaphor seemed to be appearing everywhere.

Scholars say the church was built on the remains of a Roman temple. It was used as a monastery in the ninth century, and as a church when a Romanesque nave was built in the seventeenth century. I'd also learned that a statue of Pallas Athena had been discovered and recovered close by. It had been 109 B.C. when a lake was drained. Representations of Athena show her in black.

The exterior of the church looked like a Roman temple, complete with Roman columns. As I walked along the sidewalk, with the river water tumbling and churning just below, I searched for an entrance. I didn't see the traditionally elaborate entryway with carved angels or arched doorways that I'd expected. I finally asked a passing priest, who pointed me to a simple door. I entered and walked along an unassuming hallway, then stepped into the dark of the sanctuary.

Deep inside the church, an ancient, cavernous space suddenly enveloped me. Perhaps it was my mood that made it so dark. The windows offered little light from the grey sky beyond. The darkness inside was enormous, and I was but a small dot within it. The ancient blackness seeped up through the floor with an earthen power bigger than life.

I felt relieved to see the Black Madonna shining out from a sanctuary to the left of the altar. Even from a distance, I could see a large vase of Easter lilies that felt like a beam of light. I was surprised to hear children's voices. As my eyes adjusted to the dark, I saw a group of schoolchildren and more lilies. Indeed, the Black Madonna was watching over all her children and families. A pregnant woman sat at the edge of a group, helping with the youngsters. It delighted me to see the celebration, with the woman bringing the birthing symbol to life. The church was not separate from nature, from home, from death.

I sat and listened in the dark as the children began a hymn in preparation for the Easter celebration. It was not lost on me that I had arrived at a time when the spiritual season pointed the way to death and resurrection, to birth, death, and rebirth. I was reminded of the Black Madonna's association with Isis

I finally turned to walk closer to the altar. As I approached, the Black Madonna felt imposing, bigger than life. Her face was as black as night, and I felt as though I was gazing into the face of a gypsy. I felt the contrast between how disempowered I had felt all my life and the living presence of this goddess—Mary, Isis, Inanna. In that moment I walked deep into the reality of feminine source. I felt some fear as I looked into her jet-black face, which peered out above a light blue dress. Curiously, I had not felt the same about the Black Madonnas at Chartres. Letting myself have different experiences felt important. Growing a relationship with Her many faces took time.

Suddenly my early Protestant church teachings began to register a complaint. Wasn't God only a Father? While I moved deeper into relationship with the face of the divine feminine, the old voices challenged the "She" of a spiritual icon. The children's preparations for Easter may have made this even more poignant. I knew in my heart of hearts that I was not rejecting my early Christian teachings but rather struggling to integrate the feminine aspects of God, in fact to enlarge my concept of the divine. I gazed again at her face, her beauty, and felt included, taken into her arms.

My eyes moved down to the stone altar filled with flowers and candles. Plaques painted with lilies and other vegetation surrounded the statue. I remembered that the lily is one of Mary's flowers, as well as a flower of Isis. I'd never seen images of plants surround a Black Madonna before, and it gave this one a stronger connection with nature than I'd felt with those at Chartres. There was no denial of nature in the Daurade.

I turned again to the earthen altar and its weighted solidity. Its heaviness and presence helped me to finally feel a sense of peace; the agitation of feeling alone had left me. It took entering this cavernous space for me to realize that a return to the darkness, like a burial, meant a new birth, a new understanding. In the presence of the dark Mother I felt a certain peace that pointed me to some original source. I felt deeply connected as I sat at the altar; I felt a sweetness born of presence. The Black Madonna was being unearthed in me. She was not a concept, but a dynamic relationship I could feel.

The Madonna I was encountering was herself a foreigner. She had been recovered in grottos, under the earth, in trees, as well as in sanctuaries. I, too, felt caught in the grottos of the earth as I looked deep into my own darkness, and also into my personal courage. In spite of my fear, I had risked taking the journey to meet her. I felt a sense of strength and pride knowing I had chosen to engage my internal warrior.

The children's voices continued to resound through the church. I lit a candle for friends, for myself, for those who suffered in the war, then turned and walked across the church, feeling complete. At the end of the long hall I met a nun who held the door open as I left. Her simple gesture warmed me.

A light rain began to fall as I left the church. Several hours had passed.

I decided to return the way I had come, and walked back along the river toward the main boulevard. At the corner I stopped and peered into a small restaurant. It looked warm and inviting. I bent my head under the canopy to look at the menu in the window, and the French onion soup listed at the top of the page immediately hooked me. Inside, a waiter took my coat and led me to a small table by the window. The restaurant was a perfect balance to the church, lively and bustling.

As I studied the menu, I noticed a regional dish called *bouef au daube*. Similar to a beef stew, the dish cooks over slow heat for a long time in a tightly-lidded earthenware pot called a *daubiere* in Provençal. Well, no question about my food choices—soup, salad, and a *daube*. After ordering, I listened with pleasure to the chatter of the other patrons, and the lilt and beauty of the French language. My steaming soup arrived, the cheese was melted to perfection over the thick broth swimming with onions. I felt happy and more myself as I dipped the first bit of crunchy French bread into my soup. For that moment, I felt a respite in the deliciousness of life. The beef entrée was delicious, too, and fed my need for hearth and home. A fresh salad with mustard vinaigrette completed my meal. Finishing with a coffee, my body finally felt nourished. I was glad I had chosen to stop and give myself the joy of fine food.

I headed outside and continued my walk along the river, and turned at the bridge. The rain eased a bit, and I closed my umbrella to let the soft showers fall on me as I walked to the hotel. I felt nourished in all ways as I clicked open the door to my hotel room. I rubbed my hair dry, then curled up on the bed and fell asleep to the sound of a renewing rain.

I didn't wake until late in the afternoon. I walked to the station to research departure times to Carcassonne, and soon found the information I needed. There was a train leaving in the morning at eleven. At the same time I checked departure times for Rocamadour. As I walked back to the hotel I suddenly changed my mind and decided to forgo my trip to Carcassonne. I felt a stronger call to ahead to Rocamadour.

My pilgrimage along the feminine path did require travel into the unknown. No destination addiction allowed; I had to learn to allow the process to unfold, and not over-plan each step. I knew that the deeper I traveled inside myself, the more I had to meet the unknown. But old habits were hard to change. I needed to begin again and again to be flexible and listen. The ancient holy places of the world also lay deep inside, and my wanderings were journeys to these sites within myself. I had to become an archeologist, recovering my gold from the buried layers of life.

I also knew I was not alone on the journey. I imagined my angels with me and the love and support of my female ancestors.

The next morning I phoned ahead to change my hotel reservations, then packed my bags and boarded the train to Rocamadour. I felt nervous again, filled with self-doubt. *Can I do it myself? Am I safe?* I stopped my thinking, dropped into the soft comfort of my seat, and began to enjoy the train ride. I actually fell asleep and woke not far from the Saint Denis station where I needed to transfer. Nervously I stepped out into the fresh air of the small mountain town. I had no idea where I was. All I knew was that I was supposed to board a bus. I scanned the area for a clue about where or how, and finally saw the bus sitting off to the side of the road not far from the station.

There were just two other passengers on the forty-minute ride over beautiful hillsides with freshly plowed fields. I felt the joy of connecting to the countryside, to nature, far from city life. I felt peaceful as we pulled up to the small and remote Souillac train station, where I would board a train to Rocamadour. It felt good to stand in the late afternoon sun and enjoy the fresh air until the train puffed its way to our station. I found a seat aboard, and sat enjoying the mountain landscape until I arrived at Rocamadour only thirty minutes later.

At the train station I faced another unknown—the use of French phones. I needed to call a taxi. I saw none parked at the station, so I stopped to ask a young Frenchmen waiting on the platform. Thank goodness, he spoke English. He told me his name was Jacques. He explained that he was waiting to pick up someone. Jacques suggested that he drop me off at the top of the hill above the ancient town. He told me there was a path which lead to the medieval site began. I was anxious about the "drop off," not knowing what the walk down the hill into town entailed. Our conversation was cut short as he signaled an elderly nun walking down the platform. We introduced ourselves. Soeur Jeanne had come on pilgrimage and was staying in an abbey several miles beyond Rocamadour. Jacques asked her if I could share their car just until the town. She smiled her agreement. I was grateful

Jacques turned the car uphill as we headed out of the train station. We passed a few homes and a restaurant, but were soon back within the vistas of rolling hills. We were all silent on our ride. I felt a bit anxious, while Jeanne sat peacefully with her hands folded. I envied her calm presence. It seemed only moments later that the car suddenly stopped, perched at the top of a steep cliff. I couldn't see a thing, but figured I should get out.

"We are here," Jacques said, smiling.

Once we'd pulled my suitcase from the trunk, I took its handle and rolled it to the side of the road.

He pointed downward and said, "*Sur là.*"

I noted a scruffy, well-worn path that appeared to drop off into some trees. I took a deep breath, waved goodbye to Jacques and Jeanne, and the car sped off, leaving me alone at the side of the road. I couldn't actually see the town itself, but in an act of faith I dragged my luggage behind me and headed downhill to the ancient city.

The switchback path was dark in the forested part of the trail. My anxiety grew, but no sooner had I entered the shadowy dark than the trees opened again into the sunshine. It was indeed a beautiful spring day. As I began to relax, I felt like a true pilgrim, travel worn but happy. The path narrowed as I walked the gentle twists and turns down the hill. I passed lilac bushes and trees sprouting new leaves, and wildflowers growing at the edge of the path. At the bottom of the hill I carefully negotiated rough-hewn rock stairs, and found an arched stone gate with a plaque identifying it as the South Gate. I breathed I sigh of relief, knowing I had arrived. I walked several blocks down the one-street village lined with shops and restaurants.

The exterior of the Hotel Roc was rough stone, it's feeling rustic and simple. That suited my need for a lodging I could call home for a few days. A young Frenchwoman greeted me and assured me my room was available. I stood waiting in the cozy entry, appreciating Scott's taste in hotels.

My room was tucked back in a corner, up a flight of stairs. As I unlocked the door I feared finding a small closet with a bed, but I was delighted to see a spacious room with a skylight and window looking onto a small interior patio. The bed faced the window, and was covered with a worn cotton spread. A beautiful walnut armoire sat to the left on the far wall. I hung up my raincoat and unpacked a skirt, then lay down on the bed. My body began to relax. I noticed small paintings of local landscapes and a picture of an old man with a cane walking up a street. He looked very intent. I checked the clock and saw it was 4:30 pm. I wanted to explore a bit before dinner, so I went back downstairs.

Outside the hotel, I took a right and walked along the narrow cobblestone street lined with small shops, hanging baskets of flowers, and tile roofs. Rocamadour felt ancient, even mystical, yet the tourist shops on its only street drew me in right and left. I realized how much like life it was. We set an intention to follow our dreams, make more time for walks, writing, prayer—and then we get distracted.

I stopped briefly in a few small shops that sold walnuts, foie gras, and souvenirs. Farther down the cobblestone street, I noted a strange sign saying *ascensure*, which indicated an elevator entrance. I realized why when I looked up the steep cliff. Since the houses, hotels, and restaurants were on the street, and the chapels and pilgrim sites were on the steep hill above, an elevator had been installed. I remembered reading that for centuries pilgrims had walked to this Black Madonna by climbing the hundreds of steep steps to the sanctuary. When I considered the elderly and ill people who traveled distances to see her, that climb seemed an unreasonable test. I was neither elderly nor ill, but certainly appreciated having a lift to the top, especially after a long day of travel.

I decided to briefly explore the sanctuaries above. It would feel strange not to go and honor the Black Madonna now that I was so close. I planned to walk the pilgrim stairs the next morning, but for now the elevator seemed the prudent choice. I paid a small fee and then stepped into the elevator with seven other tourists.

The elevator doors opened, and I turned left into a small garden. High walls enclosed me as I entered the Basilica St. Sauveur, a Romanesque church that seemed etched into the rock itself. I had no clue where I was going, but soon enough a crush of about thirty people surrounded me. The stone church and its vaulted arches seemed uninviting, so I let the crowd carry me along, hoping it moved toward the chapel. I followed a large family directly in front of me, and soon we stepped into the smaller, less foreboding space.

I walked to the back where pilgrims were lighting candles and offering prayers, then turned to face the altar. The roughly carved Black Madonna sat there naked, enclosed in a wooden structure, a small temple or sanctuary. Small pews curved to one side. I couldn't tell her size easily, but guessed she was about two feet high and carved out of walnut. I felt drawn to her warm brown color. I felt her power, different from other Black Madonnas. I appreciated the absence of a flowing dress. Around her hung panels of blue fabric with a fleur de lis design. It was a beautiful scene, but the noise and numbers of people in the room were unsettling, so I left.

It was a curious experience to meet this twelfth century face of the mother and then step into a metal elevator of the twenty-first century. Two women from England shared my elevator ride. After pushing a button for the "main floor," we descended through rock and earth, and I felt the momentary weightlessness as we dropped back into the fray of a modern-day afternoon. A light rain began to fall as we stepped off the elevator back out into the cobbled street of Rocamadour. Slowly making my way back to the hotel, I looked forward to the next day when I could visit the Madonna again in quiet.

I turned the key to my room and considered dinner, then decided to skip it since I didn't really feel hungry. I still had a few crackers and juice from my train trip. I felt silly dining on crackers in France, a country known for its superb cuisine. But I didn't feel like eating, so why not honor my body wisdom? It was so easy to fall into judgment about what I *should* be doing. I finally let myself off the hook of "trying to get it right." I affirmed I could eat crackers, take wrong turns, double back, and do exactly what I wanted. Perfection wasn't required; neither was an agenda.

Before sleeping that night I lay with the comforter pulled up and began writing. I felt safe in the hotel, and saw how I wanted to project my fear out into the world. It was easy to name it as a foreigner's discomfort, or to attribute it to the war in Iraq. While I was in fact a foreigner traveling alone, and my country was in fact waging war, I wanted to look more deeply to the fear. I knew that my deepest fears of trusting and allowing only developed when I pushed my comfort zones. I felt good about my travel, and while the journeys to the Black Madonnas held challenges I promised myself I would grow through them.

I woke early the next morning feeling hungry, and remembered that the restaurant just across the street opened early. When I walked out into the morning, the air smelled fresh from the rain that had cleared yesterday's dust from the damp stones beneath my feet. A deep quiet still lingered, because most visitors hadn't risen yet.

I entered the restaurant and chose a table close to the windows so I could enjoy the panoramic view. Layers of colored rock cut timelines across the gorge. Rocamadour sat perched over the Alzou River, and in this spot I felt perched above the world. As I looked over the menu and prepared to order, the sun rose over the cliffs. Pink light seemed to tremble above the rim. The dark from the night before had vanished, and I felt lucky to be exactly where I was. My breakfast arrived quickly. I was starved, and quickly consumed my plate of scrambled eggs with toast and strawberry jam. The good food and strong French coffee left me feeling ready to set out.

After riding the elevator the day before to see the Black Madonna, I knew the pilgrim climb of 216 steps would be a challenge. However, with the sun rising in the sky and the fresh smell of rain, I felt inspired. I could take the steps as slowly as I needed. I set out for the Chapel of Our Lady of Rocamadour. I didn't know what time it opened, but I wasn't concerned. I took pleasure in the slow walk through town, and understood why pilgrims in the past had made time for walking on their spiritual journeys. I headed down the one narrow street, with the gorge to my left and the steep cliff rising to my right. I felt the gentle warmth of the early sun that cast its light on the cobblestones and the cliffs.

Sooner than expected I reached the stairway, which cut its way straight up. I climbed slowly toward the first landing and then to the second. After another thirty steps, I reached a plateau where the steps opened to a narrow alley with a café and a small hotel. The hotel seemed miniature, almost like a dollhouse with its window boxes of purple and white flowers. The few café tables sat empty.

I continued up the walkway, which now switched back and forth as I climbed higher. Almost at the top, I stopped and thought about the centuries of pilgrimage to this site—pilgrims young and old, kings and queens had walked the same path. My reading had taught me about the various incarnations of Rocamadour. It was once the site of a Celtic shrine and a place of reverence for the triple goddess represented by Cybelle. In fact, a Celtic stone altar to Cybelle still rested underneath the current altar to the Black Madonna. I loved following the history back to recover the feminine story.

I rounded the corner and looked out across the courtyard, and at the grey rock rising high above, casting a shadow across the cobblestones. I stopped to rest a moment and catch my breath, aware of my sore thighs and pleased with myself for stretching my body to make the climb. The beautiful clean air and the rocky hills were enchanting, and I breathed deeply. I recognized a feeling of the unseen and invisible sacred. I felt free of my fear, and grateful.

For the first time David Abrams' words "forgetting of the air" made sense to me. His book *Spell of the Sensuous* had been a revelation, and his message was working its way deep inside my body. I saw that I had taken the unseen air and its mystery for granted. The air brushed my skin as I stood high on the steps, yet it was "absent to my eyes." I had been forgetting so much and taking so much for granted. I took another deep breath, and met the mystery of journeys in this remembering of the air. Abrams' words reminded me that our earth and its gifts of life are precious, sacred, to be reverenced.

The rock, the earth, and the very air of the place called me back to the goddess, she who was based in nature. The mother had been given many different names, all of them expressing a different aspect of her. I felt her wrap her earthen arms around me, offering life to me. I was glad I was alone to experience the deep connection. My pilgrimage, while difficult, had repeatedly offered treasures, perhaps the gold called up in my dream. The presence and joy I felt was unique, the kind of experience I could not have imagined when I began my journey. I walked the next step into the courtyard.

The chapel stood to the left. The courtyard was deserted, and I wondered if I'd arrived too early to enter. I climbed the short flight of stairs to the chapel and noticed an older man sitting in its shadows. He was bent over, leaning on a cane, and seemed troubled. Soon after a young caretaker arrived and unlocked the chapel; the elderly Frenchman straightened up and mumbled something in an irritated voice. It seemed the caretaker had arrived late to open the doors.

I entered several moments later, wanting to experience this Black Madonna in a spacious silence unlike yesterday's visit. The Frenchman walked to the rail of her altar and knelt. I felt his deep reverence and surrender. I was grateful for the quiet, a contrast to yesterday's many tourists, and glad I had waited to have a more intimate experience with Her. I sat in the rear of the chapel, taking in the beauty and simplicity of the building with its roughly cut rock walls. The earthy darkness of the church was refreshing, and I thought back to a similar feeling I had had in Toulouse. The darkness held more mystery in Toulouse, but in this small Notre Dame chapel it felt more intimate.

I wondered why the theme of darkness was woven so prominently through my quest. I longed for the beginnings of my journeying, the newness of my initial trip to Chartres where I had first met the Black Madonna. That initial journey had been more gentle and joyful. But then I knew that I had to grow a relationship with the dark, with the mystery, with wisdom. Darkness did not call up an image of evil. It never had. Instead it felt comfortable, and connected me to the deep reservoir of life. Perhaps the title of China Galland's book *Longing for Darkness* had influenced my search. One of Galland's answers says, "One longs for transformation, for a darkness which brings balance, wholeness, integration, wisdom, insight."

I stepped closer to the altar to see this Black Madonna more clearly. Illuminated from above, her dark, roughly carved wooden form sat with power. A filigreed wooden structure enclosed her. The image of mother holding her child on her lap was traditional. She wore a crown. There was presence in her simple carved wooden body. Several small gold plaques were hung on the walls around her, and depicted scenes from daily life. One showed a merchant exchanging goods with a peasant. There was a sense of the Madonna sitting among those images, supporting all life in all settings, holding each of us as we walk our life's path.

I peered through the darkness to examine a small reproduction of a boat hung high on the rock wall to the left of the altar. It was difficult to see, but I could tell it was made of wood and had a blue sail. My reading had taught me that the faithful considered this Black Madonna a protector of sailors. Why she'd been slated to protect sailors from this site so far from the ocean wasn't clear, but it didn't matter. I knew that other Madonnas in other places held similar responsibilities.

The longer I stood taking in her essence, the more I felt sad that her lineage had been written out of the sacred texts. Being in her presence helped me read between the lines and find her mystery. Like the air around me, the mystery was invisible, but I felt its truth and essence. This Madonna was powerful, no-nonsense, and vivid. The carved statue revealed a knowledge that stemmed from the earth, from source.

I went to light a candle, then walked to the rear of the chapel to sit further away and take in the whole. I felt as if I had come home; she became my ancestress. I, who had been seeking wholeness in myself, found a mirror of what I'd been seeking in her presence. I lit a few more candles for my friends and family and for those suffering from the war in Iraq.

Finally, I left the chapel, walking slowly outside. I considered taking the elevator for the descent, but when I looked at the sun shining all around me and realized I wanted to leave the way I had come. I stepped back onto the stairs to begin my walk. Although I'd climbed up with no problem, I quickly found that I feared the steep downward climb. Interesting, I thought, remembering another walk down steep stairs on a camping trip with my son's seventh-grade class. We had tramped up a falls in Yosemite and then turned to hike down the slippery, steep, and wet steps. Someone had offered me a hand then, and realized I could give that to myself now. I walked slowly, feeling how this walk reshaped me. I paused several times on the way down, feeling wobbly. Climbing up felt grounding; going down felt unnatural. Had I always felt frightened of going down stairs, or down into a cave, or down under? I realized that had. Fear rested under the skin of things, lay in the dark, grew up from dark tunnels and passages. Perhaps I needed to seek those out before the fears would be put to rest.

I shifted my gaze from the vista to the steps in front of me, and felt better as I took each one slowly, breathing deeply. I was glad when I reached the bottom. I leaned against the edge of a wall and then turned right to walk to the end of the street where another arched gateway indicated the small town's border.

As I walked I noticed a shop tucked back into the rock. It had an inviting atmosphere, and I welcomed the chance to shift my focus with a bit of shopping. The moment I entered, the sight of beautiful French linens—my weakness—made me happy. The shop had a small room upstairs that displayed an endless array of printed tablecloths, napkins, robes, and bed linens. The French provincial prints on show stunned me with a riot of colors, especially the rich Tuscan yellow and gold. I had bought little since I'd arrived in France, but fell in love with several tablecloths and a set of napkins my friend Judy would love. I had trouble choosing, and then trouble stopping choosing. When I finally left an hour later, I felt restored by beauty and also by the comfort of the mundane.

I stopped at another shop to buy pâtés and postcards, then sat in a nearby café. I found a small round table to sit and write. I ordered a Perrier and a croissant—never enough of those in my life. After writing in my journal, I took out the watercolor paints I'd forgotten I carried. I did some quick renderings of the café, finding myself drawn to the umbrellas and the beautiful rock all about me. The creativity satisfied me. When I left the café I wanted a nap, so I returned to the hotel.

I would need transportation to the rail station the next morning, so I stopped first to ask the concierge to order a taxi. Once in my room, I had to decide whether to continue on to Carcassonne or cut my trip short and return to Toulouse. I had told myself I could change plans along the way. I went back downstairs and asked the receptionist to reserve a hotel for several nights in Toulouse. I didn't know what the rest of my journey would look like, but it was clear to me I had fulfilled my journey. I spent the rest of the day writing in the café across the street from my hotel and wandering through a few more shops. I was happy with the slow pace of my day and the beauty and sanctuary of Rocamadour.

The next morning I woke around seven. A sunny day greeted me as the taxi drove me to Rocamadour station. As I stood in the middle of the small train platform, I became aware of the air on my skin and listened to the rustling of leaves, which seemed to remind me that all was well. I stayed fully in my body, appreciating everything around me, and stopped thinking and projecting fear onto my travel. What if I stopped paying court to this authority, this tending to the rules and regulations imposed from the past? I saw how this trip had brought me face to face with the distortions my fear cast on my life, like a lens bending the light. It had also helped me realize I had choice. As Hal Zina Bennett writes in his book *Lens of Perception,* "rather than attempting to escape from the lens, with all its false influences and distortions, one fully acknowledges and even embraces it." But, as he also says, we do not cling but become responsible "for getting to know what our perceptions bring to our experience of reality." I had begun the journey reluctantly, but with the good faith to face into my fear and walk through it.

I felt alone again as I stepped aboard the train back to Toulouse, but I knew as I settled in for my ride that shortening the trip had supported me. It just felt right to simplify my journey. I had used the labyrinth as a tool throughout my years of quest, and it had taught me to take my journeys one step at a time. Getting to the center was not the point, but the way I walked did matter.

My return route to Toulouse did not include a bus. I was glad to find I could make one simple transfer at Brillet. Arriving in the afternoon, I took a taxi from the train station to a large hotel in the center of town. Once I settled into my room and unpacked a few things, I headed outside into the city. After my days in Rocamadour I felt the contrast of city life, but it felt invigorating. I wandered the streets, visited a nearby museum, then returned for a dinner in the hotel. My French meal included a delicious meal of trout, salad, and *tarte aux pommes.*

The next morning I walked the few blocks to the Air France ticket office to change my ticket. Air France was accommodating, for a fee of course. They had seating available aboard the flight I would originally have taken home—same time, different day. I spent the rest of the morning ogling the beauty of the patisseries. Easter was only a few days away, and I stood transfixed at the amazing art of chocolate, which reaches another height in France. French Easter chocolate included much more than chocolate eggs and bunnies. I saw several windows filled with dark chocolate fish, something I hadn't seen before. I appreciated the different cultural expressions celebrating the Christian holiday. I admired and took photos, then bought a bag of the small chocolate fish to take home.

After dinner I returned to my room to pack and write in my journal. Tucked in the back of the book, I found the note a spiritual friend had given me. "Dark Mother, Earth fertile seeking, nurturing, remembering roots where life water springs. Calling home our yearning to dance with the Divine...healing comes in still minutes where pilgrims' footsteps trace the steps for the first time and the new life emerges from the cracks of the old."

I'd been touched when she handed the writing to me just before my departure, but the metaphors stunned me when I saw them again. I had indeed found new life in the cracks of the old.

As I climbed into the taxi the morning of my departure I felt changed, and triumphant for having made the travel in spite of my fears. I headed home to California one step closer on my quest for wholeness. Blessed by the presences of the Black Madonnas, I had met my own darkness.

Summer

"In the winter of my life, I found an indomitable summer."

—Camus

Light danced glistening off the water of the bay as my plane settled onto the slate grey landing strip at San Francisco International Airport. I felt happy to be back in California and on schedule for I counted on catching the Sonoma shuttle home. France seemed like a dream.

Sula heard me as I climbed out on the drive and bumped my dark green suitcase along the rough gravel walkway. She came running from the cool, dusty carport. I unlocked the door and put my suitcase inside before settling into my lawn chair for a serious purr-fest, time to catch up. We sat shaded by the oak tree. The warm air feathered the grasses in the field; the goats evidently were grazing at the north end. Sula, with peevish tone, informed me that though Billy had fed and cared for her well enough, it was high time I was with her. I agreed and we started our evening rituals of dinner. Travel reminds me that return home means hearth rituals. I take simple comfort in the ordinary.

My first night's sleep was long and deep, it surprised me. I woke to the world I knew--sage green bedroom wall, a cat meow, warm air and the sharp smells of an early summer. After letting Sula outside for her morning roam, I unpacked and threw clothes in the wash, then stacked travel treasures. I took pleasure in seeing the beauty of the French table linens, napkins, chocolates, pates and other gifts destined for friends. A life without travel treasures is barren. The beauty of France is, however, always carried in my heart. But then I had found pilgrimage to my beloved France a challenge. Fear had been a lifelong companion, too

157

overshadowing and constant. Why not rewrite the story and challenge fears written in my body as a child and a women. To invite change is to invite that which limits life.

The Black Madonna had called me to experience, called me to feel. Take the next step, engage trust and be receptive.

After airing the house and cleaning up I began to make a food list and pull out pots. The alchemy of cooking always brings me deep in my body. Pulling out pots, chopping block, knives and apron is transforming in itself. I feel more engaged in life when I celebrate with cooking. Off I went to Sonoma Market to fill the larder. I walked the store aisles seeing what sparked me, the beautifully stocked vegetable aisle called and I listened. "Fresh, fresh, fresh food, please."

My eyes first fell on a stack of rosy tomatoes, but then shifted to green beans and beets. In the end I chose both of them along with cherry tomatoes, squash in yellow and green, several cucumbers and red onions. I loved the visual joy of vegetables for color, shape, and texture. Food is more fun when I mix colors. As I wandered the store I also found myself turning toward the fresh fish counter. Looking longingly over the sleek salmon, I passed it by and fixed on halibut. Yogurt, black olives, cat food, eggs and sunflowers were the final touches. I felt happy and grateful to be in familiar territory.

When I returned home I set to preparing lunch. The string beans were cooked until tender, but still crisp. Next I boiled an egg and several beets, then let them cool. I feel lucky to love cooking which has become an instinctual process. What herb to use? Fresh tarragon leaves won out. After the beets cooled I cut them in quarters, chopped the tarragon, added the beans, sprinkled them with rice vinegar and salt and pepper. It is important to let the mixture marry. I then took the hardboiled egg and quartered it, sliced green onions, halved the cherry tomatoes and cut up a handful of black olives. Everything went into large white bowl and I let it sit. Hibiscus tea sat cooling, waiting for ice. While I had the stove going I decided to prepare dinner. I love opening the refrigerator and presto, dinner at my fingertips.

I put the halibut fillets in to poach, sprinkled them with lemon juice, admiring the perfect white flesh. Somehow halibut with its shining whiteness was what I needed to nourish me. I always notice the colors I choose to eat in a day. As I stood at the stove I felt the spaciousness

Hearthstories   159

of living alone; it had both gifts and challenges. Being a "table for one" person is not always acceptable; friends and family want you to be social. As I have come to appreciate my differences I have also learned to accept the differences of others. Each of us has our unique path, no right, and no wrong.

When I finished poaching the halibut I made a simple cucumber raita to serve on the fish. Raita is easy to make, simply chop cucumbers, onions and mint and mix them with yogurt and a little salt and pepper. The dressing is delightful on many things and tastes best when you let it sit awhile. After finishing the raita I returned it and the fish to the refrigerator and then sat down in the cool of the living room to enjoy my salad. Eating and preparing good food is self-care. I often catch myself not really savoring or celebrating the moment. Making time to sit down with my meal is something new. Single women have been known to eat and walk, eat and stand at the kitchen counter or eat right out of the pan.

Writing Outside

The following days brought me quickly back to my writing schedule and my summer planting rituals. One morning I checked my emails and found a flyer for a workshop given my Hal Bennett, writing coach, teacher and author. I had been alone with my writing and pilgrimage that year and a workshop sounded inviting. I hadn't spent time reading or listening to other's works and I longed to share. I also knew how shy I felt and how nervous I got when reading my writing. I knew a group would help me. It is important to protect our early creative endeavors for people often have opinions that turn out to be damaging. What also tempted me about the workshop was the fact that it was being held in the Sierra Foothills, a place I hadn't visited for a long time. Skyline Harvest, the retreat center, was in Camptonville, a three-and-a-half-hour drive north of Sonoma. Before letting my mind talk me out of it I e-mailed back a *yes*. Facing fears invited inner work again.

I looked forward to the workshop, which was a month away, and remembered my adventures the summer before at Mt Shasta. I recalled the joy of swimming in the lake and the challenge I gave myself to camp alone at Panther Meadow. Why not extend my trip and continue on to

Mt. Shasta? It would be a summer treat. There was something about the mountain—I wasn't sure what—that always called me. Why not explore?

I settled into a summer writing schedule of working early in the morning and walking in the cool of the evening. I called my friend Mary one day to join me. As the sun nestled over the west hills of the valley, we walked Gerecke Road enjoying its luscious shade. I loved the errant wild flowers that grew at the edge of the road. The dried grasses were brushed with touches of cornflower blue and dock's chocolate browns. As we walked she shared how she had been working on her new meditation web site. Her struggle, like many of us, was learning to balance work with self- care. She smiled as she said, "If I consider myself a loving person, why would I leave myself out of the equation?" I nodded with agreement and as walked uphill deeper into the shade we talked more about our history that often drove us with harshness. We parted after an hour walk; I headed home with appreciation. It was a gift to have a friend who truly listened and didn't fix.

As time approached for the workshop I realized I needed to make reservations in Mt. Shasta. My friend Susan suggested a small bed and breakfast and gave me a card of an herbalist healer friend. I liked the idea of spending time with someone who lived at the mountain; my love of herbs and different healing potions spurred me on to telephone. Denise was her name and I organized to meet her one afternoon. I began to look forward to the mystery of new encounters.

Before I knew it I was preparing for my trip to Camptonville. I packed food, clothes and my computer, and then made food to share during the weekend as well as an egg salad sandwich for travel. Everything went into my cooler and I headed out. I felt both happy and frightened as I turned the car off Napa Road. I drove east to Highway 129, and then on to Highway 80. The day was beastly hot and I was glad to get out of town, but also knew the temperatures might be the same in Camptonville.

Feelings of sadness flooded me as I left Sonoma. I was surprised by the sadness. In the past I felt excited to leave home, to adventure in difference. New feelings meant my deep freeze was melting. As I opened and trusted I became more intimate with my life. Soon I would find out more.

I relaxed into the drive and began to nibble my egg salad sandwich, put in a Celtic music CD and felt happy as I drove. I followed the directions Diane had e-mailed. It wasn't long before the four lane freeways turned into two lane roads. The smell of pine embraced me as I climbed into the Sierra foothills. Turning onto Highway 49 at Auburn I began to think about the upcoming writing weekend. Who were the people coming? Had they been writers for a long time? What would our assignments be? I felt both excited and anxious. It had been a long time since I shared my writing with others. We all have stories of someone humiliating our budding creative inspirations.

I stopped musing and paid attention when I noticed a landmark, the Lost Nugget. I smiled wondering what the *Lost Nugget* was. I had been seeking my lost gold. My directions said to turn soon after. The road narrowed and led me deeper into the country. Narrow roads often open the fear faucet; I had to trust. What if I met another car on the single lane road? As I made a sharp turn the thought became reality. The car coming in the other direction was a yellow VW, easy to see. Luckily I saw a wide patch of dirt to pull into; I let the car pass, the young woman smiled and waved. The experience relaxed me. "See, you can do it," I said to myself.

Soon after, I saw the sign that marked the road to Skyline and then the gate. I hesitated before swinging the gate open. Once through I then closed it behind me. As I got back in the car I had to take a deep breath; I felt like a door had closed behind me. It certainly was a gate to a new experience. Wasn't I only going to a simple weekend writing retreat? I knew that my weekend experience would bring me out of hiding. Each step was revealing.

I drove up the gravel road toward the house that would be home for the retreat weekend. The vista to my right included beautiful rolling hills, stands of Ponderosa pine and a beautiful view of the turquoise body of water. Goats grazed on a green grassy area. I was surprised to see a large white dog and then a black dog sharing the pasture. I found out later that the white dog's name was Justin and the black dog was named Bear. They were in fact the goats' guardians. Just beyond was a rustic barn which caught the gold light of afternoon sun, and beyond to the left was a grassy area with a willow and pond. The old family home was snuggled on a knoll just beyond; its tin roof washed with rust was comforting. I pulled the car in front of the house and stepped into the late afternoon heat.

Ice chest in hand I opened the door of the house and called out, but no one was there. Diane and Teresa lived in a house up the hill. Just inside the front door was the dining room with a lovely dark wood table and family photos and a quote from Camus: "In the winter of my life I found an indomitable summer." I stopped to appreciate his words. Could I find that summer? I then walked through to the back of the house into an old-fashioned kitchen. I put my cooler on the counter. The room reminded me of my grandmother's kitchen. The house was back in time and my Nana was ever present in my thoughts. Thoughts of her somehow connected me to the joy and simplicity of a beautiful summer afternoon.

I then walked back outside, took a right around the front porch and found a door to what I thought must be my porch room. The door stuck, but soon gave way, opening into a small but charming room, wrapped in glass windows. My gaze caught a view of stands of pine and cedar in the distance. I loved its indoor-outdoor atmosphere. A voice startled me. "I hope you find it comfortable," Diane said. We walked together back into the house so she could explain the logistics of the house. The bathroom I would use was off the kitchen, there were compost buckets to be used, and the refrigerator on the left was where I should put my food. Soon after, she left me to retrieve the rest of my luggage. I smiled as I placed the suitcase on the nubby white chenille bedspread, a sweet memory from childhood. After unpacking I lay down, looking out to my left. Outside the window was a luscious green fig tree that sheltered the room, keeping it cool. I felt I could lie in bed and whisper to it; it had a motherly fruitful presence.

After settling in I walked down to the barn and a grassy lawn area. Porcelain blue hollyhocks, red roses and a young peach tree graced the perimeter. The peach tree bore the weight of many pink skinned beauties. Directly across the road was an ancient graceful apple tree also full of its bounty. It looked as though it had been here from the beginning of time. I imagined them collecting the apples for pies. Later I learned that Teresa did just that. Below the yard was a wide pasture that curved downhill.

I took a short walk around the property up beyond Diane and

Teresa's house. The cry of a hawk accompanied me as I climbed a steep uphill road; it felt good to stretch my legs and I felt happy I had come.

I returned to my room and opened the computer to write. Writing had become a process which brought me home to myself. The computer was the canvas, my fingers the brushes to reveal my inner life and a container to keep me in flow, opening to what was true for me. The practice of expressing self, acknowledging feelings, jotting thoughts, recording important experience, helped me sort my truth. It pointed me to what I loved and what sparked me. The experience also gave me a mirror for the unseen workings of my inner being.

Writing in a journal, painting, making a pot, all are containers; they hold the old, the new and the unexplored. Making time to nurture an inner life includes offering oneself a safe place to create in.

I felt deep appreciation for the quality of land and nature about me. They reminded meal that *eco means Home*. Skyline Harvest was a place I could find home. Slowly I could begin to feel myself relax and become connected to the nature about me. John O'Donohue writes, "Beneath the frenetic streams of thought, the quieter, elemental nature of the self takes over and claims our presence. Rather than taking us out of ourselves, nature coaxes us deeper inwards, teaches us to rest in the serenity of our elemental nature." I had brought his book *Beauty* with me. His words always connected me to my Irish heritage, to that thread of wisdom that connects nature and spirit.

I closed the computer and pulled out a mystery novel I had brought along. Nancy Drew mysteries were favorite summer reading as a young girl, so I had made sure to find used copies at library sales. I snuggled beneath my covers and turned on the small overhead light. It wasn't long before I feel asleep dreaming of summer picnics and cool lake waters.

When I woke the next morning I felt the joy of a summer day spread out in front of me. I felt a bit vulnerable padding my way across the planks of the front porch to get to the bathroom, but then I gave up any ego pretense and headed for a shower. I would be alone in the house until the afternoon. The morning flew by.

Later that day I heard cars arriving. Soon the voices of women filled the house. The women were from far and near. Our leader, Hal Bennett, had arrived earlier in the afternoon. Soon the chatter of ice chests, suitcases and hellos was added. We gathered to begin our weekend with a potluck dinner. Pasta salads, tabouli salad, ice cream, bread, and roasted chicken were among the things laid out for buffet feasting. I felt my anxiety rising as dinner began to complete. The moment was at hand. Would I reveal or conceal?

After washing dishes we gathered in the living room for our first meeting. Fear gathered in my throat; I felt like a deer caught in headlights. During our round of introductions I barely blurred out, "Hello, I am Joanna. I feel terrified." What a relief, I thought, after speaking my truth. I breathed more deeply and could relax into the release I felt in being honest with the group and myself. Non-verbal support flowed toward me. Other women shared about their writing experience. Many felt challenged reading for strangers. When the evening ended I felt settled back into myself. The choice was to honor who I was in my humanity.

We gathered in the living room in the cool of the morning to hear our first writing assignment. Write in the present moment. Yes, that is what I wanted to learn! I took my notebook and was one of the first to head outdoors.

As I walked about the house I looked for a place to sit. Finally I chose the concrete steps next to the fig tree. I felt a strange fear; I knew it came from expressing myself and at the end of our writing time and then sharing. As I sat, a cloud covered the sun as I settled in. I looked up and realized that I tended to disappear behind a cloud myself. I knew my progress was slow, progress to trust, feel safe and stay connected to my body.

I surrendered into just writing in the moment. My eye caught a butterfly close by, its black-velvet, white, and gold rings offering me a reminder. Come into the moment, she beckoned. I then moved as the butterfly moved, seeking shade when the sun became too hot. I shifted to a lower step, descending into the shade, into that cooler and deeper place which also lived inside me. Vinca vines cascaded over the stairs around me as a breeze kicked up. Aware of my tight and defensive shoulders I began to listen. My shoulders seemed to act like sentinels of the upper part of my body. The tension kept me contracted in a state of being on guard. I shook my shoulders loose; I want to be free to write and relax, I said to myself.

I stopped again to notice a dark cloud covering the sun. I truly wanted to come out the shadow of fear; I wanted to move like the breeze that had kicked up, which swirled and lifted like a bird in flight. So many of my inner voices wanted to keep the control.

Time was up; a bell rang reminding us to return to the living room. Before we all returned inside we saw Diane coming toward us. She was carrying a small brown goat, a newborn named Mira who had been born early that morning. We gathered around her and welcomed her to the world; she had many mothers gazing down on her that day. As we settled back in our chairs to read I felt the comfort of our group. I read, feeling more confident and present. Small steps, I said to myself. Each sharing brought me closer to listening. Once I could let go of some of the fear I came more present in the room. I was then available to appreciate others' writings. Sunday we gathered to celebrate the weekend and say our goodbyes. There were many gifts of the weekend. I gained respect for the uniqueness of the feminine voice.

Shasta Beckoning

Once packed and in my car I headed west to Mt. Shasta, the next step of my summer adventure. Thank goodness for Diane's good directions, for sooner than later I pulled into the driveway of the bed and breakfast. I was glad my housing was close to the lake. After checking into my large upstairs room I headed for the lake only moments away. It didn't take me long to dive in and let go of everything, feeling the gift, the aliveness of the cold mountain waters. After that I headed back to my room and settled in for the night, looking forward to the adventure of the next day. I felt like a young girl in my summers at Medford Lakes where I first learned to swim and paddle a canoe. Before falling asleep I smiled, for my accommodations were a far cry from my camping experience last summer. Each offered me a different lens. I saw how the writing workshop had become another summer expansion experience. "Face the fear and do it anyway," I said to myself.

Early morning I woke with enthusiasm, pulled on my bathing suit and headed again for the lake. Taking my towel I walked to the edge of the water. I stopped to appreciate the stunning beauty of perfectly calm water. The lake had become a mirror, reflecting the sky with its cotton-like clouds. Tall trees grew from the water's depths. I couldn't tell which was above or below, everything was offered up in morning perfection.

Tossing my towel on a rock I ventured to the water. A cormorant swooped by heading south; I stood gazing at its sleek body and perfect flight. As usual it took time to adjust to the crisp cold of the lake water. I ducked my head under water and felt baptized. Lake Siskiyou was itself a holy well. My arms enjoyed the steady strokes as I pulled toward the middle of the lake; once there I allowed myself to float looking up at the majestic mountain.

Driving back to the bed and breakfast I felt refreshed and alive. After a quick breakfast of fresh peaches and toast I called the herbalist to arrange for a meeting. She had time later in the afternoon and I had the rest of the day to adventure. No question, Panther Meadow was my destination. I wanted to revisit the place I had camped last summer. As I drove the windings road to the last parking lot I passed the campground with a kind of knowing. I laced up my hiking books and breathed in the air with gratitude. My boots hit a gravel path and off I went feeling a deep joy. There is an indescribable power to Mt Shasta, especially in the meadow area. My walk took me through the stunted trees and large rock formations of high elevations, and downhill through Panther Meadow. In that sweet sanctuary I could hear the running waters and stopped in awe appreciating the beauty of a carpet of alpine wildflowers.

I hiked to the bottom of the meadow and then back up taking in the warm sun. As I drove back from my walk, I had a momentary flash of longing to live on the mountain. The thought was lost as I rounded a curve and caught sight of the stunning views west across the mountain range.

After a quick shower I went to meet Denise at her home. Her rich brown eyes and tan face were welcoming as we swung open her cabin door. I liked her immediately. We sat over tea, each sharing a bit of who we were. She then talked about her oils and herbs. Several hours passed in conversation about her living at the mountain, our love of swimming and water, and the peace we both felt in nature. When I finally left we promised to stay connected. As I headed out to my car a neighbor, June, called out. She was out watering, so we stopped to visit briefly. We met her new dog who romped on the cool grass in her yard, then said goodnight. I felt happy as I walked back to my car and felt a momentary desire to move to the mountains. I turned to Denise and mentioned it. She smiled back with some knowing.

The next morning I packed up with reluctance. I felt changed in some way. Was it the weekend, my visit to the mountain and the joy I felt swimming? I felt I was entering a new cycle. My entire drive south I spent musing. What about moving to the mountain, why not? I felt the spaciousness of the possibility, but then let it go.

I was happy to arrive home. Sula joined me as I gardened and watered, she slapping paws at errant bees and butterflies. I pulled weeds and noted the progress of the tomatoes and small purple eggplants I had planted.

One morning after giving up my writing I decided to pull out my watercolors. I was glad for my instinctual desire. I didn't have to fuss to get myself to do it. I pulled out my favorite Arches paper and poised my brush over a color. I chose yellow as my eye caught a sunflower nodding to me from a small glass vase on the table. I was anxious to take advantage of sunflower season so I decided to get serious and set up my easel. As I let go and engaged my joy of painting I sat back and realized that the painting would become a gift. I wanted to give Matt and Dawn the painting for a wedding present. It had been a year ago July that they had tied the knot.

Later I poured myself a glass of lemonade and reminisced about last year's wedding. Dawn and Matt's relationship had blossomed over several years; their wedding took place in July in Philadelphia. A California contingent went several days ahead to prepare. The day of the wedding was beautiful—a sultry Saturday. The ceremony took place in a lush green garden with an arbor decorated with flowers. The festivities flowed out of the garden into a ballroom where guests waited in line to congratulate the couple and then go on to enjoy the bounty of a wedding feast. Three sets of families and their friends joined in the celebration. There is always a certain magic and joy that radiates from such a day. My sister and I shared the happiness we felt in seeing a new generation's journey. I was only sad that I lived so far away. I set down my lemonade and called them; it was a Saturday and they luckily were home planting flowers. It was fun to catch up with them and share that I had begun the watercolor.

A week went by before I allowed myself to take notice of a small voice nudging me to move to the mountains. I decided just for the heck of it to explore the rental possibilities online. Nothing seemed right.

Meantime a dream pointed me to new understanding. My questions about the moving seem to be working themselves to the surface from inside. I dreamed I was standing in a house that had just been washed away from shore. A roaring river was carrying the house downstream. A male figure stood on the shore watching me go. I felt afraid at first of the swift moving currents of water, but when I turned to look around I saw that the house was intact. Another woman shared the house with me and was standing looking forward down the river. I was glad to be accompanied and felt at ease as I saw the sun shining. So my house was being carried away from known territory.

Days later, I had another dream. Swift water was carrying me again. This time I was without my house. Alone I tried to stay afloat and struggled to grab wild grasses. Finally I surrendered and the water carried me to shore where I could climb up on the beach. There was a hotel just up the hill. I felt safe and realized that I didn't need to struggle, the water carried me safely to shore.

Perhaps I was indeed to move to Mt. Shasta. I called Denise to touch base and share my dreams. She mentioned she had similar intuitions about a move and told me she would keep her ears open for a rental. I considered the change with a bit of caution. How would I manage in the winter, snow shoveling, snow tires? Could I take care of myself in such a place? Was I willing to give up my sanctuary in Sonoma, a place I had called home for a long time? Was ancient woman calling me to move to the mountain?

The next week, Denise called excitedly to tell me about a house rental. Her neighbor June had a rental possibility. Her brother and sister-in-law wanted to rent their house for a year. The one hitch was they wanted to rent it furnished. Was I interested and could I come to see it? Certainly, I said, but I also explained that I had been away from home and needed to catch up. Was it all right to come in two weeks? They agreed.

Surely, the mystery had claimed me. In that time of change I learned new things. Flexibility and trust were asked of me. Moving had always filled me with angst; I geared up, got ahead of myself, felt frantic. Could I stay in the moment and see what wanted to unfold? My seemingly innocent weekend writing trip had led to unimagined vistas.

It was late in July the day I left for Shasta and I felt excited. I arrived late, but Denise drove us. Once we rounded the curve and turned into the horseshoe driveway I felt a knowing. The two-story house had a feeling of home.-

Husband and wife greeted me smiling and offered to show me around the house, give me a tour. I was taken with the beautiful quality of light in all the rooms, the back porch and small but inviting back yard. One bedroom was downstairs, another upstairs under the eves along with an office area and bathroom. The house felt spacious and open. We returned downstairs and sat talking where I was reminded that they needed to rent the house furnished. Was I ok with that? As I walked around the house I noted that I felt comfortable with their furniture, art and sense of space. We were soon talking rents, snow plowing, the negatives of winter. They looked worried as they asked, "You wouldn't abandon the house if it got too cold or too snow bound, would you?" I smiled and said no, but asked for the names of people who could help me if need be. Sula was the next topic of discussion; I asked if they were open to having my cat Sula. They smiled for they were cat lovers, only recently having lost theirs. "Of course," they said. We seemed happy with each other; I took a deep breath and signed the lease and walked out breathless. I had never had any life change begin so smoothly. Could something be so easy? I met Denise for dinner that evening to celebrate and grow our new relationship. Again we promised to stay in touch and I headed back to Sonoma in wonder.

I returned home in a bit of a state of shock. It had all happened so fast. I also knew deep in my being that my soul called. The rest would unfold.

Fall

"When holy were the haunted forest boughs,
Holy the air, the water and the fire."

—John Keats

Fall hung in the air even as Indian summer offered scorching hot temperatures. Packing suddenly made my move real. I both delighted in and dreaded the change. There would be new seasons to experience in the mountains, new birthing and new deaths. Was I ready for mountain simplicity? My choice of a hermit's life would be lived more deeply. I was surprised to feel a longing for a different aloneness. The new life would show me truths I hadn't faced before. I felt tests ahead of me and the fall would bring a kind of change which would mean a deep letting go of what I had called home. The harvest season all about me reminded me to find abundance in life. To respect the turning I stopped packing to light a rich pumpkin colored candle. Simple candle lighting had come to remind me to breathe and take time.

All about me signs pointed to fall. Grape leaves began their journey from greens to beautiful yellows, oranges and reds; the last color stage of some vines would soften into dark crimson chocolate. I stepped outside to take a breath of the soft afternoon air and imagined the first altar I'd create in Shasta. Like the seasons I would move into a new cycle. The current had picked me up. Could I surrender into the flow?

Moving On

I counted the days—six weeks until departure day. An anxiety gripped me, one I knew well, which pushed and shoved me when change was ahead. The anxiety rose from fear and believed hurrying would help. I still hadn't fully claimed trust. Lists grew long. But first and foremost on the list was finding a storage unit for my furniture. The next task was putting a date on the calendar for the movers. I wasn't sure where I would be after Shasta so storing my furniture was the best option. I liked the process of clearing and sorting, and the reward of traveling light. Finding a storage locker to rent came easily; I then scheduled the movers.

Packing for storage meant first choosing what I would need in Shasta. I knew what favorite cookbooks, pots, books and fabrics I wanted to carry with me. As the boxes filled and tape sealed each closed, I felt doubt. Had I had made the right decision? Friends challenged my reasons. But then there was no reason or intellect who guided. Soul had drawn me as she had when I first traveled to France. Since then had learned to heed inner wisdom.

All in all it did seem strange to leave Sonoma, a place I had called home for over thirty years. However with Matt and Dawn settled on the East coast I felt a need to explore home elsewhere. When I phoned them to share my news I heard concern at the other end; I had to sit with doubts again. I felt as though I were giving up roots, somehow betraying the family. Did I really want to leave Sonoma life? Mountain winters were going to be hard. I felt overwhelmed at times with the process of moving itself. I wasn't getting any younger and the physical work of it asked for the limbs of a younger body.

Each day I packed and sorted. The favorite things I set aside included: a soup pot, favorite kitchen utensils, altar cloths and treasures, favorite flannel sheets, favorite mixing bowl. The task was to create hearth away from home. I knew it would be important to organize files, office materials and books. Clothes for both winter and summer had to be packed, as well as warm socks, boots and jackets. The piles added up.

One afternoon I took a break and went to my garden. The sun beat down on my head as I sat at the edge of the raised bed. I leaned into the pungent green basil and sniffed—time to harvest all the remaining leaves. My fingers smelled of the basil oils; I then harvested the remaining tomatoes. Ah, a simple lunch, I thought as I walked back inside and looked at the clock. It was actually way past lunchtime. I walked back inside to the kitchen. Vermicelli with basil pesto, freshly sliced tomatoes and cucumbers became my late meal.

Grief caught up to me as the days ticked away. I would truly miss my home in Sonoma. I would miss friends, the labyrinth, the farmers market, small things like the patch of vibrant blue morning glories that grew on the fence. I made a ritual out of each letting go. I made a visit to Friday farmers market. Would Shasta have a farmers market? I spent a leisurely time visiting each stall, appreciating the tables laden with summer harvest. I gratefully gathered my favorite peppers of yellow, red and green. My basket overflowed with raspberries, blackberries, heirloom tomatoes and more. Returning home I first set to roasting the red and yellow peppers, skinned them, added chicken broth, salt and pepper and then pureed them. The pepper puree makes a good soup base. I froze it along with the berries and peaches. There is nothing like fresh berries on gray winter mornings. All my food treasures called for a new cooler so they could be carried to my new home in the mountains. I carried with me the sweetness of the valley.

All of a sudden departure date was two days away. The movers had come and taken everything to storage except the Shasta boxes and a futon mat to sleep on, one cup and one pan for boiling water. My heart was heavy with letting go of my Sonoma home. The town had become my root, my sanctuary. But I knew from past experience that new vistas taught me to engage life with different eyes. What would follow after Shasta? Sonoma had so much history for me. Would I return?

I made time for goodbyes to my neighborhood of nature—the vines, the oaks the peacocks and goats. Liz, Carol and I had a goodbye glass of wine. I went to Bartholomew Park, giving its spirit gratitude for the gift of wild woods. Goodbyes also included a lunch with friends at The Girl and the Fig, one of my favorite restaurants in Sonoma. Good food shared with friends is my idea of celebration. Goodbyes are hard.

Sula, my ever-faithful companion, was never far away from me during those last days. She had gotten wind of the change when the boxes got stacked. But the process had come to an end and she was restless. I dreaded driving in the car with her; like most cats she despised being on the road.

The day of departure arrived. I felt exhausted but ready to go. Sula and I walked around the house saying our goodbyes. The last few trips to the car included the ice chest and my computer. I grabbed a squirming Sula and placed her in her new cat carrier. No matter the elegance of her new home, Sula started her large complaints. Cat carrier in hand I closed the door on the house, but my hand lingered. Saying my grateful goodbyes, I knew its cave-like quality had nurtured large changes. Tears ran down my cheeks as I walked down the walkway to the car. Liz came out to wave goodbye. Life felt surreal.

Dropping into my seat in the car, I started the engine. Sula howled and I cried as we pulled out of the drive. I turned onto Napa Road and headed north. Shasta was definitely the other side of the mountain. When was it that I had asked for a mountain home?

Hours later, tired but happy, I pulled into the drive on Shasta Way. I felt relief for Sula. The ride had been difficult; when she did settled down and nap she would be startled awake by a semi-truck whizzing by. Yes, we were home. Everything about my new home felt welcoming— the gentle curved semicircle, green trimmed white house, well-tended mountain gardens and front porch.

I stepped out of the car onto the stone steps which lead me to the front porch with its rocker and bird feeder. Once inside, the cool air greeted me. All the shades had been drawn; order and quiet embraced me. Directly to my right was the large white-tiled kitchen; the entry hall led into the spacious two-story open living room and dining room. Sets of tall windows let in afternoon light. Two French doors opened onto the redwood porch. I turned and headed back outside.

It was time to retrieve Sula from the car, so I swung her carrier inside. It didn't take long for her to squirm her way onto the new green carpet and begin her slow stalk of exploration. I happily opened the two living room doors to the back porch and stepped out. The grassy yard was dotted with a large maple, several birch, and beautiful specimens of mountain rocks. Stairs to the right of the porch led down to the garage; they were bordered with sage green plants topped with delicate yellow flowers. At the bottom, along the edge of the garage, was a large planting of lavender in full bloom. The bees were busy. I pulled the screen doors closed behind me to let in the fresh air, for the house had been closed up for a week.

Back inside I went to the kitchen and pulled open the blinds. As I lifted my head I caught site of Mt. Shasta, a brilliant blue sky framing the snowy peaks of the rouged and fiery mountain. How lucky was I? When I pulled up the shades of the two side windows I was delighted to see a young birch tree shelter the cove of the house. Further out, scrub brush delineated the property edge. I noticed the peak of a neighbor's house; the sight of it comforted me.

Time to unload the car and pull it in the garage, I thought. On the last load out of the garage I spied snowshoes and the big orange snow blower, a reminder of things to come. I smiled and carried Sula's things inside. "Your new home," I said to her as I set up her food and water in the kitchen. Sula sniffed and I headed for the bedroom.

The first floor bedroom opened off the living room. As I put my suitcase down I laughed from surprise, for I had forgotten the resident member of the house. A very large toy moose sat gazing out at me from his perch on a shelf above the dresser. Moose must be a totem of the house, I thought, as I recalled the iron wrought image of a moose at the entrance to the drive. I reminded myself to check the qualities of moose.

Off to the shower—water on, clothes off. Cool mountain water washed the travel dust from my body. I grabbed a fresh purple towel which hung on the rack just outside the tub. What a wonderful way to move, having everything in place including towels. I dropped my suitcase in the closest and pulled out my comfortable shirt and shorts. The outfit is comfort food, like Mac and cheese. I then padded my way back to the kitchen across the living room.

Next job was to put away the food from the cooler. Everything had stayed frozen. Sula settled in by eating an early dinner. I did the same by serving myself cold gazpacho made with tomatoes and peppers from the farmers market. Fresh rye bread toast with butter and sliced cucumber served as the accompaniment. As dusk fell around the house I melted into the large white couch. Sula came to settle in on my belly. I made a few phone calls to friends and family to say I had arrived safely, and soon after settled into bed. I snuggled into the old red and blue quilt grateful for the ease of a furnished home. Sula took the clue and jumped up to settle on my feet. Neither of us budged until the next morning.

I woke to sun shining in the window next to the bed. The sun in the mountains is twice as bright. It was a lovely September morning. I felt truly happy as I headed for the kitchen. The air was warm; the temperatures would stay so until that first fall cold snap. Denise called that morning to welcome me. After talking with her I took my tea outdoors on the brick patio just off the bedroom. I sat down in a rickety blue canvas chair nestled under the young birch and felt I was the luckiest woman alive.

After tea I began settling in by creating hearth for myself. First I set up an altar in the west corner of the house and then unpacked my kitchen treasures. After completing the kitchen I went to gather lavender from the yard for both the kitchen and the altar. I felt grateful and peaceful. I lit a candle in gratitude to the owners, prayed for a gentle fall transition and for creative fires to be strong.

The morning flew by. I wrote for several hours in the afternoon and then headed to Lake Siskiyou for my first swim. The water was as delicious as I remembered it. I found a new place on the far side of the dam to swim; the rocky bottom took negotiating, but soon I plunged under the cold water and felt the deep cleanse that only fresh lake water gives. The swim helped me arrive as did a drive up Barr Road and down through the center of town. I drove slowly past a video store, a deli, and also stopped at Berryville, the organic grocery, to buy fresh raspberries, cucumber, salad greens, and lemonade. What a day! I felt happy as I closed the door of the garage and stepped into the house, feeling it was home. Sula was stretched out on one of the living room windowsills. She had found her spot.

New Community

One morning around dawn I sat writing. My habit is to light a candle, say a few morning prayers and turn to my writing. I liked the new mountain schedule of waking with the sun and sleeping when it turned dark. I drew deeper in love with the in-between times of dusk and dawn. That morning I climbed out of my warm comforter, pulled on my green flannel robe and pulled the shades up. The first grey light of morning filtered through the French doors. The bedroom became a favorite writing room for it provided more cocoon. I pulled the shades "to this opening of the door of day" and then returned to bed. Sulfa perched at the end of the waffled quilt comforter. She suddenly sat attentive, her ears twisting like radar. I wondered if she heard a rascal squirrel or two, they were abundant in the neighborhood.

As I turned to look, out of morning mists a face appeared. At first I was frightened, but then I sorted out the head of a small grey fox who had poked her nose against the glass. She seemed to be saying, "I have been waiting, you are finally awake." I was in shock and delighted; I laughed. Was there a neighbor fox? I felt welcomed and confirmed in the mystery of my mountain journey.

I found out later that this particular fox was a neighborhood fixture. She had to approve of the new resident! The fox stayed for only a moment and then slipped back into the morning mist. I laughed and knew she was a gift. As I do sometimes I went to look in *Animal Speaks* by Ted Andrews. The book is a treasure house of information about the life and qualities of mammals, birds and insects. Each creature reminds us to listen and learn. He suggests that one quality of the fox includes its ability to shape-shift.

My world had been shape shifting that was sure. I was glad I did not feel afraid, and grateful to have been greeted. I returned to my writing, carrying the mystery and magic with me. I finally stopped halfway through the morning. I showered and stretched and felt pleased that my writing had become my art. I saw how I had begun to honor my creative expression more and more.

One afternoon several weeks into my move, I finally felt ready to connect with other people. I had been given the number of a neighbor. Her name was Susan and she was a friend of the owner. I had met her briefly on my last stay. When I called I got an answering machine, but she returned my call later that evening. She recognized my name and suggested I might enjoy a neighborhood yoga class.

"It is the perfect place to meet other people and hear about other events," she offered.

"I will be there that evening and introduce you, so come."

The next week I walked up the street to the corner house with anticipation. I stepped into a warm carpeted room where I introduced myself. The class was a wonderful opportunity to meet people who were seekers themselves. Over the next months I looked forward to gathering with my new community and growing back my flexibility and strength—mountain life called for it.

It was late one afternoon in October when I caught a shift in the weather. The crisper air meant winter was on its way. I closed my writing files and started the car for the short ride to Lake Siskiyou. I had a particular fondness for the lake and the path that wove around it. The path was nurturing to me; it became a way to feel at home in my new life. As I walked the narrow path, I breathed in the wonderful scent of pine. One of the many trees I passed had hundreds of small pinecones around the bottom of its trunk. I always collect pinecones, but didn't have a backpack with me to fill. So I decided to return another day. I imagined the different sizes of cones in the large wicker basket on the raised hearth. The smallest cones would help in fire starting.

I turned around to catch the warm rays of the sun and caught sight of a woman paddling a kayak. I smiled to myself; kayaking had been an unfulfilled dream. Thoughts of kayaking or canoeing on any lake had been written in my body as a child; they were memories of fluid peace.

Later in the month I began to connect to my own rhythm of life again. My first seasonal ritual was pantry stocking. The house had wonderful shelf space, one especially large one for stocking foods. I had prepared and brought with me lentils, black beans, rice and kidney beans. However, I knew that with the long winter coming I had to take my food stock more seriously. I thought about the snows ahead and knew that candles, matches and wood were needed. A few other items needed were dry soups, tomato sauce, potatoes and nuts. I began with the firewood.

Stacking Wood

It took several phone calls to locate some wood. Most of it had been purchased and already stacked in the summer months. I finally found wood for sale at the local community center. Two days later a large mound of wood filled the far edge of the driveway. I committed to stacking thirty minutes a day until the last log was in place.

One afternoon several days later, while stacking my wood, I got a surprise call from a woman I had known many years ago. Mary had seen me in Berryville. While surprised to see each other after two years, we recognized our shared love of quest and the sacred feminine. Mt.

Shasta was a place to deepen our journey. We had exchanged phone numbers. Now she was calling to ask me to join her at the headwaters. The headwaters of the Sacramento River were a local treasure; I gladly stopped my wood stacking and said yes. Over the short time I had been at the mountain I had heard it was one of the most sacred and magical spots of the area. She told me to meet her at the rear of the city park.

Later I learned that this land was once part of the hunting grounds for the Wintun, Maidu and Okwanuchu Indian tribes. At the beginning of the 20th century, Big Springs was designated as the location of the headwaters of the Sacramento River and contained a water wheel. It was the city's first source of energy.

I felt happy as I waited to share adventure. Mary arrived, carrying two water bottles. I had forgotten mine. We walked a short distance back toward the hill listening to cascading water, a musical sound. I walked with the joy of a pilgrim who goes to reverence a sacred spring. The flat stone plateau came into view first; bubbling water and dancing water grasses met us. As we stood on its edge our gaze went to the source. Water was pouring out of two small gaps in the earthen hill. The water flowed down into a narrow stream.

Both of us were fascinated and sat down on a small green bench to take in the spirit of the place. There were fairies all right, and the spirits of water all about us. The purity and freshness were palpable. We sat in silence, smiling, until we heard voices. A young couple came with large water bottles to negotiate the rocks and shallow water. Water bottles in hand they stepped on flat rocks to fill their bottles. Water from thousands of feet up the mountain flowed into their bottles; they smiled and left. I imagined the water as it rippled through streams, ran deep inside the earth, came up to surface and then returned to the depths.

Mary and I went to the edge and pushed our bottles under the surface of the magical liquid, offered a prayer of gratitude and said our goodbyes. My experience at the headwaters that day would be something I returned to and never stopped treasuring. Each time I went I filled my bottle, reminding myself of the many gifts of source. I felt the wellspring of the place; I wanted to claim that place inside. I knew exactly how our ancestors prayed and gave thanks for its life-giving gift.

As Mary headed uphill to her cabin, I headed into town to explore. Since Mt. Shasta is considered California's most sacred mountain, the bookstores are full of both traditional and esoteric spiritual writings. Visitors and locals alike enjoy the treasures of herbs, crystals, healing bowls and unique books. I recalled my camping experience and the woman who was gathering sage on the mountain that afternoon. I often burn sage leaves after I clean my house. In honor of her I wandered into a shop—no sage. Further down the street I found a bookstore that sold sage gathered locally. I was happy to learn from the storeowner of a local woman who gathered it. She spoke to me of other plants growing wild and of the native tribes involved in restoring and caring for the native plants. Everyone worked together to keep the mountain a place of sanctuary. When I lit the sage I offered a prayer in thanks for the gift of my time at the mountain. I also honored the gifts of Princess White Feather, my first teacher at age two. For five years of my life she cared for me. Her gifts were many; she was the one who set out the tone which would draw me to journey. She was the face of ancient woman who had called my soul.

The next morning I pulled on a pair of gloves and set to stacking wood again. I had promised myself I would finish. As I filled my arms, I heard a voice calling, "Hey!"

I turned to see my neighbor, a white-haired man, waving from his driveway. "I'm Jim. Can I help you?"

I hesitated before saying, "Yes, thank you."

Jim arrived, an elderly gentleman wearing work gloves and warm jacket. I looked at him with a question, but he set to work right away. We both set to hauling and stacking the wood under the eaves of the garage. When we were close to finishing I felt my back complaining. I smiled at myself for I had initially been worried about his back. He seemed ready to continue. Over wood stacking I learned something about him; I learned that he was in his eighties and that a year ago he had lost his wife to cancer. He was a bundle of energy; I knew instantly we would become friends. I looked forward to hearing more of his life story, took his phone number and promised him a dinner in exchange.

October brought squirrels scurrying about gathering their acorns. The temperatures had dropped, which inspired me to make heartier food. I decided that macaroni and cheese was a perfect comfort food for the day. It serves the creamy, cheesy longing that comes in cold weather. Good mac and cheese takes a bit of time to make, but it is more than worth it. I began to prepare it that morning so I could enjoy it for a late lunch.

As I wrote that morning I was inspired by the luscious smells that warmed the house. Later I spooned myself a healthy serving, one with lots of browned crunchy macaroni on top. I always make an effort to eat my food slowly, especially with comfort food. I sat eating and watching the maple tree and her brilliant leaves. I hadn't been up close and personal with a maple for years. Over the fall I had been watching the subtle changes. One half of the tree started its shift from green to red leaves; the second half followed. Mountain life was a gift. Several days later I felt sad to see that the tree had lost many of the leaves—a wind had come and blown them about the lawn. Another lesson in letting go, I thought.

As the daylight shortened, I felt how much I missed Sonoma. It was new to have feelings of loss. Letting my feelings filter into life grew my aliveness and presence. While I phoned to catch up with friends regularly, I still felt the void. A friend came to visit for a weekend soon after. We spent time hiking, visiting the headwaters and enjoying good food. Her companionship filled me and I went back to being happy on my own. My writing thrived in the quiet of mountain life; I was able to connect deeply. Perhaps I was less scattered and distracted. Leaves fell, winds rattled, the mountain and I moved into each moment together.

The inner turnings of winter approached. It was the time for descent, facing into my truths, deepening my writing and opening to darkness. Mountain life was more rugged, and while I appreciated the difference, I missed the gentle feminine quality of the Sonoma Valley. Sharp mountain peaks replaced rolling hills. The landscape called me to build strength, perhaps more masculine aspects of self. Mt. Shasta in particular seemed imposing to me. Was it because of the rocky landscape, the wild tree topped vistas? I wondered what the inner work of winter would reveal, especially when mounds of snow closed me in. The year had brought so much change I felt a bit dizzy from it. Yet I was strong and available to myself in new ways. The mountain would teach me to let go of fragile images of self.

As the winter approached the weather intensified. One evening howling winds woke me. I tossed and turned, listening as the wind shifted around the house. Grateful for warm flannel sheets, I huddled under my covers, recalling how some friends found the wind exciting and invigorating. I feel uneasy with wind; my molecules come unglued. It was then that my mind could spin disaster stories, which included power outages. My flashlight was close by, so I stopped my crazy thinking—Hey, I have plenty of food, a wood stove and neighbors if I needed anything.

The mountain provided me with proving ground. I lived closer to the elements. My new cocoon of nature was not to be trifled with.

Yes, there I was in the mountains. I was surprised; but a hearth life held me in Her cycle of change. The mountain would not tolerate the disconnected me. The rugged, wild and empowered self wanted to be claimed.

Fall Recipe (Comfort Food)

Comfort foods are for all seasons. It helps to know as the light recedes that we have a pot of food warming. This is the ultimate hearth food.

Mac and Cheese
1 pound of elbow macaroni cooked
1 quart of milk
1 stick of butter
½ cup of flour
4 cups Gruyere cheese grated
2 cups of white Cheddar grated
1 cup of breadcrumbs or Panko flakes
salt and pepper to taste

Preheat oven to 375 degrees. Heat the milk in a pan with the butter. When the butter is melted, whisk in the flour. Add hot milk and cook until thickened. Add cheese off the heat with the seasonings and macaroni. Mix and put into a three-quart casserole dish. Sprinkle with breadcrumbs. Bake for 35 minutes. (This recipe comes from Ina Garten.)

Year Three

Winter

"The greatest friend of the soul is the unknown."

—John O'Donohue

Winter in Mt. Shasta brought more than I had expected. I felt wonder at the changes that had brought me to beauty and frigid cold. The mystery was living me. I grew into a life that required unfamiliar actions such as snow plowing, shoveling and buying snow tires. The long winter days alone challenged me to engage in deeper listening. Regular bouts of loneliness touched me, but living on the mountain gave me a chance to grow. My perceptions refined as I became more closely connected to fox, clouds and the flow of mountain streams. Writing called for shelter, so did inner exploration.

The dark days of winter continued to invite me to its potential. The mountain winter also taught me to appreciate various shades of grey. My rental house, thank goodness, was warm. Living as I did in someone else's home, with their belongings, offered me a strange comfort. Yet I also felt confused and a bit bereft—but light—without my own belongings. What was important to belong to? Mountains were considered to offer spiritual opportunity. Letting go became a large part of that opportunity. I wasn't sure what else I could or would give up. I had let go of home in Sonoma, my friends, and the known. The unknown offered possibility.

One November morning the temperature suddenly dropped; I'd heard predictions of snow. It was Thanksgiving week and I looked forward to sharing the holiday with Denise and her family. As the holidays came upon me I felt a poignant loss being so far from both family and friends.

187

The course of my life over these last years would teach me the gifts of holidays shared with unexpected friends and family.

I felt a chill in the air. It was late afternoon as I walked upstairs for a heavy sweater. Just the day before I had moved to the small bedroom tucked under the eaves of the roof. It was the warmest place in the house. The upstairs northeast-facing window had a direct view of Mt. Shasta, blanketed in snow. The mountain looked radiant. By day the sun would often glistened off it; by night radiance was created by the moon which shone on its white peaks illuminating the pitch-black darkness.

The darkness sustained me. I felt grateful for the spacious house. My upstairs bedroom opened out to the office balcony and a small bathroom. The joy of morning showers included the gift of looking out the window; at a slight angle I could see Black Butte. Black Butte is a cluster of overlapping black lava domes. About 10,000 years ago, when Mt. Shasta erupted, this dark peak was left after the lava flow cooled. The peak is sometimes mistaken from Highway 5 as the mountain itself when the high peak is shrouded in cloud cover.

I am reminded that "the created world is holy" and that the sanctuary of all landscape offers us wombs of transformation. While the volcano is dormant on Mt. Shasta I knew that the fires subtly affected life all about me. The last time I lived with similar forces was in Hawaii. When I thought of Hawaii I thought of the indefinable power which lived "under the radar" of the physical world. Mt. Shasta was one of those places where the forces of life invited the individual to listen and surrender. There was legend, which spoke of the connection between Hawaii and Mt. Shasta. Fire had grown me over the last years; I was curious about its role in my mountain life.

Snow Struggles

As evening approached, I became aware of the feeling I sensed as a child before it snowed. I remembered when my sixth grade English teacher asked all of us to memorize a short poem. Our instructions were to choose poems from a list of authors and then recite them. It was the winter of sixth grade and I chose a Robert Frost poem. This single fragment came to me: "Whose woods these are I think I know..." I laughed remembering that it snowed the very next day. Years later I trusted my memory to help me recite the whole poem, and so I did.

To honor those childhood days, I prepared a simple dinner of tomato soup and grilled cheese sandwiches. Nothing like the delicious tastes of creamy red tomato soup and its compliment of crunchy toasted bread, oozing cheese of choice, and Fanny Farmer pickles to add more crunch and sweetness. I felt the excitement of a small girl that evening, a feeling of joy. My beloved Sula sensed the change in weather too and looked up from her permanent home in the black leather chair next to the wood stove. Perhaps she also sensed change.

I settled into the large white couch which I had adapted with my aunt's green handkerchief quilt. I turned on the television to check the weather report. Yes—snow! Before curling back up on the couch, I stoked a blazing fire with the pinecones I had gathered and the wood I had shared stacking with Jim. The large two-story living room was hard to heat with the small white enamel wood stove. I was glad to have the option of central heating. But that evening I treasured the stove where it sat center stage on a platform at the south end of the house, the tall black stove pipe soaring toward the roof.

Fire building on the mountain took a bit more work than in Sonoma. But somehow that evening I found the process invigorating. I loved walking out into the freezing night, gingerly descending the stairs to where wood and kindling were stacked. With wood piled high in my arms I negotiated my way back up the slippery steps. Stomping my feet at the door I then carried my load inside and stacked it on the hearth platform. We were ready; Sula and I fell asleep, lulled by the sounds of a crackling fire. It had been a long time since I had fallen asleep by a fire.

Hours later I woke up with a start. I was surprised to see that it was eleven o'clock. Like a child anxiously waiting for Christmas, I opened the front door and turned on the porch light ready for any small fleck of white. No snow! It had been way too many years since I had seen snow. The closest snow one could see in Sonoma was snow that sprinkled the tops of the higher hills. Well, the quickest way to morning was sleep, so I gathered myself up, turned off the lights, and with Sula skipping ahead headed upstairs.

Morning arrived and although the shades were drawn I felt the telltale quiet that indicated snow. I got out of the warm bed slowly, like a young girl awakening to Christmas, walked to the window and pulled the first blind open. My heart leapt at the sight of the winter wonderland below me. Large random flakes swirled with the wind. A white blanket of silence lay in front of the house. It looked as though several feet had fallen. I felt lighthearted as I watched the falling snow, and then another feeling arose. I felt the snow wrap around the house, settling me inside.

I pulled on my robe and warm socks, walked downstairs and pulled out the chicken I had set to cook in my soup pot. First things first though, fill the kettle and set it heating. A dark green can of English Breakfast tea sat on the counter waiting for me. The wraparound counter on the wall was covered in white tile. I had made the kitchen mine with a few of my favorite cookbooks, a framed print of in dark greens and gold's, a cobalt-blue hand juicer, and small glass bottles. These favorite belongings created home and helped ground me and remind me of my love of color.

After tea, I began the process of pulling meat from the bones. The flesh was cold, but juicy. I discarded the bones and skin and skimmed the fat off the broth. My hands knew this ritual of food preparation, the chopping, the ritual soup pot and soup making. I loved my soup pot's solid heavy frame and shiny, brushed metal. This pot signaled soup, warm and scented. I cut large chunks of carrots, quartered an onion, chopped celery, and added thyme, salt, and pepper. As the pot heated and bubbled I pulled up a stool and watched the snow gently land on the young birch limbs. White on white. The house slowly took on the smells of good things, of closeness and intimacy. I smelled the sharpness of the chicken as it cooked, its aromas filling the house. Soon I would have "chicken soup for the soul." Its goodness was a gift, as was the beautiful snowy morning. A good day.

I breathed deeply into my body as I slept and woke over the remaining days of that week. I woke to a sameness of the continued whiteness. I began to learn about the nuances of a white landscape, becoming aware of the deep contrasts. The empty and barren branches of deciduous trees appeared black. The wild manzanita bushes that covered the edges of the property were laden with snow and looked like chunky snowmen. I could not help but contrast the differences in my seasonal life. Sonoma winters always brought green grasses and misty landscapes.

I stood at the back door. Snow covered everything except the stately pines in their dense greenness. A bit of morning sun had melted the frozen water clinging to low branches. The sturdy structures of maples and birch out the back door showed their emptiness. Their limbs seemed to mirror the bones of things, without cover, naked in their winter presence. Everything was quiet, everything curled in. The stark landscape taught me a new way of seeing, but the emptiness, the deep quiet, agitated me that day.

I squirmed at feeling trapped when I saw the driveway buried under snow. It was too early to plow. I headed out into the snow. Suddenly I heard a snowplow gearing down as it rounded the corner off of McCloud. The snow scraping had started. I both cursed and praised this mammoth machine. It meant a clear road but also a large pile of snow dumped at the end of the drive. I dreaded cranking up the orange monster of a snowplow. It sat waiting in a challenging silence. I had only received instructions on using it once.

I avoided the machine and set out for a walk. Just bundling up and venturing outside into the cold and wind felt like an act of bravery. When I had reported some of my adventures to friends they laughed and called me "mountain woman." I watched the white of my exhaled breath and listened to the sound of my crunching boots.

It was natural for my thoughts to turn to Christmas as I trudged home. Snow, trees and lights were part of a picture postcard winter from childhood. I wanted to create a lovely holiday for myself. How? I imagined large windowsills in the living room, decorated with candles, pine branches and pinecones. A bowl of oranges on the dining room table would bring color and joy into my new Christmas setting.

I stopped imagining and set to snow clearing. I put on my warm heavy gloves and headed to the garage. Could I do this myself? The large orange machine must be faced; I knew I had to learn its tempers. I had two neighbors within walking distance. I hoped my neighbors Phil and Margo were home. If I needed help I could call on them. They were born and raised on the mountain. Snowplowing was like leaf raking to them. My fear of not knowing rose up as I tentatively started the process.

I had to get beyond "I don't understand machines" to put the gears in place, turn the key on, and give it the right amount of gas. Oh, yes, there was gas. My nerves got the better of me and I fumbled. I felt embarrassed and inept, but I didn't want to call for help so soon, so I tried again and again. I walked around in the driveway making a plan to plow down the left come and back the right. Thank goodness the drive was blacktop, a sturdy base.

As I walked the drive I saw Phil out beginning his work. Somehow this gave me confidence. I went back into the cold garage and started the strange machine. It charged out of the garage with a mind of its own, almost a "lets get on with this." So with me trailing behind, the snow blower led the way. Part of getting the knack of it was to remember to turn the blower in the right direction. The snow was supposed to be blown to the sides of the drive, not in the center. Two passes later I got the rhythm of the task; I didn't dare stop but was proud of the large clear swath I had cut. Before long the drive was completely cleared. Carefully returning the blower to its place in the garage, I walked out to enjoy my accomplishment and then saw Phil and waved. I had passed the test.

Inside I showered to warm my frozen toes and hands. I stoked the fire and considered again my newcomer status on the mountain. I was still learning to drive in snow. My spanking new snow tires helped, but the thought of traveling down the mountain or over the pass for the holiday was beyond me. Traveling by air anywhere meant a risky drive north to Oregon or a long drive south to Sacramento. The unreliable mountain winter left travel very much in question. I couldn't help but feel sadness being away from family on Christmas, but I was glad to stay put. Traveling would mean setting up hearth and home in strange places. This was a good opportunity to challenge myself, to flex my ability to trust and know home was inside. Learning how to nurture myself didn't depend on place but on my commitment to give myself what I needed.

Alternative Celebrations

Thick snow still covered the ground the day before Thanksgiving. I had made plans with Denise for Thanksgiving. She had invited several friends to gather at her home. She was in charge of preparing the turkey, the rest of us were bringing different courses. My contribution was to be dessert. So I headed to the store to shop for chocolate *pot de crème* ingredients, stopping first at the hardware store. I bought boot crampons to keep me safe on the driveway. In spite of warnings from friends I had not walked carefully enough on the drive; one minute I was standing, the next I found myself on cold black ice. Ouch, I cried that day. Crampons are snow chains for the feet. I amused myself when I went to purchase unknown equipment. Buying the crampons meant marching into the local hardware store and pretending to be snow-wise. The locals saw the foreigner coming and had knowing smiles on their faces. I had to finally give up on pretense even to find them in the store. Who knew that two Thanksgivings ago when I was flying over Mt. Shasta, I would end up actually living on the mountain?

Thanksgiving arrived, blanketing the mountain with another few inches of snow. The night before I had pulled out my pot to make the chocolate *pot de crème* recipe, which came from my friend Judy. The ingredients included one cup of semi-sweet chocolate chips, one and a quarter cups of light cream scalded, two egg yolks, orange zest and three tablespoons of brandy or Cointreau (orange liqueur). The dessert is easy to make. Once the milk is scalded put the chips in to melt, then place everything in the blender, process, and pour into ramekins or small dishes.

Dinner started at four so I headed to Denise's house on time, driving right behind the snowplow. Luckily her street had also been plowed and I could park the car. I negotiated the slippery sidewalk to the front door. As she opened the door the delicious smells of roasting turkey and wood smoke blended into a perfect Thanksgiving welcome. Friends introduced themselves as we settled by the fire to get acquainted before the timer went off. Last minute dinner preparations called.

We heated mashed potatoes, gravy, and cooked fresh green beans. An abundant table of delicious food welcomed us as we gathered to offer prayers of gratitude. We fell silent as we began to eat, but soon after conversation resumed. Dinner conversation ranged from writing, to a teachers conversation about her class, cost of gasoline and more. We groaned as our meal came to an end. Someone suggested a walk. The snow had stopped falling earlier, so several of us bundled in coats and stepped out into the quiet of the snowy evening. The town seemed strangely silent as we crunched along breathing the crisp night air. Thirty minutes later, after a few songs—one of them appropriately being Silent Night—snowballs and hill walking, we returned gladly to the warm house. Piping hot tea and dessert completed the evening, which everyone loved. Who wouldn't, unless you hated chocolate! I said my goodbyes soon after dessert and headed home with leftovers, grateful for a Thanksgiving of many blessings. Sula curled next to me as I read a book of Barbara Kingsolver's. Earlier in the week I had found the book on the upstairs shelves. Having access to someone else's library on a cold winter night was a gift.

Another overcast winter day left me feeling buried indoors. I knew it would help if I got myself outside for a walk. Winter solstice was approaching. I missed the chance to walk the labyrinth on solstice in Sonoma. Walking reminded me to honor the spiral of life and honor ceremony, nature's womb. While I loved the rich darkness of the season I also felt the isolation. Pre-holiday rituals of Christmas would normally include shopping in Sonoma and the tree lighting ceremony in the town square. I missed friends and family. The newness of the mountains has worn a bit thin. So if I didn't have a labyrinth what would I do?

One dark evening I sat by the fire musing on the very first winter of my quest. The labyrinth had inspired me to take my change one step at a time. As I sat recalling the spiral walk, I imagined each step on the path. I knew that my steady course of listening had inspired change, exploration and self-care. Each meeting inside myself brought me ground, trust and presence. I had chosen freedom by facing into my fears. Yes, I had chosen freedom above all else, but still in the moment I felt the challenge. Action was needed, which meant an evening walk, something I had not done. Mountain evenings are especially dark. There are no streetlights to interfere. Would I challenge myself to take a short walk and appreciate the bright winter stars?

Yes. So I bundled up and set out the front door with my high boots. The dark was pitch black and the thousands of pinpoints of stars felt close enough to touch. I crunched my way over the plowed part of the driveway and out to the road. I stepped gingerly so as not to slip. I headed down the street where no dogs would be out. As I found my stride I leaned my head back to view the dark womb of the night sky. Looking in wonder, I felt the enormity of our universe. The womb held possibility, births. I was reminded that stars had announced births for eternity. I wondered what and/or who was being birthed in that moment. I felt a special kind of grace that evening as I slowed and turned back toward home, grateful for the gift of walking on that winter night.

Warm inside the house I made a plan. Instead of my labyrinth walk on the shortest day of the year I decided to ask Jim to help me cut some greens. This would put holiday magic in my new home. The next morning I called him and asked for his help. He said he had just been outside cutting a few bottom limbs from an elder pine in his yard. Would I like those? I felt grateful for his generosity. I walked the snowy drive to his house and met him. We carried three large limbs back to my house. Dropping the limbs at the garage I asked him to come in for tea and pancakes. I made a pot of black tea and a simple meal of fluffy pancakes.

I had prepared the pancake batter earlier, thinking of a winter solstice celebration. Eggs, sugar, baking powder, baking soda, buttermilk, butter and vanilla were the ingredients. The owners of the house had left a wonderful griddle. I had come upon it in the back of the pot shelf one day and knew it would be fun to use. After oiling the griddle I started the pancake making. Four small pancakes fit beautifully; I waited for telltale bubbles before turning them. Ultimately I finished with a nice stack of cakes. We filled our plates, poured generous amounts of maple syrup and sprinkled the cakes with sliced almonds. We both agreed that pancakes were too often forgotten; we agreed to nourish ourselves with them all winter.

Christmas drew closer. Another large snowstorm piled more of the white stuff. By then the snow had reached above the window ledges in the downstairs bedroom. Snow also mounded to the top of the back porch steps. I went out to shovel a path out the front door to the driveway. The right side of the house seemed more protected—the winds didn't mound snow so deeply, so I could shovel to keep the path clear. It was exhausting and finger numbing, but once I shoveled, the warm sun would help melt off the lower pack. Since before Thanksgiving I had gotten used to the blower; my orange monster had become a friend, ensuring my connection to the rest of the world.

One morning the snowplow dumped an especially large mount of snow. I set about my task with vigor, but the snow blower stopped dead in the middle of a large drift. Frustrated, I stopped, tried to restart it. It wouldn't budge. I gave up and sat in the snow, a few tears trickling down. But soon after I heard the telltale sound of my neighbor Phil setting to the same task. The challenge in the moment was to ask for help. I got up and went to ask. Soon his deft knowledge of snow blowers and packed snow dismantled my fears and taught me strategies for mastering them.

Even though the day was bright and sunny, melancholy shrouded me. I called Denise to celebrate the snow before Christmas. We planned our first snowshoe expedition. The owners had left their snowshoes out for me to use, so I gathered them up, packed my backpack with water, snacks and sunscreen, then drove off to pick up Denise. The winding drive up the mountain always thrilled me, but I was nervous about what we would find. Luckily the road was plowed. Both of us marveled at the snow packed on the side of the road which measured to the top of our car. Tall pines looked like sentinels with their white coat of arms. The sun caught the crystalline snow and flashed light between the shadows along the winding road; we turned and smiled at one another.

At Bunny Flats we climbed out of the car and took in the view of snow-covered hills as far as we could see. We then surveyed the possibilities for a beginning route. Our decision was to climb up, then head down and over, heading south. It was a stretch to get used to the snowshoes, but once accustomed we felt exhilarated being engulfed by the beauty and warm sun. I felt the joy of movement and the clear fresh quality of morning air. The crunch of our shoes, the laughter of skiers, and the songs of a few birds accompanied us as we walked along the top edge of the deep snow. We stopped along the way to enjoy our chocolate and nuts, unpeeled our scarves and felt warm under our heavy coats. When we finally climbed back to the parking lot we were tired, but rosy cheeked and happy.

What a day! The sanctuary of nature walking cured any blues or grays hiding in me. After dropping off my friend, I drove home with new appreciation for the differences of being in winter's landscape. It wasn't likely I would have found myself on a mountain slope snowshoeing if I hadn't come. Surprises and change are miracles.

Moving to the mountains had brought me a new appreciation for simplicity. I had to give up experiences I took for granted, which included momentary shopping distractions and quick fixes. Nature drew me to untapped places in myself and taught me patience.

Several mornings later I stood at the kitchen window looking out into the front yard. I suddenly caught sight of a covey of quail running across the front yard. They were the only sign of wildlife I had seen besides a few squirrels who raided the flat-pan bird feeder on the front porch. The green tray was easy to fill and I found it fun to watch the occasional squirrel jump onto it for a breakfast of sunflower seeds. As I watched the quail I counted twelve gray heads as they bobbed to safe territory in the scrub manzanita, leaving behind tiny footprints of life. I was revived by those gentle morning gifts. Small gifts are the best on stark days.

Christmas Day arrived, and although yoga friends had invited me for dinner, I chose to stay home. In the morning I talked with my sister and brother-in-law who were visiting in Florida. In the afternoon I spoke with Matt and Dawn and several other friends in Sonoma. My neighbor Jim stopped by briefly to bring me his famous Lund chocolate bars. I was grateful for his friendship. He handed me my present and went on his way to a family dinner in Dunsmuir.

There was something pleasurable about the simplicity of that Christmas day. I missed being with family, but I knew there would be other holidays. How to make the day special alone? The sun was shining. I made sure to have special food; I lit a candle. As I sat looking around the beauty of my home I smiled at the special mountain gift of pinecones and tree limbs. I had dried orange slices in a low oven all morning, and then strung them on fine gold thread inherited from my Aunt Annie. The orange circles hung from the branches of the pine and gave me pleasure. The day was spacious and simple.

I settled into preparing my Christmas dinner. My first course was salad with oranges, pecans and goat cheese. The salad included endive, finely chopped and toasted pecans, sliced oranges and some pieces of goat cheese to put on top. I made orange vinaigrette from orange juice, shallots and oil that gave the salad a lively taste. I had decided to make a fish soup for the main course. Soup included a can of tomatoes, chopped onions and fennel, carrots and pieces of fresh halibut. I added oregano and at the last minute a bit of dill. For some reason the whole process felt ancestral, Scotch-Irish in its simplicity. I mused on that as I savored my soup.

Later I gave myself the gift of preparing chocolate *pot de crème* for dessert, and saved that for when the stars came out, when I also relit a ceremonial fire. Christmas was on a Thursday that year and as the day came to an end I was grateful. I thanked my angels who had guided me to the mountain. I saw how my move was offering me new understanding about loneliness. I saw that loneliness as a sign that I had not come present in the moment. When I separated out from self I lost my connection. I also felt compassion for those parts of me wanting to be connected to family and friends.

The next week I continued the holiday celebration by inviting a few friends for dinner. The scent of roast chicken with parsnips, carrots, onions and potatoes filled the house. Jim, Susan and Ted came, bringing wine, figgy pudding and chocolate. We sang a few songs, shared stories and ate till we felt our buttons pop. I felt happy for the joys of the holiday solitude and for the group celebration. The following week I settled back into my writing and quiet, reminding myself that the dark still held potential.

Winter brought dreams. One night I woke from a frightening dream about a dark ghostly man. I remembered having come across other dark male figures in dreams. The dream masculine was directly or indirectly shaming me. I felt disempowered by these aspects of my psyche; I felt they wanted to prevent me from pursuing my own path. Over my lifetime I had distracted and betrayed myself with ghostly lovers. My inner fantasies had connected me to creative men; in the end I choose men in the outer world who mirrored these images. But then I betrayed myself by depending on them to spark me; the seduction could be intellectual or sexual. When I gave in to the game, which of course I played also, I knew I was lost. I began to see the patterns of my encounters. These encounters included creative men who mirrored my creative talents. The tangle of these webs resulted in low self-esteem. The outcome always led me to give up my own knowing for the male's superior expertise or knowledge. My early sexual abuse played a role. Fear, passivity and negativity replaced the power and mystery of life. A series of dreams followed that showed me how run I was by this negative masculine. I felt angry as I watched myself stand by passively. Why didn't I stand up to these characters? Standing up for my unique feminine voice was what was needed. I had to challenge the shame-based voices. Those voices were also mirrored in women friendships, for much harsh resentful criticism had come from my mother. Transformation was needed.

As December flowed into January, I felt my usual January fears. Something about the New Year and the unknown made it easy for me to go to the negative. The challenge was to look to creative expression to replace the anxiety. I knew many women who shared the struggle to find ground in themselves.

Matt and Dawn telephoned midweek to give me news. Big news! They had decided to move back to Sonoma! Their plans were still forming, but they wanted to arrive sometime in June. The timing would depend on the sale of their home. My voice squeaked back with delight as I digested the good news. I couldn't help but feel a grandchild might be on the way soon.

I danced away from the phone with anticipation. Would I be returning to Sonoma? A new year was filled with possibility and spring would come. But I wasn't in Sonoma and there were still months ahead of me.

Winter Recipe

This seasonal treat is a favorite dessert of mine. I love its texture and sweetness.

Apple Crisp

4 Granny Smith Apples
¼ cup of apple cider
1 teaspoon ground cinnamon
$1\,^1/_2$ cups oatmeal
$^3/_4$ cup light brown sugar, packed
$^1/_2$ pound cold unsalted butter, diced

Preheat the oven to 350 degrees F. Butter a 9" baking dish. Peel, core, and cut the apples into large wedges. Combine the apples with the apple cider and spices. Pour into the dish. To make the topping, combine the oatmeal, sugar, and cold butter in the bowl and mix with electric blender. Mix on low speed until the mixture is crumbly and the butter is the size of peas. Scatter evenly over the apples. Bake for 45 minutes until the top is brown and the apples are bubbly. Serve warm.

Spring

*"As we relate to the world with a new sense of connection,
we often experience a second wave of feminine spiritual
consciousness. We come to recognize the innate holiness of the
earth, the sacred dwelling in nature, matter, and body"*

—Sue Monk Kidd

Water

Spring came to the Siskiyou Mountains, so differently from its arrival in the Sonoma Valley last year. I was continually learning to accept change. The weight of a long winter reflected in tightness in my shoulders. My body wanted a long walk away from the confinement of high snowdrifts. Denise had telephoned to suggest a walk to Moss Falls, a place I had wanted to see. We both needed to feel the sun on our faces. The snow was beginning to melt and we both looked forward to adventure. We made a plan to meet late one morning.

It was February. My distant Sonoma Valley home I knew would be full of the scent and beauty of cherry blossoms and acacia. I felt the joy of change recalling that Matt and Dawn would be moving to California. June wasn't that far away. My heart hoped for grandchildren sooner than later. A new generation would be writing their stories.

I dressed for our outing in layers. Mountain weather can be fickle, turn on a dime. As we drove south to Dunsmuir, we smiled to each other and felt like pioneers. Our destination was not far. Denise took the first exit in Dunsmuir and then drove us along the river road. She stopped the car in a small parking lot; we got out and pulled our sweaters on. I was surprised to see us headed up railroad tracks, an unlikely beginning to finding waterfalls, but I was open to adventure.

Our feet crunched on gray rocks between steel rails. The bright sun shone on our faces and warmed our bodies. I felt like Huck Finn. We walked quite a while up the west side of the river. Trains once traveled this route to bring summer vacationers. A train still stops in Dunsmuir, although I'm not sure which line it is. We walked at a slow pace. The river rushed below us; snowmelt churned and picked up the red soil.

At high noon we removed one layer of clothing. I loved the feeling of comparative weightlessness. Streams poured down the hills from our left, emptying their fill into the river. Two deer headed downhill to drink from the river but stopped when they spied us. With short bounds and fluid strides they rushed out of sight.

After what seemed like an eternity of rail and rock walking, we rounded a curve. Denise pointed to a path just on the other side and soon we were headed down to the river.

I heard the sound of crashing water and turned to my right to see an astonishing wall of water cascading straight off the top of the hill. The water was woven with vibrant green moss and short grasses. Torrents of it tumbled from the rim above. The white water below was propelling everything along. Large craggy boulders were landing pads for small birds. Amazed, we both watched them dive for food and then resettle themselves on the rocks. The power and mystical quality of the place left me dumbfounded.

I walked along the river's edge and then crouched down on the sandy bank breathing in the moist spray which seemed to bless me. After moments of just being, I became aware that the tightness in my body had dropped away. I felt the freedom and coolness of the water. What joy to feel the swooping and flowing grace of the day. Denise smiled as I walked back to join her. "Thank you," I said. -

When I arrived home I showered and settled into some writing. I was aware how full of life and at peace I felt. Just a few months at the mountain had given me experience of the innate holiness of the world. I agreed with Sue Monk Kidd that my healing brought new awareness, that awareness opened me to a deeper relationship with life. The voices of Moss Falls spoke to me of flow and source, a truly feminine offering.

As I grew closer to a feminine sense of self, I came to honor the gifts of receptivity and intuition. I wanted to stop dominating my life with standards imposed from outside which invited me to respond to the voices of self-doubt. The voices were mirrored in others' judgments. I had been there myself, but as I claimed more of myself I didn't need to be right any longer. It was a challenge to give up the old habits.

As the month unfolded I felt the cold inside and out. The snow still wrapped the house in its whiteness and asked me to embrace more of myself. March finally arrived with the hope for snowmelt, but spring did not bring a thaw. Finally one morning I heard rain tapping out its sounds on the skylights. I hoped for snowmelt. The warmer weather would chip away at the banks of snow still piled high around the house.

I headed outside with my parka for a quick walk to clear my mind and smell the freshness of the cleansing rain. I took one of my comfort hikes past a bubbling and churning stream just a short distance from the house. New rainwater and snowmelt had filled the stream. I stood at its edge just breathing in the tumbling flow. The water was so alive I couldn't help but bend down and cup my hands, raising the water to drink.

Heading home later I felt appreciation for my mountain landscape. More and more I came to honor the differences in each tree and stream of my neighborhood. I felt the truth of David Abram's words that "each place had its own dynamism, its own patterns of movement, and these patterns engage the senses and relate them in particular ways...it has its own intelligence..." Of course I hadn't taken time to experience these truths before. There was such bounty and reward in listening for the essence of each and every aspect of life. Inside the house I stoked the fire and heated a big bowl of tomato soup. I stood watching the rain fall and puddle into the bird feeder on the front porch while enjoying my soup.

I sat by the fire later with tea and pulled several books from the stack. I had been rewarded over the recent years reading about my Celtic roots. Celtic spirituality had given me a new model to bring spirit and matter into harmony. The resurgence of Celtic Christianity held hope for evolving consciousness and inspired new understandings.

I went to the altar to light a candle in gratitude for the rich knowing I was gathering. I grabbed two books on Ireland and went back to the fire. My favorite pages spoke to me about the traditions of visiting wells for blessing and prayer. The power and presence of such traditions somehow lived in my soul memory. I realized that my recent experience at the stream followed that tradition; I had felt blessed by the swiftly running waters. Next I opened an Irish travel book. Pictures of rolling green hills, ancient ruins, rock walls and turf fires delighted me. Was it time to go to Ireland? Travel to Ireland was a roots journey. It did seem like a missing piece. I felt the call from the bone. Reading about my heritage was one part of the experience, but it was time to step foot on Irish soil.

As I considered travel to the land of my ancestors, I wished I had heard more stories. Stories connect us. I recalled again how I had loved spending time with my grandmother drinking tea or looking at old albums. My grandmother's death had been confusing because no one had talked about what death meant, nor given me time to grieve. That was the way of those times. Much later in my life, when my grandfather passed away, I was far away. At the time I was totally disconnected from him. I didn't miss him, but wished I knew more about my heritage. If I were returning to Ireland I wanted to take the opportunity to heal with my family, especially with my mother. Just thinking about Ireland brought up so many emotions I didn't really understand.

Dark Shadows

My relationship with my mom was complicated. Alzheimer's complicated my feelings. Her long-term nursing care in a home in Illinois near my sister had weighted on both of us. I was grateful to Barbara for caring for Mom. She had taken on the responsibility of paying bills, checking the medications she was given and visiting her regularly.

Opening the family chest of memories triggered hunger. I found myself in the kitchen making one of my favorite comfort foods, cinnamon toast. I recalled winter mornings seeing my mother mix the cinnamon and sugar and sprinkle it on warm toast. I carried the toast and a cup of tea to the sofa and enjoyed the first sweet crunch of toast. As I sat enjoying, I remembered I had packed an album of childhood pictures and went to pull it off a shelf. Its faded blue cover and white tasseled cord were aged. The bottom of the book sported a colorful collage of toy soldiers, a clown, and a bear. It had that 1940's design sense to it and easily pulled me back in time. I opened to the pages of faded photographs. As I turned the pages and looked into the face of a distanced and sad three-year-old self, I pondered with knowing; my childhood pictures showed the truth. The pictures I leafed through included a formal photograph of my Irish grandmother and grandfather.

My Irish grandfather William had been born in born in Belfast, married my Scotch born grandmother Margaret and then came to the U. S. to begin a new life in Philadelphia, Pennsylvania. My mother was one of four children. My Aunt Annie who had recently passed away was the eldest. My memories of both my grandparents included a lively Irish humor and a strict hand. There were also dark secrets and unresolved feelings connected to my roots. Ireland held both light and dark.

While wrestling and distancing from my heritage I opened to the dark secret which I had rarely spoken about. My conflicting feelings about my grandfather didn't reveal themselves until the late 1980's. Over many years I had labored with depression and behaviors typical of women with molest in their background. I had also spent years deepening into my body, feeling, growing and healing the spiral of my history. Each spiral of witnessing opened more cell memory. After years of work healing the molest wounds with my father I assumed I had faced the past. However, more life changes and another round of inner work revealed more.

One day in the therapy process I had strong recall of my grandfather's hands. The experience was profoundly visceral, an emotional cell memory. His long white hands were frightening to me, not only because I recalled they were the hands of a butcher but also because they carried some ghostly quality.

The process of recall of molest by my grandfather took some time, but then I understood my long-standing fear of him. I could see why I was so alone in my feelings of distrust. I was the only member of the family who seemed to feel this way—wasn't he always charming and funny, an Irish twinkle in his eye? Wasn't he a man of religion, a church-going, loving man with such vision? Well, no, I didn't see anything funny or charming about him at all. I knew a truth about him.

The memory recall was traumatic but also helped me face so many unresolved feelings. One outcome of facing into my history was the opportunity to understand some of my habits of not speaking and of silence, one of them being my mantra of "I don't want to tell you." Another understanding shed light on our family dynamics. It was the knowing that my mother had also been molested as a child. What followed was another thought—my grandfather had also been molested as a child. I dropped in that moment into a deeper understanding. Suddenly the few stories I had heard later in life about an alcoholic uncle of his fell into place. Molestation was part of our family history! I had inherited the family secret. However, the secret began to feel like a dark cloak weighing me down. I wanted to go to Ireland and release this cloak. I no longer was willing to carry the shadow history of my family.

To take a step toward healing in that moment of understanding I carried several pictures of myself to the altar; I lay them gently there as an offering for the tenderhearted girl who still hid inside me. It was time to call her out of hiding and begin the healing process, accept, forgive and transform at the deeper level.

Over the years I had negotiated some of my frozen emotional world. Abuse takes time to heal. One starts at the edges of trauma. I looked back to my 1940's and 50's upbringing and recalled how little was said, how few emotions were expressed. I often thought of my father and his repressed feelings. He was actually more emotional, more open and sensitive, offering us more feminine values on one hand. Yet I also knew that his heart condition related to his unexpressed anger and pain. I needed to resolve more of my past, and Ireland offered a new lens.

A couple of days after looking in my album I discovered a treasure of a book. Self- nurturing on the mountain usually included a stop at Village Books. Bookstores were like mountain hikes to me for they offered adventures. While exploring I found Christina Baldwin's book called *Storycatcher: Making Sense of Our Lives through the Power of Story*. Baldwin's book put my process into new perspective. I was writing to make sense of my life. I was also writing to find my truths, to recover that essential self. I saw through her suggestion that it is important to offer new stories to the generations that follow.

I thought about my role in the story. The telling of our story offers insight, healing and much more. My writing also challenged the history of family silence, but I felt I had a long way to go. I liked Baldwin's reminder that our story is about "forgiveness, about compassion, about questioning."

I was more than ever determined to heal with my mother. Our story was unresolved. I still felt anger toward her, yet withheld my feelings. I became restless thinking of her, my body fearful of her cold and distant presence. A walk always opened me so I grabbed my coat and headed down Shasta Way.

I took the cutoff across the railroad tracks. As I walked I pondered travel to Ireland and the unconscious emotional patterns of my family. A shadow still hung over me like the dense shadows of the thick forest canopy. I smelled the dampness of the snowmelt, inhaled the fresh air and brought new breath to my story. I felt refreshed after walking.

When I returned home, I heated rice and lentils that I had made a day before. Spring had not shown herself in our markets yet so I kept to my winter menus. As I settled into a chair in the bedroom, the sun came out. I pulled a chair up to catch the late afternoon rays, continuing my thoughts of Ireland. As the sun warmed me I knew I wanted to go to Ireland.

I felt lucky to have money to travel, but it felt strange to consider leaving the mountain. The trip just to the airport was a long one. San Francisco International was too far away. The other option was to drive to the Sacramento Airport. That trip would take me three hours or so. Well, first things first. I wanted to find a group to travel with. After last year's travel on my own, I needed the support and guidance of others. Other plans to leave the mountain would have to include finding someone to come and stay in the house with Sula. The logistics began to feel overwhelming, but Ireland wouldn't wait another year.

Travel Preparations

I woke with excitement the next morning and began my travel exploration. I recalled a newsletter I had saved, searched and found it. Listed half-way down the page was an Ireland trip guided by Phil Cousineau, author of *The Art of Pilgrimage*. The trip sounded inviting. It included travel on the West coast of Ireland—unknown people and destinations, ancient ruins, a visit to the island of Inis Mor—and ended in Dublin. Being in Ireland with a pilgrim-conscious leader would make travel even more meaningful. Soon after, I called for a brochure.

While I waited for the mail to arrive I considered the travel options. I couldn't think of travel to Ireland without visiting my mother. Then the thought came to me that I should visit Scotland to honor my grandmother. I had just a year prior heard from a relative that she was born close to Glasgow. If I was making a roots journey I wanted to include Scotland—but where to go?

It didn't take long for me to remember the island of Iona. The island lay in the Hebrides, just off the west coast of Scotland. Just the sound of the word Iona called me. Iona in Gaelic means dove. Yes there was a soul calling, something beyond words. Iona had crossed my sights several times before. When I had searched it online the first time I found out how long it took to travel to the small island and quickly gave up any idea of it. The second time I recalled talking about Iona was with Elizabeth during our picnic in Chartres; she had mentioned her travel to the sacred island with her husband, had even mentioned the name of a hotel. What was it? I went online and discovered it. Yes, the Argyll Hotel. It would certainly be easy to fly from Dublin, our last stop during the trip. Should I or not?

When the papers arrived I liked what I saw. The ten-day trip would focus on the West Coast of Ireland and then end up in Dublin. I was happy with the travel itinerary which included ancient sites, monasteries, modern towns, Irish music and much more. I began to put a rough plan in place. The plan included a visit to my mother, ten days in Ireland, and then two days on the island of Iona. I doubted at first, fearing it was too long and I would have no one to care for Sula. I thought of Mary, and while I recalled she didn't particularly like cats, I knew she would enjoy the beauty and spaciousness of the house. Perhaps I could warm her to the idea by inviting her to visit for tea the next day.

I made scones; we sat talking and enjoying ginger tea. I mentioned a tentative plan to travel and asked her if she would house sit and care for Sula. She said she was delighted to help, would enjoy coming and staying. I felt good with the plan and took the next step to schedule air travel. It was still March and the group travel in Ireland would not begin until May 4, so I hoped for decent airfares. I called Scott to ask about reservations for hotels in Illinois and Iona. First things first I thought; I needed to secure my place on the Ireland trip.

The final papers sent to me included names of people who would be traveling in the group. I noticed several women from California. One in particular I decided to connect with. Her name was Dawn. It would feel good to have some connection before the trip, especially since I had planned to travel a day ahead of the group. I knew my body, mind and spirit adjusted more easily if I had alone time first. Visiting my mom would be emotional and I wanted to give myself space to have my feelings.

With my timing clear I called Scott to see what he had come up with. My flights included departures from San Francisco, Chicago, Shannon, Dublin and Glasgow. It seemed a big order, but having the support of his travel wizardry helped. Everything was in place.

Ireland had been a longing for several years. I knew my return to the land of my ancestry would give me a mirror. Frank MacEowen speaks richly about longing in *The Mist-Filled Path*: "What we long for speaks volumes about who we really are. Although surrendering to our sacred longings can sometimes be quite a painful soul-stretching and soul-tempering process—our longing, with its unique quality and energy, is also a magical state to befriend, for it is a trustworthy guide." I moved toward my longing to know my roots.

Spring signaled her presence when the Shasta lilies began peeking their heads above ground. I set about my ritual of spring cleaning. The corners of the spacious house needed tending. I took the cozy quilt and pillows back downstairs out of the loft bedroom, moving myself into spring headquarters. I looked forward to actually seeing earth, seeing the bricks on the patio, throwing open the French doors and smelling spring roses. I washed and polished the wood floors. I cleared the altar of winter pinecones and twigs and replaced it with a small nest found on a forest walk. Cleaning out the old gave me a chance to receive the new. Going to the corners of our life and tending them heals. Out of that tending arises authentic story. Baldwin reminded me of an important reason to write. She writes that "only by telling each other our authentic stories will we come upon our wisdom and make the new road map we need for survival."

I felt good about the inner work I had done over the years. I also gained deeper appreciation for the fact that the last third of our life is an opportunity to sort life and refine understanding. Life process asked me to deepen and honor even though the work was not easy.

One turn brought me face to face with more feeling. About three weeks before my departure a spring cold put me in bed. I was like many other women in my family who were intolerant of sickness. It was my fault in some way that I was ill. Illness was a sign of weakness rather than an opportunity. I finally settled under the covers and brought compassion and awareness to the cold. The colds I get are not mild sniffles: I have a lumberjack sneeze and painful sinuses, run through boxes of Kleenex. My eyes were sore and puffy so I couldn't do any reading or video watching. I finally gave in and took an Epson salt bath to relax my body.

As I sat in the tub I thought about colds. They usually signaled emotional backlog. I had put off feelings during this time of preparing for Ireland. My visit to see my mother was what sat most heavy in my heart. I had successfully avoided my feelings about my visit. It had been easier to focus on the travel to Ireland. But if not now, when? I had to face my fears.

I turned to my writing to help me focus. I felt at odds with myself, still blaming her for being a less than model mother. So many childhood habits of blaming, of keeping my heart protected, still blocked and limited my life. My habit was to keep people away from the inner me. My mother had been the number one person locked out. I felt pain, anger and resentment. Just acknowledging that truth helped me drop into questions about my visit. I didn't really want to go, but also knew it was time. I spent several days growing confidence to actually speak to my mother and to open to levels of risk by sharing feelings with her. As a child I was raised with strict rules and prohibition. There was no speaking back to a parent, no direct communication in my family. I had also chosen silence to keep me protected. Many of us have the experience of sharing and then have the information turned on us, used against us. But that silence no longer served me, it stopped my flow of connection to others.

I had to grow again into claiming my voice. I knew healing asked me to commit to speaking directly with my mother; it didn't matter that she couldn't hear me. I called and spoke with a friend in Sonoma to have her witness my commitment. It felt good to have support. Soon I anticipated the visit with more openheartedness.

When I felt into my visit I saw the wisdom in visiting my mom alone. My sister was going to be away. The visit would help me listen more closely to my truths. As Baldwin suggests, healing the lineage through story is "not about adhering to someone else's version of historical truth." It was important to be authentic with myself. It was important to unearth the unresolved and bring it to light.

I set about packing my clothes, taking into consideration May in Chicago, Ireland and the island of Iona. In the end I packed a warm coat, sweaters and then lighter spring clothes. It was fun to consider all my destinations. I also planned my pilgrim bag well with gifts, writing paper, books, watercolor paints and papers.

Our leader, Phil Cousineau, had suggested we take small things from home to give as gifts. I had tucked postcard pictures of Sonoma in my bag before leaving in the fall, and I always had a stash of lavender sachets. I packed these items with care. Our travel included stops at several wells dedicated to St. Brigid so I also planned by preparing offerings. I felt connected to her since celebrating St. Brigid's feast day the year before. At that time I had forged a link with her strength and forthrightness. It was her fire of commitment and the water of her wells that I looked forward to visiting. I invoked her help in my journey to visit my mother. I wanted to be a modern pilgrim walking in the footsteps of my ancestors. I recalled the well tradition of tying rags or ribbons and decided to make them.

I approached this ritual process with gratitude, for it made the travel feel more alive and intimate. I had brought a small box of cloth with me. When I started rummaging I found scraps of Guatemalan fabric saved from a weaving project. The fabric was vibrant with blues and reds and yellows. I took out the gold thread I had saved from my Aunt Annie's sewing box and began. First I cut the fabric in twelve-inch lengths and braided the cloth with gold thread. I did this with a conscious heart and felt my love of fabric wrapped in my gifts. Cloth of any kind inspired me. I loved linens, dresses, handkerchiefs, quilts—all were lovely heritages to bring forward into new generations. My feminine cloth braids would be my offering to Ireland. It felt as though I was carrying my female heritage with me. When I finished the braids, I liked my results and lovingly tucked them in my suitcase. I was ready to go.

Spring reminded me of new birth and the opportunity to be connected in deeper ways. I hoped Ireland would open the gateways to deeper experience. I wanted to experience the land and connect to the land of my ancestors. I recalled reading that in times past the kings were married to the land through ceremony; the ceremony and intention joined him with the Goddess and the land belonging to her. Considering the sacred marriage I realized that I had been focusing on the feminine so long that I had forgotten about integration. I also needed to work with healing my inner masculine. I had avoided the male aspect of my journey. Each day I prepared in small ways. I began to look at my years of relationship with the masculine. My wounds had taught me to distrust men. However, over the years having a working relationship with Hal Zina Bennett, my editor, had taught me trust. While still afraid of men, I wanted to risk connection. I hadn't realized that travel would offer a safe opportunity to see where I stood. Slowly I was stepping into presence through creative exploration and I felt stronger.

I began to see the wisdom of choosing a male leader, one grounded as a teacher, writer and pilgrimage leader. If Irish genes had silenced me, Irish fires would restore me to speak and honor my truths. The healing process would continue.

I stopped my musing and set about my last bits of packing. Pilgrimage meant giving myself new thresholds for change. Being with a group of people was going to be a challenge for me. I knew I mistrusted my ability to set boundaries. My patterns were to withdraw and be guilty about my needs. Self trust and awareness would help me honor those boundaries. Perhaps the trip would offer me the practice I needed to live centered in the hearth of my essential self.

What would Ireland bring? Just before leaving I phoned Matt and Dawn to catch up and say goodbye. They delightedly shared that they had just sold the house and were putting their own travel plans in place for June. I felt happy and told them I was considering moving back to Sonoma and would certainly come home to greet them. I promised to connect when I returned to California.

Spring Recipe

When I come home from inner or outer pilgrimages or adventures I drop back into rituals, which give me, back a sense of home and hearth. My favorite comfort ritual is making warm toast and a hot steaming cup of tea.

Tea and Toast

Choose your favorite crunchy bread. Pull out the butter. Choose a favorite jam—blackberry or orange marmalade is mine—or soft cheese like cream cheese or goat cheese. Toast the bread, slather on your topping of choice, and then take your slowly brewed tea and sit by the fire and muse.

Pilgrimage III to Ireland

It was early May when I boarded my plane at Sacramento International, headed to Chicago's O'Hare Airport. The pilgrimage I was embarking on held much potential. It would be my last travel for some time. The journey process invited healing; I felt the ancestral threads draw me to new stories. The first spiral of my travel asked me to step into one part of my unhealed landscape of relationship. The next turn of the journey would take me to the physical shores of Ireland, to the land of my heritage. The mystical island of Iona, Scotland would follow.

It was late afternoon when I settled into my seat. I was confronted with simultaneous feelings of dread and longing. I was not sure how I would feel when I saw my mother. It had been eight years since Alzheimer's had claimed her mind, and the disease produced a kind of limbo. The last time I had visited was Easter a year ago. Yet, while she seemed less herself she also became more herself. She carried a quality of peace. For most of my life I had resisted her, feared her anger and bitterness. Since committing to speak my emotional truths I felt dread. But I distracted myself from these feelings. It was easier to distance; there were logjams of emotions waiting underwater and I didn't want to feel them. I opened a book I had brought with me, an Irish mystery called *Master of Souls*. The series is written about Celtic Ireland in the 7th century. Sister Fidelma, the main character, is a powerful woman and sleuth extraordinaire. My friend Kathleen had mentioned the series when I told her about my journey to Ireland. Kathleen and I share the love of mystery, Ireland and transformational quest.

The book distracted me but didn't stop the low rumblings of deep sadness and anxiety. A friend had commented that my mother was a frail wheelchair-ridden woman who no longer could affect me. She questioned the source of my fear; but fear lay deep in my cells and would not be talked out. At the time she had said this I knew she meant to be supportive. The fear didn't cease because the disease of Alzheimer's had taken my mother's mind. I felt ashamed that I had not healed the past and let in the light of forgiveness.

My plane landed in Chicago an hour-and-a-half later than scheduled. A thunderstorm with torrential rains and flashing lightning heightened my anxiety. I then smiled for a moment, for actually it was a perfect backdrop for my visit. The weather mirrored my stormy feelings. Time to be who I was, be in the moment. I was a woman who had learned to accept travel anxiety and allow vulnerable feelings to arise. I didn't have to cut them off, pull up my bootstraps, or act as if I weren't afraid.

My car rental was waiting for me. As I pulled out of the airport the sky was dark. I was used to being greeted by my sister and I felt the loss of her presence. I had rain and thunder at my back. Nevertheless I headed to Naperville with hotel directions in hand; the drive would take me about thirty minutes. I turned on the radio to a classical music station to ease my fears. The rain blurred my vision. My heart felt heavy.

The truth was that my mother was the last person I wanted to see. I felt vulnerable, without defenses. What would I say to her? I felt pain just imagining her in her wheelchair. The week prior to my travel I had talked with my sister; she told me she hadn't seen much change.

A large part of me wanted to turn around and head back to a hotel close to the airport where I was to catch a plane to Ireland in two days. But I kept my hands steady on the wheel, headed for a Marriott closer to my mother's nursing home. Alzheimer's had mellowed the bitter woman I had known as a child. Mother's anger had confused and frightened me. What part of her heart and psyche had been wounded and by whom? These thoughts of compassion were new; I had, for such a long time, felt comfortable in blaming her. Allowing the healing was a process. Could I let go of thinking of her as my mother and see her as a woman?

As I met my own feelings, I knew seeing her would release me from the past. I began thinking of her life as a young girl and then woman. Certainly her own childhood wounding had molded her. I was surprised to feel this truth. I also considered the fact that she was the only woman in the family who had children. Why was that? Her two sisters married but never had children. What were her truths? As I began to see beyond the mother-daughter bonds, I could release the story that limited.

The rain stopped as I finally pulled into the Marriott hotel. I felt relief as I checked myself in; it was late, eight o'clock. I took a long hot shower and fell into bed. I awoke in the morning to the sun peeking through the dense maroon curtains. The curtains were metaphors for the history which blocked a life of aliveness and joy. Glad for the sun, I dressed with an open heart, still feeling unsure. I drove into the center of town and found a small restaurant that advertised morning specials. I had told the nursing staff I would be there around ten. Since it was just 8:30 I looked forward to a leisurely breakfast. My choice was easy, eggs over easy and rye toast.

As I ate I recalled Sunday childhood breakfasts prepared by my father. My sister and I loved to wake up to the smell of bacon that enticed us out of bed. Breakfast always included eggs and toast, Tailor's ham, or sausage. It was a breakfast that provided the proper protein, my mother would say. Cream of Wheat with brown sugar, a pat of butter and milk was our other option. Yes, that was the '50s.

My waitress smiled as she offered me more coffee. I sat intent over my journal. She asked me what I was writing. I told her I was writing in my journal and had come from California to visit my mother. She smiled again and left as the bell rang for her to pick up the next order. I was grateful for her relaxed openness; I was contracted and tense. She reminded me to relax.

I wished I had brought sunglasses to hide under for I felt raw; my feelings were running back and forth in time. What was I to do with all the feelings? I wanted to cut them off.

The world I had wrapped around me as a child was an intellectual world. I wrapped up in mind, dissociated from my body. I retreated into studies and spending time alone. I saw others live from their mind. The price was high however, for it meant overriding needs. I stopped feeling hunger, stopped feeling cold, or fear. It was easy to silence myself when I felt anger. Generational rules stopped my self expression. Perfection and mind became important.

I definitely felt afraid in that moment in Naperville as I remembered Mother's harsh retorts. I had always felt intimated by her presence. She dressed to perfection and seemed distanced in her beauty. The wicked stepmother image comes to mind sometimes when I imagine her face full of criticism, her face tight and her eyes staring at me. I wished to disappear when she spit out, "You'll survive. Stop being a baby. I'll give you something to cry about." The little girl inside me longed for her mother to enfold her, stroke her face and give her encouragement. Yes, it was true, I hadn't listened deeply enough to the small girl inside who felt despair and pain.

My mother was a person of her times and heritage. She had been raised with a strict Irish hand, bound by rules of conduct and tied to pleasing men. As a young mother she had listened to what Dr. Spock told her and later instructed me in the importance of giving the stage to men. She was also a feisty wife. She submitted but raged. I knew she wanted to have a job outside our home. Many women of her generation were not allowed to work; it wasn't acceptable for it reflected badly on the husband's ability to provide for the family. I put down my pen and then paid my bill at the restaurant. I still had time to wander around the small town of Naperville. On my ramblings I found an Indian restaurant and a small flower shop on a side street. I went into the shop to buy flowers for my mother. While the shop was small, there were many choices. I couldn't remember my mother's favorite so I chose yellow daisies.

I then headed for the nursing home just south of town. As I approached the road I felt comforted by the budding trees and smell of spring. As I turned into the circular driveway, Manor Care's formal brick buildings gave me some kind of solace. Yet as I parked I dreaded walking through the door. I wished that my sister were there with me. There was comfort in her shared presence; simply walking into the home together was a silent support.

The nursing home was well kept both inside and out. A green lawn, old trees and shrubs graced the grounds. There was a crisp coolness to the day, which included a feeling of bursting out. I considered taking my mom for a walk in her wheelchair, but then thought twice because she wasn't really an outdoor person. Once inside the front door I felt comforted by the traditional furniture and colonial feeling of the appointments. It mirrored the physical world of my childhood. As nursing homes go it is well kept, and felt fresh and clean. I gave my name to reception, then pushed open the large doors. I clutched my daisies as I walked the long hall to Mother's room. I nodded hello to several women in wheelchairs. Seeing them added to my dread.

When I opened the door to Mother's room my body resisted. I paused. I didn't want to be in that room. Taking a deep breath, I continued through the door. Mom was tucked in bed with her head resting on her pillow. She looked frailer than the last time I'd seen her. Her blue eyes were so pale! But her skin was still beautiful. That both surprised and saddened me--her beauty seemed to stand up against the greater reality.

I put on a cheerful face and sat at the edge of the bed. "Hi, Mom, how are you?" I handed her the flowers. She didn't really respond. I said, "It's spring, Mom. I thought you would enjoy some flowers for your room." She stared ahead. I felt the longing again, the longing for a response. Just then a nurse came in and offered to go and get a vase. For a moment I felt the grief of seeing my mother in the home, so vacant and alone. I wondered where she went when she wasn't here in this time and space. I also knew I was afraid of becoming her in a home myself. But I quickly shut out the thought. She finally looked directly into my eyes, but the hoped for recognition still wasn't there. Yet there was a blessed quiet in her, very different from the anxious and dictating woman I had known.

When the nurse returned, she handed me the vase. "It is time to take your Mom to her bath, I am afraid. Will you wait?"

"Yes," I said, asking how long it would take.

"Not too long," she said as she got Mom out of bed. "She still has beautiful skin, doesn't she?"

"Yes." I smiled. "I noticed it myself when I first came in the room."

"Ok, Peg, time for your bath today. You can come back and visit with your daughter after."

I was glad to hear the nurse speak to her as an adult.

When they left I sat gazing around her room. Suddenly, a picture of my grandfather caught my attention. On the wall directly above it was a watercolor of our family home. The combination of photos hurtled me back to the early '50s. I remembered my grandfather visiting one winter in January. My sister was around six when we moved into our new home that fall. Our Pop-Pop, as we called him, had come for a weekend. A large storm brought a couple of feet of snow and later on Saturday the high winds brought an electrical outage. We all sat around the fireplace roasting hot dogs on twigs, staying warm with sweaters and blankets. We played in the snow the next morning since school was canceled. The memory was a joyful one, which surprised me considering my history with him.

This vivid recollection of my grandfather was not something I was used to feeling. Perhaps the slow work of getting back into my body was in fact leading me deeper. I was startled back into the present moment when the nurse returned with Mom who looked more alert. The nurse had dressed her in slacks and a blue blouse. She sat in her wheelchair with reserve. I turned to her and asked if she wanted her hair brushed. The nurse left, saying that lunch would be served at 11:30 and the dining room was down the hallway to the left. I felt better when I saw Mother looking fresh and more alert. I took her hand and again asked her if she wanted her hair brushed. She did not answer. I felt uncomfortable with her. I realized how rarely I had touched her; my mother's body was strange to me. The legacy of fear, the lack of physicality, had taken its toll on both of us. She didn't answer but I brushed her hair gently and found some cosmetics in a drawer. I put a bit of blush on her cheeks and applied a little lipstick. I pushed my edge of fear to touch her in ways I wasn't used to. But being comfortable wasn't what the visit was about.

I realized now that I probably had hardly touched or hugged Mother since I was a little girl. My adult hugs had indeed been perfunctory. When I finished her makeup I thought how in the past she would never be seen without it. She didn't know at the moment anything about makeup or looking good; what a relief to give up the pressure to look perfect, every hair in place.

Lunch still was a ways away so I sat and picked up a Mary Oliver book I had brought along. She is my favorite woman poet, a woman who risks writing deeply of beauty and loss and presence. As I read I thought about my heritage, about claiming our lives, about the unique journey of my mother's life. Oliver's words reminded me to live my own voice; I was on quest for that voice. Why was I so afraid of being myself? How appropriate, I thought, and sat for another moment. Certainly other people felt the same way.

I finished reading just as the nurse peeked her head in to remind me it was lunchtime. I wheeled Mother down the hall with reserve and turned into the dining room. Her lunch included a glass of pureed foods and ice cream; I gave her a few spoonfuls of ice cream, one of her favorite foods as I remembered. During the meal I made conversation—one way. She still did not respond or appear to recognize me. I had to stretch out of old habits of not speaking about my life. I began to share about the upcoming trip to Ireland. "Mom, guess what? I'm leaving for a ten-day trip to Ireland! I am happy to be able to connect with our ancestry and to step foot on Ireland's soil. I wish I had found out more about Nana and Pop-Pop's lives."

Thinking back to that time, I now realize that I felt ashamed of my feelings of confusion, my mixture of up and down feelings. I was supposed to be the elder daughter, taking care of my mother, not wading into the past. I still felt there was some way to be, something acceptable that included being sociable and happy, not sad, not angry. Feelings make life messy, my family system had droned.

As I sat there I considered my Mother's life. How was she mothered? Suddenly I found myself having more and more compassion for her. Perhaps it was seeing the photograph of my grandfather and knowing the values of their era that shifted me. I again considered the fact that she had been molested as a young girl.

In recent years I'd had the chance to look back at my own parenting. I saw how I also distanced, how I set too rigid rules rather than inspiring my son to thrive. We all do the best we can. I hoped to grow my compassion and understanding about all of my life experience.

After the last spoon of ice cream I wheeled Mom back to her room. I felt opened but tired. Was I ready to speak my truth to her? What was curious about breaking my silence was that she could no longer hear me or respond. There was so much unspoken between us. I didn't feel ready that day to open and speak my pain, but I still had tomorrow, one more day to spend with her, so I decided to return to the hotel.

I slept restlessly that night and woke in the morning with the memory of a dream that immediately spoke to me about an emotional truth. My dream of having to walk across an endless frozen landscape mirrored my life experience. In my dream I asked for help from strangers, but they turned their backs. What a perfect image, I thought. My inner landscape was frozen and I was trying to negotiate it alone. I felt the deep fear of aloneness with a terror I must have felt as a little girl. I saw myself inside a house I had made of snow. The fear of being alone froze my limbs.

I felt rooted in place. I shook myself out of the fear and punched a hole in the snow house. I broke through the walls and saw two men below. I called out for help, but they turned their backs. I felt shock at their indifference and then crawled out of the house onto the level below. No one was there but I somehow felt better.

As I reflected on the dream of feeling frozen, I recalled other dreams where I was negotiating frozen landscapes without help, climbing up, over or through something, always looking for warmth. It was difficult to face into the real aloneness I had lived most of my life.

I felt loss for both of us, about the challenges of life and the tenderness needed to foster well-being in children. The deep longing to connect called me to make the next step. To name the frozen landscape was to speak of choices, the choice of control and order or the choice of the rich texture of human life that could be messy, not frozen into perfection. That frozen life took great energy to keep in place. Besides, I wanted warmth, hearth, center, life, flow and joy.

I wrote my dream in my journal, then dressed and went immediately to the nursing home. As I headed down the hallway I saw mother sitting in the living room, dressed in her grey slacks and green turtleneck. I left the inner space of my dreaming world and recalled her beauty as a young woman, especially her curly auburn hair which set off her fine features and delicate frame. I was glad to see her dressed and up in her wheel chair. I had hoped I could take her outside for a walk in the spring air.

As I walked down the hall I met another woman whom I had seen in the dining room. I briefly said hello and wondered if her mother was in the nursing home with Alzheimer's also. I longed to talk to someone else. There were so many people going through this same experience with their parents. Twenty-four million Americans have the disease. This gave me some relief as I thought of others, knowing they shared the heartbreak of the illness.

I felt a sudden quiet come over me as I took in the beauty of the living room. The small white and blue flowered wallpaper was of the same generation as me. This felt like home. The setting could have been back in the '50s. Light was shining in through a small window, the setting accentuating Mom's delicate frame. As I walked toward her, I said, "Hi, Mom!" She smiled broadly at me. Her pale hands reached out for mine. I walked toward her in slow motion, not believing my eyes. For that moment, she recognized me. I reeled in confusion, but in the moment she was my mother, the mother I had longed for! I took her hands and bent down on my knees to greet her, my emotions running wild. As I knelt down the tears ran down my face. I finally said in a quiet voice, "So glad to see you, Mom." The voice was the voice of a child, a young adult, and a mature woman who was deeply happy. I remained smiling in joy; my wish had been given. Hello, Mom! I wanted to run around the nursing home telling everyone. Moments later, she slipped back into another world.

I felt joyful as I wheeled Mom for a walk in the fresh air. After a gentle stroll around the grounds we sat together on the front porch. The maples were beginning their leafing and rhododendrons were blooming in the distance, pink and flowery. We sat in silence, until I noticed she was rubbing her eyes and ears. I instantly remembered she often had spring allergies; she was responding to the spring pollens. I wheeled her back inside.

I was still feeling the glow and disbelief of the experience when I left the nursing home, just after lunch. I headed to the Indian restaurant I had noticed the other day, and enjoyed a vegetable curry that was warm and comforting. I took a short walk after lunch, staying with feelings of gratitude. Soon after, other feelings flooded in. I began to feel anger rising in me. What other voices wanted to speak? I had to let go and allow what wanted to be expressed.

As I drove back to the nursing home I knew I had to honor myself. Feeling free to express myself was a focus of my pilgrimage to Ireland. I hadn't thought about it that way before. Old voices also warned me to keep quiet, suggesting I was spoiling the day with my negative feelings. I knew the time was right. I saw that Mom was in the living room, napping in her chair. I began by reading to her quietly; she woke up but didn't recognize me. Now or never I thought. A waterfall of awkward words flowed from my mouth. "You were cruel. Why did you call us crybabies? We were just children! I hated you. And what in the hell did you think you were doing as a mother?" I felt my body tense and simultaneously felt the need to explode at her by leaning over her and shouting in her face.

I stood up and then sat down again, fuming and raising my voice. "Why did you treat my sister and me as slaves, making us wash the cellar steps while you sat smoking menthol cigarettes and reading the newspaper like a damn queen? Where was your humanity, Mother? What about that time you threw a fit about me reading, lying in the grass? I ended up with grass stains on a pair of shorts? Who cares?" My words flew out of me in a loud whisper. On and on I went. My stomach churned.

The last question I asked of her with deep pain in my heart was, "Why in the hell did you say you wished I could be like Valerie, a friend who was a cheerleader? What kind of mother tells her daughter she wishes she were someone else other than herself?" I finally sat back, afraid I would break down in sobs. Not in the nursing home!

I know I must have raised my voice on that last question, for a few nurses walking by turned their heads. They probably had noticed before and were waiting in the wings. My mother sat silently in her chair. The nurses went their ways; I calmed down and slowly wheeled my mother back to her room. I went to the ladies room to splash water on my face and gather my wits. I returned and said goodbye to her. But my hello that day was what I had come for. As I left the nursing home I stopped to ask the staff about the recognition I received that morning. They suggested that over the hours I had spent with her she had begun to recognize me by the tone of my voice. I smiled and left.

Ireland Arrival

I felt shaky as I boarded the Air Lingus plane late in the afternoon. I settled into my window seat as the plane lifted out of O'Hare Airport headed east to Shannon, Ireland. My heart felt both lighter and heavier. From my window I watched Illinois fade into the smoky afternoon light. It was difficult to sit still for I was filled with emotions, all of which sat close to the surface. The joyful surprise of my mother's greeting still flowed through me. An inner door had opened into a room of gratitude, yet I still felt loss. I wished I were on a flight home to California. I would have felt safer feeling my feelings in the known territory of my cave-like house. At home I could crawl under my covers and just be. Would I have stayed with the cascade of feelings or not? It was easy to bypass feelings, drift away, distance, distract. The process of "know thyself" was a pilgrimage, one which at that moment was difficult. The joy made my anger complicated, because I had had that moment of my mother's presence. I couldn't blame her anymore.

I knew the soul held the larger picture and wanted to include everything. Ireland became an inner landscape to be walked. Ireland pilgrimage had begun with deep emotions connected to my mother line. Of course the spiral to feminine healing asked me to heal. I had distanced from the feminine in her and myself; feelings and intuition were portals back into Her presence.

The land of the Goddess, Ireland, asked me to walk her soul story. She had mantled the peoples of Ireland since the beginning of time. I was returning to feel her sheltered presence and power. I sat back letting the feelings soften and move where they would. My thoughts turned to my upcoming travel, the mystery yet to unfold. I would be joining my group the next day. How would it be to carry this experience into my travel? How was I going to feel around a male leader?

I had been so inspired by our pilgrim focus that I had not considered how comfortable I had become around women teachers. My safe choice would have been a female leader, someone who held similar focus and beliefs as I, perhaps someone who would have offered more Celtic tradition. Hadn't I for so long been claiming back the more feminine earth-based tradition of Celtic spirituality? I had wanted mirrors to reflect my journey, a mirror to restore my relationship with myself, a female person. But then I realized that claiming back my creative fires was an important aspect of my quest. The journey included both male and female parts of me. My intention was to bring balance back into my life.

When I considered my history with the masculine I felt blocks. These blocks related to the sexual abuse, but at this juncture also called me to heal and take back my potential. Would I fall into old negative patterns of self-betrayal, of giving up my power, during my travel? Creativity was a chosen path, one which celebrated mystery and one which asked me to walk dark passages to find the gold.

But then why hadn't I integrated the fact that I was working with a male editor? Hal Zina Bennett had supported my process of discovery. His books *Write from the Heart* and *The Lens of Perception* had given me many gifts. As a teacher and editor he had challenged me to claim my voice and craft my writing. The process was an antidote to the roots of shame, self-doubt and fear. Yes, I hadn't trusted women to support me. That was an interesting note. Having just visited my mother helped me feel that truth. She had felt too insecure to validate or guide me back to myself. Games sadly called for competition in those days. Support replaces competition when we claim our value and self trust. I took a deep breath in recognition. If Irish genes had silenced me, Irish fires would restore my essential truths.

Voicing my feelings with my Mom had shifted me. But in that moment, sitting on the plane, I felt emotionally exhausted and wished I had separated the trips. But there I was on my way to Ireland. I took down the rough grey blanket from the overhead compartment and wrapped up to give myself some comfort. I was happy when dinner arrived and I could distract myself with chicken, rice and grapes. I realized I needed to heed the fact that I was in transition. I was moving from a *here* to a *there*. Slowly the *there*, Ireland, began to take on a darker hue in my mind. Of course I knew the dark was necessary, it was part of the balance of pilgrimage. Both light and dark must partner. I didn't really want to know what was ahead.

I fell asleep dreaming of a group of wanderers in a grey fog. When I woke I felt like the wanderers. My body longed for a shower and breakfast, and I longed for the feeling of waking to a new day. We weren't far from landing in Ireland though, and I looked forward to seeing Shannon from the air. The next day I would be meeting my group. I considered whether I would put on my social mask for the group. Don't be messy with feelings, "put on a happy face" part of me barked. Did I recognize that as the voice of my mother? Part of me did. But another part was still too frightened to truly be myself. I knew I had made progress, but still didn't trust others with that world. If I was getting to know myself over these years, it was slow process. The transformation was still in the cocoon stage. Nevertheless I had to let go and let the process be what it was. I was flying over Ireland.

As we circled and then descended into Shannon Airport at 6:30 AM I caught sight of the beautiful vibrant green Irish countryside. I remember the sun glancing off the airplane window; I forgot my exhaustion and looked down with delight. The green hills infused me with spring joy. I wished my Mother could see this. I lit an imaginary candle in my heart, to honor my entire line of Irish ancestors; foremost was Margaret, my mother, and my sister, Barbara.

As I walked through customs I asked a taxi coordinator to call a cab to take me to my hotel. He looked at my red hair and blue eyes and smiled saying, "Welcome home." I did feel welcome, but uncertain. I climbed into the taxi and breathed, hoping to ground myself. My taxi drove me to a hotel close to the airport. I was glad to have accommodations close-by because the next morning I would return to Shannon to meet my travel group.

I dropped my baggage in front of a small oak desk inside the hotel, smiled and took my room key. The hotel felt old—Ireland lived in its walls. I had expected a sterile airport version with non-descript rooms. I wearily climbed the stairs to the second floor, found my room and unlocked the door. A window with cheerful, white sheer curtains greeted me as I entered. The room was a good size, tucked under the sloping ceiling, and felt welcoming. A tufted brown chair sat in the far corner of the room, with a small table light to its left. The bed looked comfortable and I longed to fall into it, but I knew the gift of staying awake from past travels. Anyway, I was hungry, so I put my suitcase down and headed for the longed for shower.

Water always grounds and refreshes me. After the shower I felt human again and was happy the hotel had a restaurant. I headed for breakfast. The dark wood-paneled dining room felt comforting, as did the real Irish breakfast buffet. The feast included pork sausages, bacon rashers, eggs, black pudding, and brown soda bread. I took a small taste of everything and inhaled my first cup of Irish black tea.

It was still very early but the dining room was warm and friendly. I noticed only one other guest, an older man. As I looked at the weathered Irish face of this older gentleman, I caught the twinkle in his eye. I turned back to drinking Irish tea and enjoying my food. Some of the Irish breakfast was familiar and some not. Black pudding was the *not*; its name simply didn't inspire, nor did a small taste. But I so loved the ritual of participating in a culture's food. Eating an Irish breakfast brought me to their hearth story. Food was a joy and helped me engage with my body.

Excitement and exhaustion caught up with me as I finished my breakfast. Too tired to take in any more of the hotel I returned to my room, undressed, and sank under the blankets of the soft bed. I felt happy to be sleeping in Ireland and did not wake until many hours later. Dusk had fallen. Just about the same time a maid knocked on the door to hand me fresh towels. I thanked her and went to shower again. I felt groggy, so cold water revived me. After my shower I realized how I felt depressed and so did a few yoga stretches. The heaviness lifted.

Afterwards I made myself some hot tea. I loved the difference of

Irish hotel rooms being set up for making tea instead of coffee. I always travel with my favorite tea bags and snacks, which help me feel at home. I unpacked my almonds and raisins, nibbled my snacks and drank tea, enjoying the cozy chair.

I settled into the lumpy chair. Its age and worn fabric provided solace like a child's blanket or teddy bear. I still felt between worlds. To give myself a container I opened my journal. I moved my snack closer, took a sip of hot tea and imagined myself at home. It was like wrapping myself up with a lovely warm wrap. As I began to write I came home. Journal writing had become a way to witness and make sense of my life. Over the years of both journaling and writing the manuscript I had come into more intimacy with self and the world about me.

As I wrote I witnessed my truths. It was normal for my body to feel disoriented, spinning a bit from strong feelings, time change, and the truth that I felt less than happy about being in Ireland. I was surprised.

Of all places I knew that Ireland was the place to speak my story. Yet the past had kept me silent. I wrote in my journal: "I feel some court over me, I am sitting in a court and being judged, people have written letters of recrimination, my family members have ostracized me and are sitting in the gallery laughing, I am sitting in a court centuries old."

As I wrote I found a point of entry. Ireland felt like a pointing finger, a place where I had come home, but where being myself was forbidden. I was wrapped in a cloak of dismissal and regrets. The feelings crossed ancestry lines. I was bridging a gap, traveling a trajectory of Irish women's history. I felt gifted by that awareness, but sleep drew me back to bed. I closed my journal and fell into a deep sleep.

I didn't wake until the phone rang. It was 5:30 in the morning. My wake-up call was right on the dot. I heard a lovely Irish lilt at the other end say, "This is your wake up call." I lay in bed to look around the strange room, feeling disoriented. My body was out of sync still. Yet there I was in Ireland, the journey upon me. It would be an hour or so before our ten-day pilgrimage began. Before dressing I went to the window, but soon stepped back quietly, for tucked in the corner of the roof was a nest with a mother bird and her chicks. She was feeding them. I smiled. What a lovely image! I was reminded it was spring, the season for birthing. I packed my clothes and set out on the new leg of my travels.

Luggage in hand, I left the hotel and headed out to meet the taxi. I had asked the taxi driver from yesterday morning to pick me up. There was comfort in that small detail and I felt happy—uncertain, but happy to be setting out. The taxi dropped me in front of Shannon Airport. Suitcase in hand I searched for hot tea and found a small table where I waited. There was hardly a soul about except for the gift shop clerk. When I saw a grey-haired Irishman rush in I took notice. Niki, one of our coordinators, had previously suggested that I look out for our driver, Billy, who would be meeting the plane. I took my tea and walked up to him asking if he had come for the American tour group. "Yes," he said, "I am Billy."

I smiled and introduced myself, but I did notice how protective I felt.

"Any news about the plane?" he asked.

I told him no so he turned and headed back out to move our van out of the loading area. I suspected the same rules held in Irish airports about not leaving unattended vehicles.

Just as the plane landed, Billy returned. His Irish blue eyes and twinkle of humor reminded me of my family. Irish humor was my grandfather's and aunt's gift; I think I was passed by when that gene was handed out. As we waited I found out that Billy lived in Northern Ireland. He briefly mentioned his family and the fact that his wife had died of cancer a year ago. I offered him my condolences.

I found it unnerving waiting for the group to arrive. I wrapped my trench coat about me and doubled the tie on my blue scarf. The twenty pounds I had put on over two years felt uncomfortable. I noticed that the anticipation of mixed company brought out the voice that needed me to look good, be intelligent and desirable. I was in new territory and old habits wanted voice. I noticed how easily I could fall back into unconscious behaviors. I told myself I didn't have to put on any mask.

Going on pilgrimage always sounded pompous, but I didn't really experience it that way. It was easy to think of it in overly serious and aloof ways, yet this outer journey to Ireland had so many inner destinations. I had never felt so clear about the process of the outer supporting the inner and the inner being enhanced by the outer. I made a mental note to "remember that everyone on that trip is part of what I call me." Those mirrors, I knew, may not always be comfortable, but that was the mystery of life. I also felt glad for the container of group process and the support of guided travel. By the time the door burst open and travelers began pouring through I felt more at ease.

When the plane arrived Billy and I went to greet everyone. Soon we began to see faces that certainly belonged to fellow pilgrimage travelers; many were women my age. I thought I recognized Dawn, a woman I had spoken with on the phone. Included in our conversation had been Dawn's description of herself—short brown hair and blue eyes. The conversation with Dawn had comforted me because she had seemed sensitive to the mystery of pilgrimage.

Last came the group leader, Phil Cousineau, and Collette, who was to lecture during our travel. I recognized Phil from his picture on the brochure. I had chosen the trip based on the fact that he was the author of *The Art of Pilgrimage*. From his website I had learned of his extensive experience in travel. I had been impressed as I read about his twenty books, about the fact that he was a friend and student of Joseph Campbell. He also made films, photographed and taught classes. His many credentials and talents would certainly be gifts to all of us. At the same time I felt intimidated. My fear was giving over power to creative men. So many of us had bowed to authority outside ourselves.

I looked forward to meeting Collette, our lecturer. She had been born in Ireland and would offer special understandings of Irish history. I was happy for the balance of masculine and feminine.

I walked over to Dawn, introduced myself and gave her a hug. I then introduced myself to Niki and finally our leader, Phil Cousineau. I was taken by his good looks and warm handshake, but knew my truth of feeling vulnerable with strangers. What would our group travel bring?

A bit of disorder and chatter filled the room as our group assembled. With baggage gathered, money exchanged and our van ready, we climbed in to begin our ten-day adventure together. I felt nervous and suddenly very hungry and realized my last meal had been yesterday's breakfast. I was happy to hear our first stop would be an inn where we would share breakfast. I anticipated the joy of sharing a meal together.

Ballyvaughan and Beyond

Our white van headed west to Ballyvaughan, a fishing village that sits on the coast of Galway Bay. The village would be our first home base on the ten-day tour.

It was still early when we stopped in a lovely inn for our breakfast. I sat with Dawn and Lynn. The latter, I learned, was connected with the University of California at Santa Barbara. Dawn and I talked briefly about Northern California. The two of us found out we both loved the Sausalito ferry ride to San Francisco. Delightful what virtual strangers can find in common!

I was happy to be sharing an Irish breakfast that day. I still felt overwhelmed with feelings and was afraid to share too much. But hearing about other women's lives was refreshing. Our group seemed revived after a filling Irish breakfast. Later we climbed back into our van and headed to Ballyvaughan where we would be staying for several days. Our trip offered us time to experience each place, come as a pilgrim. I was surprised and happy when we pulled up in front of our lodging, a beautiful inn with yellow and white flowers bordering its front walk.

The air was cool but spring was bursting out in Ireland. As our group entered the inn we received a warm welcome from the owners. Inside we found a peat fire burning in the inn's fireplace. I walked to the fire and put my hands over it to warm myself. I still felt on edge—a chill from the past. In spite of the chill, I was nurtured by being in front of an Irish hearth. Hearths were no longer just images in a book. I breathed deeply and smiled. I recalled the first winter I was reading Mara Freeman and had come on the word. *Hearths* had become more than a word I loved. They had become a guiding light, a place to return to again and again. They truly became a nurturing symbol of feminine presence and a visible altar to Her qualities of warmth, compassion and transformation.

After finding our rooms and unpacking, several of us took a walk around the village. The weather warmed up as we strolled along taking in thatched roofs, small shops and the gentle curve of the bay. I felt at home in the simplicity. The town invited us to enjoy every nook. We peered into shop windows where local crafts of pottery, woven cloth and jewelry delighted the eye. A woman named Carolyn and I took special joy in discovering that local crafts were part of the life of the village. Our small group walked and talked with each other. Carolyn and I found a common interest in art and for the rest of the trip would share stories, meals and walks.

After our walk I returned to my room for a nap, for I was still adjusting to the time change. My body needed rest. I also knew I was tired from the emotional journey I was on.

When I awoke I felt much better and headed downstairs. Our first dinner felt wonderfully festive. The intimate dining room was set up with two tables for us, and from there we could hear the fire crackling in the adjacent sitting room. A bountiful dinner, served with beauty and warmth, included poached salmon, fresh vegetables, and lemon sorbet. It more than satisfied our hunger. We all tried to talk at once to share some of ourselves. I also listened to catch snatches of conversations across the table. Catherine, or Cacky, as she called herself, came from Louisiana and brought with her a wonderful drawl. Included in our travel family were also a mother and her teen daughter. Jeanne and Colleen lived in Pennsylvania and had come to explore their ancestry. Our only other male member was Steven, who joined in comfortably; we were grateful for his presence. Both men would give us masculine balance and perspective.

The weather the next morning had turned grey. A few of us met for a warming breakfast, while others slept in. Soon after breakfast we gathered in a room off the lobby for our first of many morning circles, setting the tone of "sacred and mindful" travel. Phil offered us a poem to help us focus. I was happy to hear him speak of the various stages of a pilgrim's journey. That first morning he asked us to write about our personal call in coming to Ireland. In certain ways my call seemed obvious: I wanted to reconnect to my roots; I wanted to walk the land.

Later during circle we were also offered the question, "What is the sacred seed of the day?" I loved this metaphor. I thought about planting seeds; spring was the perfect season of the year for it. Birthing and blooming, I thought to myself, as I remembered the mother and baby birds in the windowsill of the hotel. Yes, tend to the seeds of the journey by staying connected to the ancestor thread. I asked myself what wanted tending and what new life was growing in me.

So much of my search had led me back to the sacred in nature and the sacred in the cells of my body. Had my ancestors forgotten their connection to the land? Certainly my grandparents' loss of their homeland had affected their relationship with the whole of life. My search over time had brought me to reconnect to that which had been lost or buried. I felt the unraveling of the unhealed past, the splits and the need for the balance of the hearth principles. I was standing on that hearth in Ireland.

I felt again the importance of embodying my truth through the physical; my fear ran me out of myself. So the first order of the day was to stay in my body. That became a focus each day. Toward the end of the morning the discussion led to the word *threshold*. I felt an inner knowing. That was my seed word: *threshold*. We were reminded that the *threshold* in a home is the space between the inner sanctuary and the outer world. I wanted to become the threshold bringing the inner and outer worlds together. Someone suggested that thresholds are places where the spirit world comes through. In Ireland they are called *thin places*, places to meet the invisible divine. Standing on a threshold also meant new beginnings to me. Yes, that word was the seed I wanted to carry with me. Ireland herself seemed like a threshold.

Soon after our invigorating discussion we finished our circle and gathered our belongings for our first day of sightseeing. Time to test my resolve to take care of myself. To support my need for quiet, I climbed into a seat with Carolyn. In the short time that I had known her, I had come to feel certain she could be present in silence if need be. Once settled into our seats we sat together quietly as our bus wound up into the rocky hills. Our first stop was the Burren, an ancient landscape close to the hotel.

Soon after we stopped at a desolate hill. I wondered what could be of interest there. Once outside the van we slung our backpacks over our shoulders, turned left inside a small gate and then headed up a rough path. Once we gained some height we could see ancient plateaus of rocks about us. The Ice Age landscape, once a seabed in Neolithic times, had become windswept plateaus. Planks of limestone lay on the surface, but later I learned that under some were caves and rivers that filled up when it rained. I felt disappointed at the sight of the austere grey rocks, but suddenly the sight of flowers and ferns growing between the rock crevices surprised us all. Carolyn pointed out a flower named "Rosy Rock Rose." All eyes were glued in wonder at white orchids, blue, yellow and pink flowers sprouting here and there. I marveled at the contrasts and the unexpected joy of seeing flowers blooming out of the harsh rock. As I climbed further up I recalled the words of John O'Donohue: "...wild landscapes remind us of the unsearched territories of the mind." I felt the truth of that, but it was more than the mind; it was the unearthed landscapes of our complex human history and wisdom. The Burren fascinated all of us.

As we walked further up, we came upon heavy rocks called *dolmen*, dated from around 2000 B.C. These tombs dot the Irish countryside. A picture of this site had been reproduced on our brochure. There was a mystery I had felt even in the picture. But in that moment, actually there in Ireland, I was standing in front of my history. We stood in front of the large stones which made up the Poulnaborne Dolmen. The tomb is made of one large capping stone, delicately placed on top of three large stones. The ancient builders were masters and we all wished we knew more. The top stone seemed to reach a height of about six feet. How did the builders put these immense stones in place?

Several of us walked closer and took turns standing under the capstone. When it was my turn I stood feeling the cool air from below brush my face. Was it death I felt? I was standing at a threshold, no question; dolmens held indescribable energies between worlds, that unusual space where time goes away and you feel you are participating in a myth or story. I realized how visiting such ancient places inspired a connection in me and opened me to the wisdom of the ancient peoples who were my ancestors. Dawn took her turn next and stepped out from the stone with tears rolling down her cheeks. "No words," she said. I knew that the experience on the Burren challenged my preconceptions of Ireland; it was indeed an unknown landscape.

I felt a pull to take out my watercolors; my paints could explain more of my experience than words could. Hesitant at first because no one else was painting, I began because I knew I would regret it if I didn't take advantage of the moment. I chose a rock close by to sit on and began to place color on my small pad and then draw lines to delineate the image. I had never painted anything with such weight—it seemed foreign to me. I also photographed the delicate flowers that against all odds found their way through the hard rock surface. I felt like one of those flowers, finding my way up from under hardness, from under the frozen landscape of my childhood.

Our group stayed on to experience every nuance of the unique Burren landscape. I saw the difference of coming as a pilgrim, not just as a tourist. If I had come by myself I wouldn't have stayed so long. It took *presence* to be in the large emptiness of that land. Alone, I would have gotten impatient and stopped connecting. I appreciated the time to absorb the experience. I thought back to the morning circle at our hotel and our discussion of thresholds. I might not have used that word myself for this landscape. Being immersed in the landscape of the ancient rocks of the Burren and standing at a 2000 year old dolmen pushed my normal sense of reality. It was satisfying to imagine the ancient peoples who planted, built shelters, and birthed children. Those early citizens of Ireland had to be very connected to earth and her cycles.

How did so many of us lose touch with those rhythms of harmony? I thought again about the wonderful words of John O'Donohue's—*clay body*. His writing about the land, about the clay of life, gave me pause. The life I sought held balance and integration, and honored uniqueness. That uniqueness, while unexpected, was shown me in the Burren. *Clay body* and *unique* were bells to wake me. O'Donohue's words sounded out: "In your clay body, things are coming to expression and to light that were never known before, presences that never came to light or shape in any other individual. You represent an unknown world that begs you to bring it to voice." I had copied these words to put in my art room last year. Yes, return to Ireland did ask me to honor the light that reflected the great unknown of the world.

When we returned to the inn I chose a soft fabric chair near the fire to write in my journal. I found it difficult to stay focused enough to record but a few notes; I loved the gift of enjoying the hearth away from home. As I relaxed into the chair I realized my body and soul had caught up. I settled in and took out my notes which reminded me of Beltane, an Irish mid-point celebration. It was the season of the year to celebrate fertility and sensuality and honor the marriage of the goddess and the King. I considered the inner aspects of my masculine and feminine often still in conflict, but I let those thoughts go and remembered that spring was inviting me to build inner fires.

The tradition of building fires was also used to purify and make people ready for the new cycles of the year. As Mara Freeman puts it, "Fire was an interface between the human race and the divine." Beltane was full of life, a time to make offerings to bless livestock, assure safe journeys, bless childbirth and new marriages. The sacred fire of the community was carried into individual homes to their hearths. These rituals marked new beginnings and I was there in Ireland at the time of new beginnings.

I sat warmed by the peat fire and felt the interweaving of past and present threads. I fell asleep quickly that evening, and next morning I awoke suddenly from a dream that disturbed me. Filled with emotion, I joined the morning circle. I knew from my dream group the power of sharing dreams, so when we were invited to share, I jumped in. In my dream I walked down a few stairs from a center room. A male poet stood at the back of the room and criticized me for coming downstairs. I told the man that I wanted to see the silver paper in the beautiful oak cabinet. He seemed angry.

I stopped speaking and felt uncomfortable, but was glad I had shared. I didn't get much response and realized a familiar family feeling that was one of being unseen. I felt frustrated as I acknowledged my lack of self-esteem. Still, I was glad to have taken a step in voicing my inner life. I realized that I shouldn't have been surprised by the critical male figure in my dream. I also knew that people's anger had stopped me from standing up for myself. I knew this dream was no fluke. It was a curious first Ireland dream. What were the seeds of that dream?

The challenge was to confront those parts of myself which stopped me from being fully myself, to own my creative power. I felt I was standing at another threshold of opportunity. Yes, it was spring and my creative potential wanted birthing. As I thought more about my dream, it became a point of transformation. How would I transform the inner male critic and take back the silver paper placed in a drawer? That silver paper had been there all along, waiting for me. I wasn't going to step fully into my story unless I retrieved it.

The dream was an invitation to challenge myself; the male poet was the challenger. I smiled knowing the silver represented the feminine.

Women and creativity was a singularly important topic for me. I looked at the long journey I had been on. I had been releasing and letting go, questing inside and out and at the same time writing, all of which offered me not dissimilar answers. So many times harsh marks and intellect put down the tendered soul poem, the heartfelt act of gathering a bouquet or sharing a tender fearful place. Art was the place to take hold and transform the old. The games of judgment killed the dream, the potential. Part of that expansion had taken me to a pottery class, another had asked me to pick up my paints, and another had inspired me to create a hearthful home. But there I was my second night of pilgrimage; Ireland asked me to look. Recovering my voice meant not only speaking my feelings with my mother, but also facing into self-denial and shame. It was time to become empowered. Women birthed, created and inspired. Who could not marvel at the wisdom and power of women's gift to birth children! Would I have the chance to be present at the birth of my grandchildren and experience the miracle of new life?

Our group left after morning circle for our new adventure. Before leaving for our morning sightseeing we took time to gather our things. I waited at the hearth and wrote for a short time about fear of men, for I saw hesitation in my dream. I felt fear of disapproval. Other women can probably relate to this experience. The smallest frown from my father would stop me in my tracks. A perfect example of my internalized father was a voice I heard when painting a wall in my art/writing room. I had forgotten. I recalled the day vividly. I had paintbrush in hand to stroke a deep vibrant orange paint on the wall. When I filled my brush and put it close to the wall my hand shook. I stopped and realized my father was standing behind me. The voice spoke inside me: "Bright orange. Are you sure? Isn't it rather strong and bold?" I had loved the color of the wall when it was finished. It was bold and alive. After painting that wall I received a variety of responses. "Nice but I couldn't live in it," was one of them. All those fears so familiar stepped in—self doubt, fear of being too expressive, too much in my feelings, not perfect enough, out of control, too bold.

I looked back to the history of creative expression in my family. Since Dad made many of the aesthetic decisions in our home, he was everywhere. His voice was the authority, so to speak. Where was my mother in all of this? She seemed left out. During childhood I felt her passivity and self-doubt. The cover was her need to control and bully. I didn't know what she really wanted. She fussed and fumed a lot, but never took action. I knew that both the masculine and feminine voices of my childhood could be disabling. My feminine passivity would bring me to collapse, turning my back on my accomplishments, creating despair; as time went on, negating and disowning my gifts were acts I would continue on my own. All women know these negating voices; we are more than those voices.

I closed my journal and joined the others to set out for the Cliffs of Moher and St. Brigid's Well in Liscannor, two sites not far from Ballyvaughan. I felt lucky as we drove up the coastline; the day was clear and sunny. Everything stood out in bright relief. We arrived at the cliffs, a stunning meeting place of rock, water and sky. The hills in some places reach a height of 390 feet above the Atlantic Ocean. The churning and crashing waters below reminded us of the immense power of nature. The vista with the sun illuminating the deep oranges of the sandstone cliffs inspired all of us. Our cameras were clicking as we leaned into the strong winds. I was glad when we set out for our next stop. Since reading of Irish wells I looked forward to our visit to Saint Brigid's Well in Liscannor. Wells had taken on deep meaning for me since my first pilgrimage to Chartres. I felt the multilayered symbolism. I knew the gift of water and understood why wells and holy places were connected. Soul knew the path home.

Our van took us to the parking lot in Liscannor. We set out to find the well but first stopped in front of a life-sized modern statue of Saint Brigid enclosed in a glass case. I felt surprised at the stiffness of her image. The statue was created to honor Saint Brigid especially because the well was a favorite pilgrimage destination and part of a cemetery. Once in front of the memorial I felt uncomfortable and was glad to leave the glass case with her statue behind. I was relieved to hear the sound of trickling water. A small cave entrance invited us in to drink. I felt its everyday sacredness as we bent our heads to enter the narrow passageway.

The moist air and cave-like space were nurturing. Along the sides of the walls were narrow ledges full of offerings people had left for the saint. Small statues, photos, votive candles, toys and rocks graced the small sanctuary. Only a few of us at a time could fit inside. I stood reading the petitions for miracles that people had left and shared in the human need to pray. My gaze landed on a picture of a small boy on crutches. It somehow reminded me of an uncle of mine who had a withered arm and limped. I was always afraid of him as a child because of his strange disability. He was no longer alive, but I asked for forgiveness for my insensitivity and forgave myself for my fear.

In that moment I also prayed for my mother, offering her my reconnection to the Irish tradition of healing wells, and wished for health and happiness for my sister Barbara and her family. I then placed the braided tie of cloth I had made at home on the rough stone. It was my offering. I recalled the ball of gold thread which I had chosen from Aunt Annie's sewing drawer. It was a fine cord she probably used at holiday time. I loved carrying that and a beautiful hand embroidered tablecloth home after her funeral. That thread was braided in the tie. The braid would weave our worlds together and bring forward ancient wisdom. The multicolored braid lay mingled with other offerings, even though cloth ties or *clote* were traditionally tied to bushes or branches outdoors at wells. I asked for courage to drink deeper of the waters of creative source. I committed to walk out of what felt like crutches of generations of fear and let my steps be true. I thanked St. Brigid for her guidance and presence in my life.

The earthen walls of the small sanctuary reverberated with a true feeling of source, of womb and the feminine. For the years I sought the wisdom of the sacred feminine I had not been disappointed. Her compassion lit the difficult passages. Her hand drew me to her rich black icons, and places of sanctuary. At the moment I was standing in a cave. My right hand held cloth, touched stone; my heart whispered prayers into the cool air of the cave. I recalled the words of Caitlin Matthews: "Wisdom kindles in them by exposure to the old places of holiness where the earth speaks clearly." It was there in that cave that earth did speak clearly. Ancient memory bubbled up from below for those who would hear.

Our group left the moss-covered sanctuary and wandered uphill to the adjacent cemetery, then returned to our bus. Writing in my journal on the way home I mused on another of Caitlin Matthews's offerings: "Brigid shares with black virgins the ability to bring life back, she is associated with blackness which stands for the healing power of nature." It was the deep blackness that held possibility for me. I recalled my experience meeting the Black Madonna at Rocamadour the year before. Each new experience grew me deeper into life. What a rich day I! I was glad for the seeds of change pilgrimage offered.

On our ride home I closed my journal in time to join in a group sing of "Danny Boy." My Ireland dream voice tapped me on the shoulder again. Was I ever without that judge standing in the back of the room worried about what others thought of my singing voice, especially the males with us. Over the day I had noticed how distracted I had become by the two men in our group. Stephen seemed to be a spiritual man, sensitive to pilgrimage travel. Why was I not relaxing? Instead I watched myself give up my confidence and power. I began to see that my dream was working itself out in my waking hours.

Compassion was a key as I navigated my truth. My true power lay in presence and in my willingness to feel and speak my truth, give up the fears. I could then let go. I was in the land of my ancestors where I shared truths with generations of women behind me, not only in my family but also in the ancestry of women around the world who were rewriting their stories.

I felt somewhat overwhelmed by the constant challenge of the trip. I actually wished I drank, but joining the group at the pub that evening felt more threatening so I gathered my writing and headed for my room and a soak in the tub. Ireland unexpectedly had indeed become a threshold, a place to meet an inner challenge. My limits and blocks were the last thing I wanted to experience on a spiritual journey. It was easy to over-identify with the light side of spiritual quest, to forget that the darkness is a different kind of path to walk, one which frees us. The dark is a place of mystery, a fertile ground for recovering our gifts and owning the truth.

Negotiating a very private and interior journey made me vulnerable, even more so because of my unavoidable external connection with others. I was still afraid to share too much of myself. Could I trust? Were feelings honored? Was my traveling family a safe place to be open? But why was I so concerned with what others thought? I recalled the image of Saint Brigid in her glass case. I felt like her, glassed in by a box of fear.

Just before gathering my papers up to go to dinner that evening I felt cold. I went to sit in the lobby at the fire knowing I had to break out of the box. What had stopped me from standing up and accepting myself? Only lack of self love, only fear of meeting the "stranger" myself. Love blew the ashes into flame. Love asked me to accept. Love asked me to stock my soul fires, my creative fires with self love. I considered my inner fires. In the days that followed I felt lighter as we traveled. We stopped for picnics, visited ancient monasteries and old cemeteries, walked a sandy beach, enjoyed an outdoor Irish dancing festival and much more. Just before heading north to our hotel in Galway we stopped to visit a monument raised in honor of famine victims. This set a new tone in me; a powerful door opened and continued to open. Visiting Galway became a chance to feel grief and surprisingly to look deeper into my shadow.

Galway and Inis Mor

Galway sits at the northern tip of Western Ireland. We arrived late in the afternoon. The city was a strange contrast to the windswept waters, mystical Burren and rocky coastline we had been traveling. Our large modern hotel felt awkward, but I also knew that difference inspires new perspective. We unloaded our luggage, settled in our rooms and then set out for dinner.

The plan for the evening was to have dinner on our own and then return to the hotel for an Irish fiddle concert. Carolyn and I found a cozy Indian restaurant close to the hotel, dined on curried vegetables, rice and a delicious mango dessert. Our concert began about seven when we gathered in the hotel conference room. The conference room proved to be less than inspiring for our musical evening, but once the young men and woman started warming up, all the formal business tone of the room and hotel fell away. The Irish music carried us back to a warm earthen-floor cottage we had visited earlier in our travels. The music lit a fire in our hearts and got our feet tapping. The players surprised us with hour after hour of music. About a half-hour into our concert I became aware of the stiffness of my chair. It seemed incongruous to be sitting and not dancing. However I was too shy to get up, too self-conscious to simply move my body. I realized as I sat there that this music lit up my very cells, but I wouldn't move. I was afraid to. I felt locked in ego.

I felt like a stodgy older woman, afraid of making a fool of myself. I knew the self- consciousness came from being with men. But the truth was I felt delight and joy. Since no one else was dancing I sat glued to my chair, but managed to let go and join others whose feet were tapping and hands clapping. I recalled Niki and Collette's wild abandon the day when we had stopped to enjoy an outdoor Irish festival. We stood outside on that warm spring day, watching as local Irish young and old danced. I had felt as stiff then. That evening challenged me again. Let go, I thought to myself. The whole evening was a gift and ended with rousing applause

As I settled into bed that night I reflected on the fears and shame which still ran my life. It was frustrating to feel the joy of the Irish music moving through me, immediately followed by fear... fear of letting go. My uptightness was not only connected to ego but also to fear of letting go and opening into a sensual life. I promised myself I would buy Irish music to take home with me. If I couldn't dance in public I could dance at home.

We rose to a lovely misty morning. I looked forward to several lectures which Collette was giving that morning. Collette had been born in Ireland and I knew she would offer us wonderful stories.

We gathered in the same conference room as last evening. I felt a bit embarrassed as I sat down with Carolyn, knowing myself to have backed down from the dancing in light of a few men in our group. However, I also gave myself space to acknowledge and know that pilgrimage brought us unexpected gifts of our truths. Carolyn and I both looked forward to hearing about the life of a modern Irish woman. Her life was a rich tale of presence and commitment. Collette began her lecture with the story of Maud Gonne, who was born in England in 1865 of an Irish father. She was still young when her mother passed away and her family returned to Ireland. When her wealthy father died in 1886 he left her financially independent. For her entire life she worked for Irish nationalist causes, wrote newsletters and founded a literary society with the poet William Butler Yeats. Maud Gonne was also known as Yeats's muse. She refused several of his marriage proposals. I felt inspired by her fiery and committed life.

At the end of the lecture Collette shared with us her intention to make a film about Maud Gonne's life. I felt her excitement and looked forward to hearing more about it. Collette's intention for creative fulfillment was exciting to me, as was her desire to use film as a medium. As a young woman I would have loved to see such a film about the successful life of Maud Gonne.

The lecture that followed held a different essence. Collette introduced the name "Magdalene Laundries," a term I had never heard before. The subject turned out to be shocking to all of us. The most shocking of many facts we heard was that the last laundry had just closed in 1999. These institutions were opened to house fallen or promiscuous women. Women were sent there to live lives of repentance. The Catholic Church was the arm that sanctioned the horrific quality of life in the laundries.

These women were basically considered a threat to the moral fiber of the community. All ages of women were placed behind stone walls to live and die there. The Church's idea was to keep the women in silence, offering up their lives to prayer so that their sexual sins could be washed away in the laundry.

Collette told us that a movie was being released about this shadow history of Ireland and the Church. The film, called *The Magdalene Sisters*, shows the cruelty and injustices of the laundries. I felt the mirror. My own abuse had generated a lifetime of shame and fear. While I had not lived behind those stone walls I still lived out the "soil of shamed silence." Many women and men know the feeling of being treated as though we were invisible. I felt how sharp and subtle the prison, that which kept me fearing my female sexuality and my creative fires. Male voices inside could not keep me from the silver paper of my dream and the divine essence of myself.

When Collette finished her talk I felt angry. I no longer wanted to carry the shame and blame. It was time I returned the heavy dark cloak, time to give it back to those I had inherited it from. On the Irish side of my family it had originated with my grandfather, but I knew he himself must have experienced the same shame, inheriting it from those who went before him. However far back the shame went, it would stop with me. Secrets and abuse, shaming and fear of sin were to be left behind.

We walked out of our lecture a bit dazed but strong. Carolyn and I took a walk to clear out emotions and breathe in fresh air. Hearing the story stirred up a lot for me. But on our way back to the hotel we found a beautiful fabric store. Irish linen was part of the beauty of my heritage. We went inside the store and bought several things. I chose Irish linen napkins and a handkerchief. There was joy in carrying new linens home with me. My own love of fibers and weaving gave me a chance to share another aspect of my life with Carolyn. We returned to the hotel to pack and get back on the road.

Soon after, we left our modern sanctuary and headed for a ferry that would carry us from Galway to Inis Mor, one of the Aran Islands. Once on board the ferry I felt lighter. I loved riding ferries and stood with Collette enjoying the misty fog blanketing the water. We didn't have time to talk much but I suggested a short ceremony to ground her creative intention. She smiled and suggested we talk later; she suggested we do it when we visited Yeats Tower and Lady Gregory's Estate. It would be a stop after our stay on Inis Mor. The wind picked up as we landed on the island's rocky shore. We headed to a pub for a light lunch and then set out for our afternoon activities. I used my watercolors to make quick sketches of the island.

I noted how I had actually used my watercolors more than my pen, recording my memories in paint, beyond words. I saw the importance of using paint; I saw how I became closer to the image and its essence. I reminded myself I was learning intimacy, an intimacy outside the limits of mind. I also realized how unaccustomed I was to sharing my inner world, definitely not used to honoring my experience and expression. While Ireland called me to use my voice, it also invited me to speak from a non-verbal, intuitive plane. I saw another opportunity to go beyond the family history of silencing and being tight lipped. I realized that Ireland's colonization had something to do with not speaking directly or truthfully. I felt how truth had gone underground; the original wisdom had been lost to fear.

Our afternoon that day included a visit to the island museum where we watched a video of the island's history. It told the whole story of the rugged life of Inis Mor's citizens, showing the hardship of times past. The simplicity of life, even now, was appealing as we watched the bicycles and enjoyed the fresh island air. I was also glad I was not one of the island women I saw in the film hauling seaweed up steep hills. All people who lived on the island had to be strong and resourceful.

Later that afternoon we settled into our lodgings, a small bed and breakfast that sat at the edge of the bay. I climbed upstairs to my room and sat, taking time to myself before dinner. Dusk was falling over the water as I pulled a chair up to the window and mused. Directly in back of the hotel were the ruins of an old cottage. The disarray of tumbling stones only suggested the home which originally stood there. I had no idea of its age. I thought of the family or couple who had lived in the cottage long ago. The isolation of the cottage triggered my memory of our visit, days before, to one of the many monuments dedicated to those who died in the Great Famine of 1845. It was not difficult to feel the fear and pain of Irish families during that time. Groups of people left their homes and walked miles in search of food. Some found food, others perished. The day we visited the monument we sat on an outcropping close to the river where Irish citizens had perished after being refused food. History reports the deaths as a million.

Still feeling the sadness I opened my heart and just let my imagination flow. What remained of the old cottage was one short wall; it suggested a fireplace. As I took up my brush to start painting the rocks, the tumbled ruins began to form themselves into a hearth. The rocks then formed a bed; my instinct then was to stroke in red orange flames. I recalled reading that when a flame went out in the hearth Irish tradition considered the cottage dead, soon to turn to ruin. I wanted to relight the fire in the hearth of this ruined home. The symbolism was strong and mirrored my inner journey. My small painting took no more than ten minutes. The intuitive process of titling a painting often reveals more of our individual process. I was surprised when I wrote, "Resurrection of Brigid's Flame." I felt the joy of the entire process, closed my pad of paper and then dressed to join the others for dinner.

The next morning at circle I shared my painting. At that point we had only several days left to our journey; I suddenly felt grateful for the opportunity I'd had over our ten days to share and express myself. My dream had challenged me to step into the room and reclaim the silver, an individual feminine yes woman journey to claim her voice. I was equally surprised by the support I had received. This mirrored my own willingness to shed my blanket of fear. The truth was that I was the only person stopping myself; the inner masculine who disapproved was part of me. I needed to claim my silver.

Yeats Tower and Dublin

After our gathering we spent the morning visiting historical sites, all powerful, all reminding me of the depth and breadth of Irish history. We took the ferry to the mainland. Once ashore we headed east toward Dublin. We had several stops to make before we arrived later in the afternoon. On our way to our first stop, which was to honor one of Ireland's most famous poets, William Butler Yeats, Collette stood up to tell us of a change in our itinerary. Her first words included the fact that we would visit the town of Kildare. We were going to actually include Saint Brigid's well and cathedral. I was delighted to hear her news and had been disappointed that Kildare was not included on our original itinerary. It meant a lot to me to go to Cill-Dara, "the church of the oak," where St. Brigid had built her abbey. I loved the coincidence of my intuitive painting and the synchronicity of our travel destination.

As we rode along I began to plan a ceremony to honor Collette. I wanted to be proactive and support her creative process. We had candles and our intention to honor her, I thought. When we arrived at Yeats Tower I asked Collette if she still wanted the small ceremony; she smiled and agreed. I spoke to our leader about making time on our schedule.

Yeats' Tower is located close to Coole Park, or Lady Gregory's estate. The tower or Thoor Ballylee served as home for him and his family. His literary life was woven with his life-long friend Lady Gregory. Lady Gregory is well known for her work supporting the Irish Literary Revival which began in the late nineteenth century. The Revival was very significant to the Irish nation because it rescued the Gaelic language and redeemed Irish culture. William Butler Yeats was very involved with this revival and co-founded the Abbey Theatre with Lady Gregory. What I loved hearing next was how she had walked about gathering folk tales and stories of the peoples living in Galway County. Her volumes of these stories were published in the early 1900's.

It was misty as we climbed out of the bus and walked toward Yeats Tower. The weather had cooperated in setting a lovely scene for our visit. I immediately felt supported by the beauty and sense of wellbeing in the natural setting. The spirits of those who had come there before certainly lived on. We came upon the tower after crossing a wide creek. The tower sat next to flowing water and was surrounded by trees and walking paths. We inadvertently arrived on a day when the tower wasn't open, so we were unable to go inside. However we stood on the bridge facing the tower and listened to Yeats's poetry. We listened to the beauty and grace of his words and honored his spirit.

Right after the readings I set up for the ceremony for Collette. We had talked briefly about it and the setting seemed perfect. Our group circled around Collette. Niki set out some candles, helping to facilitate. Our group stood on the bridge in front of Yeats Tower and lit a candle. I guided a short ritual invoking the blessing of the land and the Irish ancestors, especially writers and women who took action to witness and honor the creative process. We held her creative dream to produce a film about the life of Maud Gonne in our circle and sent out the intention for its success, inspired by Collette's commitment. It felt good to support another woman's commitment to claim her creative vision.

After our short ceremony we walked out into the beauty of the natural setting. My body felt happy to be back in the beauty of nature. I needed the balance of trees, so I wandered off by myself to paint a small grove of beeches. As I sat down on a rock wall peering into the magic of the place I recalled Ireland's Druid history. The Druids venerated the native trees of both Britain and Ireland. I so loved trees and recalled how different virtues were associated with different species. I always felt sheltered by trees and understood why ancient people worshipped in groves. Groves of trees were used for sacred ritual, prayer and meditation. I recalled my beloved birch limb resting on the beam of my ceiling. I had created my own place of worship back home in California. The experience had given me such joy.

I recalled that beech, while not native to Ireland, had been linked with words. The first book, according to Fred Hageneder, was made of small beech boards. It replaced scrolls. I turned to the beech to find my own center again; I smiled, for I had been drawn mysteriously to the grove. Hageneder had noted in his book the inspirational gift of beech— finding one's own center.

I sat on a low rock wall and listened quietly as my body relaxed into the quiet. I could feel the magic of places like this, where nature thrived and a human could feel more connected to the unseen world of tree life. I took out my watercolors and waited for the right moment. Brush in hand I began painting with a soft green. I let the natural curve and direction of the tree trunks reveal themselves to me. I was painting that which wasn't visible.

I surrendered into the movement of life, my paintbrush barely touching down on the paper but giving form to the essence of trees as I saw it. I felt I kept being drawn deeper into the mystery of the dance of nature and spring's flow of life.

Our group set out after lunch for Dublin. We sang along the way; this time I stopped myself from judging and joined in with full voice. Arrival in Dublin signaled the end of our journey. Many of our group members would be heading home to the U. S., only several of us would be going on to other destinations. I was feeling ready for a solo voyage to Iona, Scotland. Once settled into our hotel Carolyn and I decided on sharing dinner in the hotel. We were both feeling overloaded with travel. We had a simple dinner of leek and potato soup and a unique Caesar salad served with mayonnaise, then headed to our rooms for an early bed time.

I awoke early the next morning, anticipating our trip to Kildare and the mystery of the prehistoric site of Newgrange. Kildare was our first stop, where we would meet up with Sister Mary Moneghan who was to be our guide. Once out of Dublin and in Kildare our van wove through a quiet suburban neighborhood and stopped at a modern home. I looked forward to honoring Saint Brigid with Sister Mary guiding us. The home houses Solas Bhride Centre, a Christian community focused on the traditions of Saint Brigid and Celtic Spirituality.

A gentle-faced woman met us at the door and showed us into a quiet room with a small altar and a colorful hand-painted picture of Saint Brigid. As we settled into chairs I felt relief to be in the context of a feminine tradition. A simple altar with candles felt nurturing. There was a quality of hearth and home about the sanctuary. Mary shared some history about the abbess Saint Brigid and then invited us to sit in prayer.

After a ritual and our guided prayer Sister Mary and our group climbed back into our van and drove to the cathedral located in the center of Kildare. The cathedral was the original location of Saint Brigid's wooden church. I stood briefly in front of her cathedral but was more interested to see the fire pit located at the north end of the cathedral ground. I was happy to actually see remains of the fire temple. Once the others came out of the cathedral we all gathered and stepped down into a small stone enclosure. I imagined the ritual service of the nineteen nuns who came to tend the fire in ancient times. In that moment I felt proud to be connected to women resurrecting Brigid's fire, wisdom and compassion. I was grateful as Niki and Collette guided a short ceremony by lighting a candle and offering a prayer

As I walked out of the fire circle I realized the gift of the ritual. I committed to tending my own flame of creativity. As I crafted a more soulful life, I appreciated meeting the faces of the sacred feminine, those from the past who were keepers of the wisdom. I knew that the resurrection of feminine wisdom was important for our world. Keeping silent was the old way.

After our visit to the fire pit we walked to a pub nearby for lunch and later continued on to the beautiful meditation garden of Brigid's Well. The approach to the well area required a few words as road crews were repairing the road; Sister Mary got us on our way. We all stepped out of the van into a carefully tended garden with its prayer route. Ritual helped ground me in my relationship with Brigid and I was grateful for Sister Mary's commitment and her sharing with us. The gentle green landscape, carefully tended garden and gentle flow of water softened me. The small garden was a pilgrimage process in itself. Our guided prayer route ended when we stood at the well and Sister Mary guided a prayer. I completed my honoring by tying my last cloth braid on a branch of a tree close by. I put my hand into the cool water and drank; I honored the female members of my family as I drank, especially my mom. Somehow I knew she received my gift. Our ritual over, we then left the garden, drove Mary home and thanked her for her presence.

Next stop was Newgrange. Since Newgrange is a historical site popular to many visitors, tickets and time slots had to be planned for ahead. I was excited to be visiting this Neolithic monument, believed to be over five thousand years old. I had seen pictures of the large dome structure sitting on a hill. It was a marvel of ancient architecture.

Historians consider Newgrange to be one of the many types of passage tombs. A passage tomb is the term used for burial chambers dating to Neolithic times. A portal dolmen like the one we visited in the Burren is one type. Newgrange is the variety of passage tomb which houses several chambers off of a main burial room. Newgrange was discovered in the 17th century, but its restoration did not begin until 1964. We all felt lucky to have the opportunity to visit this ancient site known for its expansive dome roof of turf and stone.

We waited our turn to be bussed to the site. The contrast of bus and Neolithic wonder was somehow incongruous but necessary. Our bus pulled up in front of the massive structure; it was larger than I had expected. Once on the path to the site, we walked with awe. Our group wandered around the ancient site while waiting our turn to enter. I walked with Collette and Niki, appreciating the bright green grasses and expansive blue sky that framed the enormous structure.

Walking along that day with the clouds shifting and the sun shining invited respect for those who went before. The mound itself lay before us stretching about 250 feet across and rising about 40 feet above us. Stark white quartz curbstones edged the bottom of the exterior; a green turf and stone roof rose gently above.

We broke up into small numbers to enter the sixty-foot passage. As we waited to enter the domed structure I examined the two large rocks carved with triple spirals. I thought about the hands which had carved the lines. After falling in love with the labyrinth I had become attentive to the symbol of the spiral. It was considered the ancient symbol of the Divine Mother or the Goddess. The interweaving of the pattern reminded me to hold life in balance and to honor the Mother's patterns.

Finally our guide led us inside around the two large entrance stones to walk the red soil path to the center chamber. The passage is the same route the sun travels as it shines on winter solstice. Cool air greeted us as we walked along the floor and down the narrow earthen passage. The sides of the passageway were carved with smaller spirals. I couldn't help be aware of the spiral of life and death. Walking the passageway was like walking a birth canal. As we stepped into the center room I felt opened, the room felt like a womb. I had hoped I wouldn't feel claustrophobic and I didn't. Rather the earthen room was deeply feminine; the dark somehow enfolded me. Surprisingly I felt at home and I could understand its use as a burial chamber or for ceremony. I wished we knew more of its history. Moments later our guide reminded us of the winter solstice alignment. She proceeded to turn off the lights. We stood in the pitch black for the moment. Then through modern technology a light simulated the rays of the sun traveling down the passage on winter solstice. The light flowed down the narrow passageways into the dark chamber. I felt held in the womb as the light came toward us. There was a mystery and a slight fear. But as the light came closer I felt touched somehow. The earthen ritual was clear—the sun impregnated the earth womb of the goddess. The sun's fertilization offered new life. Yes it was spring. I was aware that the seeds I carried inside wanted to begin their growing cycle.

I walked out of the chamber feeling new. My legs felt a bit wobbly from the experience, but I held onto the depth of my experience. What rests in the dark, what births from the dark and what is recovered from the dark?

Soon after we headed back to Dublin. I felt saturated with experience. My body still recalls that walk into the dark chambers of Newgrange.

When I need to feel a container for new birthing I walk that passage in my imagination. It lives in my body memory. I walk to reconnect to the Mother. Newgrange also gave me a powerful experience of being in the dark. My soul had prepared me and I loved the mystery of that process. Being willing to go underground was a way to transform.

It was strange to be back in the van heading into 21st century Dublin. Once back at our hotel Carolyn and I took time together by taking a walk about Dublin. It was our time to say our goodbyes before dinner. We promised to stay in touch and continue our sharing. Our last evening festivities included attending a play at the Abbey Theatre, after which we would celebrate with dinner.

After visiting Yeats Tower and hearing of Lady Gregory's role, going to Abbey Theatre held special meaning. It was part of our literary travel. The play that evening was called *Blackwater Angel*. I found it to be powerful and moving. Its themes explored the mystery of the gifts of a healer, his struggle with his gift, loss of it and his meeting of a young woman who sings like an angel. The play brought me to tears, but I felt less uncomfortable expressing my feelings with my group members. Seeing that Irish play reminded me of the importance of our living stories.

Our farewell dinner followed soon after the play. The restaurant was full of celebrating people, some of them the theatre crowd. While we waited for our table I noticed beautiful lacework framed and hanging on the wall. The sight of delicate lace mounted on a black background was stunning to me. The delicate Irish craft inspired beauty and reminded me of the threads which wove the mystery of all people's lives

Our group gathered at a long table together, we raised our wine glasses and expressed our gratitude to Phil, Collette, and Niki who had made our travel inspiring. I appreciated the enormous amount of work and coordination the trip had taken. It was late when we all climbed back in our van for the last time. As we arrived back at our hotel for the last time, I said my goodbyes to everyone, thanking them for sharing the travel. I was taking an early morning flight to Iona, Scotland while the others would be leaving later in the day.

I was glad I had risked becoming part of a group process. Ireland had become a ritual space where I let go. I had been nurtured in the pilgrimage circle and was glad for the space held by Phil Cousineau, Niki and Colette. Ireland had offered me a chance to grow and let go, to be nurtured at wells, to meet the face of St. Brigid in Sister Mary and be inspired to stoke the fires of my heart.

Pilgrimage to Iona

It was early morning when I clipped myself into my seat as Air Lingus left Dublin and headed to Glasgow, Scotland. The day would be a long one, for from Glasgow I would travel west and arrive in Iona, a small island in the Hebrides. The last time I boarded a plane I was arriving in Ireland; Iona offered me a new spiral.

I was happy to be flying solo again. It wouldn't be until very late in the afternoon that I would arrive in Iona. While a bit travel weary from ten days on the road I knew the island would offer me simplicity.

As I settled into my seat I thought about the first time I had heard the name Iona and my soul lifted. However at that time I had found the travel to be too long and unnerving. But since then I had grown in my capacity to explore. Iona, the mystical island off the coast of Scotland, awaited me. While I felt uncertain, the spirit of adventure called me. I engaged trust and imagination.

At Glasgow Airport I hailed a cab for Queen Street Station. As the cab wove across town, I remembered my grandmother and the information my Aunt Peg had given me about Nana growing up in a town close to Glasgow. Where did she grow up? I invoked her memory. These memories included afternoon teas, her small city garden, her love of books, and our Sunday ritual of shelling peas on the back porch. Nana had patiently taught me how to squeeze the pod just right to release the tender peas. My grandmother had died at age 63, when I was seven years old. I was close to 63 myself as I began travel through her homeland. I gazed out the taxi window as we pulled up to the train station.

Before purchasing my round-trip ticket, I stopped to buy film, and an egg sandwich since I'd had no breakfast. I took out my itinerary to review the route. The first leg of the journey out of Glasgow started with a three-hour train ride to Oban. There I would catch a ferry that would take me to the island of Mull. On Mull, I would board a bus to Fionnephort, and finally catch another ferry to Iona. It was paramount I bring patience as a travel companion; I was glad for my writing paper and pen.

As I waited for the train to depart for Oban, I settled down and took out my journal to digest the Ireland pilgrimage. I kept checking the time, impatient to leave and be on the way. But then travel had taught me to be in the moment, allowing the journey to come to me. Finally the words I wanted to hear were spoken, "All aboard. Those passengers traveling to Oban please board on track number two." I walked the platform looking for my car number. I noted my transition anxiety, similar to what I felt during seasonal shifting from winter to spring. The challenge, I knew, was trusting. I felt calmer when I found the car. Lifting my suitcase aboard, I finally settled into my seat, looking forward to Scotland's vistas.

The mystery of the trip wrapped me in a soft pleasure. As the train gained speed outside Glasgow, I settled into the slow rocking movement of the cars, allowing myself to just sit back and be carried along. The mystery of the trip was broken up into gentle steps. Arriving slowly at a destination gave me a chance to appreciate the journey. I didn't feel so pushed, picked up and dropped suddenly into foreign territory. There was indeed more mystery in the slow progress to Iona. In the past I had found it stressful to hold the tension of the unknown. While I still felt twinges of fear, I was slowly becoming comfortable with the journeying process.

Fears were natural as I stepped out; but I sought freedom. When I actually considered the false belief that the destination was the end, I laughed to myself, because I knew it just meant another beginning.

My fellow travelers on the train included young and old. A young mother, her redheaded daughter and terrier dog sat across the aisle from me. I noticed for the first time that people traveled with their dogs. In the seat in front of me was an elderly Scottish woman dressed in a green tartan hat and coat. Feeling at home, I leaned back and took in the countryside.

As the train meandered through Glasgow and further out of town, I delighted in the abundance of rhododendrons growing seemingly wild along the tracks. They reminded me of childhood springs in my southern New Jersey town. They signaled abundance, their large pink and white flowers full of new life. I leaned into the window as the train sped by bluebells poking their heads above tall grass. The train rocked along, the landscape opening out to rolling hills and inland slate-toned lakes called *lochs*. A low mist shrouded the land, blanketing my journey with the unrevealed. I loved the spaciousness of the day-long trip. Sitting gazing out into the mist quieted my mind. The travel helped me learn to relax into the spaces between things. Entranced, I sank further into my window seat.

Inhabiting my life had taken me down many roads. I had found reward in marking each piece of those roads and experiences fit with another, and felt joy in connecting the dots, perhaps the work of aging. Coming present was a goal. I was surprised to see how travel had revealed fears I wouldn't have encountered at home. Ireland had taken me to rocky hills where I walked the dark of the past. What gifts would Iona bring me?

But how were the two linked? There were many interweaving threads. I thought about my grandmother who had been born in Scotland. Perhaps in that moment the train was passing her town. I carried her blood in my veins. There were many historical threads that wove Ireland and Iona, including the link of the Druids and then the Irish Christian named St. Columba who sailed from Ireland with twelve monks. They arrived on Iona in 564 A.D. He had founded a small monastery that became a jewel of a center for Christianity in Scotland. I imagined their harrowing trip by small boat, through rough seas and possibly even storms. I considered the journey my grandmother took when she left Scotland for Ireland to marry my grandfather; then as a young bride she left Ireland's shores to take the long trip to the U.S. I had new appreciation for the risks they took coming to unknown shores. Scotland felt like a coming home.

I considered other threads that linked Iona and Ireland. Having just visited places sacred to St. Brigid in Ireland I considered her legends. One places St. Brigid the abbess in Iona. Her presence in my life catalyzed my travel and deepened my reverence for the sacred feminine and creative fire. Memories of her wells, Kildare and the synchronistic painting I had done in Inis Mor flooded back. I felt the gift of her protection and invoked her inspiration as I stepped closer to claiming my voice. My fears were raw materials to be melted down and reformed. I was stoking the fires to forge change.

The three-hour train ride from Glasgow to Oban was softened by a few cups of hot tea. An older Scottish man with a blue vest pushed a cart along the aisle inviting us to buy tea and sandwiches. The warm tea nurtured me. My eyes softened, catching only small snapshots of the lochs, an occasional castle looming in the distance, or a red truck driving over a hill in the distance.

To receive the gifts of new travel I needed to let go of where I had been. At the same time I took the time to digest what I'd experienced in Ireland. It didn't take long to sink into memories of the Burren and Inis Mor. The outer journey to the rocky landscape of the Burren had surprised me. It had mirrored my own rocky grey inner world. Walking its territory asked me to consider the beauty of life that had found its way through the rock. The Burren had also brought me face to face with death. Wasn't it important to include it rather than turn from it? The harsh life of the windswept landscape seemed to teach endurance and surrender. I had myself been tempered by harshness and challenged to thrive. Yes the outer world journeys were inner world invitations. The possibilities were endless; each was a jumping off point for another.

I was surprised when the PA in our car announced that we were approaching Oban. I gathered my luggage and stepped onto the train platform. Though I could smell the sea in the distance, the reddish brown walls of two buildings prevented me from seeing it.

Oban sat at the edge of Car Sea, which lay to the right and left of me. Oban means "little bay" in Gaelic. The seaside town wrapped itself in a horseshoe shape about the bay. There was a feeling of summer holiday about the place. A large, older hotel called "The Queens" sat about a half mile down the street. I could see it through an interesting orange-flowered road divider. It looked like the kind of place one came for summer vacation with the family, yet the stone architecture felt formal, not clapboard, not similar to towns at home. The ferryboat dock with small sailing and fishing boats painted blue, red or grey, dotted my view. I enjoyed the sea more than anything. Travel weary and overloaded with images from Ireland, I took little interest in the shops. However, I found pleasure in seeing the ruins of a castle that hovered in the distance like a protector of the town.

The ferry to Mull would depart in an hour, so I wandered the streets, grateful to stretch my legs and be refreshed. Before standing in line to board the ferry I spied a blue awning covering a small fish stand. Fresh fish and other goodies inspired, but a small voice reminded me to buy something. I chose a salmon salad sandwich *to tide me over.*

My grandmother's words floated by and hovered above the water.

She had offered me compassion and humor. While I had lost her at a young age, my early years had been infused with her own fires and willingness to be a pilgrim in new territory. I could liken this experience of traveling in Scotland to a rock wall that had fallen into disrepair; though it no longer stood tall, seeing it restored built foundation and links with ancestry. Traveling in Scotland honored her. I walked along imagining her joining me. Taking a bite of my sandwich, I felt happy as the cool air began to blow about me. A few clouds were gathering in the distance. I loved the smell of the sea air, and the adventure of travel by ferry always felt magical.

Soon it was time to join others lining up to board the ferry. I was surprised by a large number of people who seemed to appear out of nowhere—children with knit caps, adults toting baggage, blue, orange and purple coats, backpacks, the ring of English and Scottish dialects, smiling faces all headed aboard.

Soon the line moved and we all climbed the gangplank. I found a seat close to the windows on the lower deck and listened to the clunk of cars as they moved into the ferry hull. The sound woke memory of the ferry I used to ride to Whidbey Island in Washington State. The name of the ferryboat I was riding that day was the *Caledonia MacBrayne*. It sported two large lounges and full cafeteria that served ferry faire—fish and chips, burgers and pastries. I headed for a tea and then returned to my seat and joined the other passengers who sat musing, reading papers or watching the dock slip away as the boat turned west.

As the ferry chugged further from shore, I felt uncertain again. I had gotten used to traveling with others. I reassured myself with the thought that traveling alone is a different thrill, with intuition and trust as companions. I would risk this adventure on my own and continue to build self-trust. I reflected on my first pilgrimage to Chartres, where I walked the ancient labyrinth. I remembered the joy as well as the self-doubt I had experienced. Each pilgrimage had expanded my potential and opened new doors of understanding.

Forty-five minutes later our ferry landed at Craignure on the Island of Mull. As I made the slow trek off the ferryboat, I spotted a bus waiting at a distance. Up close I could read the name Fionnephort on its destination sign. That bus was my connection to the other side of the island. There, wherever *there* was, I would board another ferry. After reassuring myself again I climbed aboard and settled in a seat with my luggage overhead. I watched with curiosity to see who boarded the bus with me. There were finally eight of us who traveled across Mull together, locals and other pilgrims like myself headed for Iona.

The island landscape of Mull initially seemed desolate, but after my eyes adjusted to the simplicity I began to appreciate the rough craggy rocks, equally craggy sheep, and wild oxen, who all grazed on scrub brush. The unfamiliar landscape fascinated me; green hills were backdrops for what seemed to be just rocky soil. When I looked closer I appreciated the subtle tones of purples and rusts, while water flowed in rivulets here and there throughout the landscape. We made several stops to drop off the Mullions, as I guessed you would call the local residents of that island. A half-hour later the bus pulled into the parking lot at Fionnphort where a ferry waited. Iona was actually a stone's throw across the water. A cold wind focused me and suggested I pull on my beautiful hand-dyed indigo-blue sweater brought as a treasure from Ireland. I felt sheltered in the sweater and boarded the ferry.

The wind had picked up as the sky darkened. As I approached my destination I began to feel like the weary traveler I was. While the sky had darkened, a light shone in front of me—Iona, a "small jewel" lighting up the horizon! A soul call had been sounded long ago, and that day I was arriving.

I bundled up in my blue coat, pulled my hood up over my face, and wrapped a warm scarf around my neck. With firm grip I held on to the rail as the wind whipped and the cold rain began to pelt the deck. Fionnphort, the small port town, slipped behind me, the gangplank dropped ahead of me and I was there. I instantly fell under the spell of that mystical island. Bundled in my coat, my wheeled suitcase bumping along behind me, I walked down the narrow street to the hotel. I pulled open the heavy plank door of the place and stepped into an old inn where a great hearth and blazing peat fire welcomed me.

Inside I was glad for shelter. Surprisingly I felt at home immediately. The hotel had the hearth quality I looked to, a sign told me the inn was built in 1868.

The smell of the peat fire warmed my heart and soon a young Scottish woman with dark hair greeted me. She knew I had traveled all day and quietly took me to a room at the top of narrow stairs. I loved my small room immediately. Its windows looked out on a yard. The room was cozy and my body smiled as it saw a beautiful claw foot tub tucked under the bathroom window. "Dinner service starts at 5:30," my Scottish hostess said, then smiled and closed the door

The small room was a delight; a warm white throw graced the bed. I wanted to fall into it and sleep, but then considered a hot steaming tub. Moments later, hot water and fragrant rosemary bath salts awaited me. I climbed into the steaming tub and soaked the long travel day from my bones. It was then 5 PM. As I soaked I looked forward to taking back my own rhythms, giving myself permission to make this pilgrim exploration my own. I let my mind go blank, feeling nurtured as I settled into the warm water. Tired but relaxed from my bath, I climbed out and took a fluffy towel from its rack. Soon after, I lay down into the soft yellow sheets and fell asleep to the sounds of the ferry as it clanged its bell and prepared for departure. I awoke an hour later feeling amazingly refreshed. As I dressed I noticed a pamphlet that lay on my bedside table telling me that the hotel served organic foods.

I realized I hadn't heard anyone pass my room and was curious to see who would share the dining room with me. The hotel had only sixteen rooms and a small attentive staff. As I descended the stairs I heard fiddle music playing softly. It put me in the mood; I was actually in Scotland! A large fire burned brightly in the fireplace and set a lovely tone in the dining room. A young hostess seated me at a small table close to the fireplace. The fire blazed behind me and from my chair I looked out on the descending dark of Iona's evening. For awhile only two English women my age or older sat at another table. We shared the quiet beauty and warmth of the room. I ate fresh fish caught that afternoon and salad greens grown in the garden behind the hotel. The risk of the long journey was already proving to be more than worth it.

After dinner I took a short walk. The rain had stopped but I needed to pull my hood up to stay warm. I noted how the sturdy stone homes of Iona suggested simplicity. The imposing cathedral, now lit in the distance, loomed in sharp contrast to the windswept hills and buttoned-down village. Soon after my walk I returned to my room and tumbled into bed, looking forward to exploring the island the next day.

I awoke to sun streaming in the window. Tired not only from yesterday's travel, but also from the ten days on the road in Ireland, I put my head back on the pillow. Since the island was so small I didn't feel pressure to rush out to see everything as I often did in cities or larger places. To make my pilgrimage my own I realized I needed to nurture myself and listen to my tired body. This meant giving myself the luxury of spending much of the morning in bed. I wanted to catch up on my writing, take time to reflect on my experiences in Ireland. I felt the importance. I also reveled in the gentle silence and space of being on my own.

I was reminded of rock and earth on the island. As I looked out my window a hill rose in the distance and reminded me the rocky landscape and I were alike. They were the bones of earth not just old rocks. I was part of that bone. I was also made of the same elements. I knew that my heritage had diminished the clay of life, made the bone, blood and skin something to rise above. The diminishing was based in fear.

As I lay in bed, I heard the clank of cooking pots below and felt the excitement of new adventure ahead. There was the sound of another clanking which announced the arrival of the ferry. I don't know what it is about ferryboats but they certainly spark my imagination. I wanted to stay snuggled in bed but I also wanted a cup of tea. So I pulled on my blue sweater and khaki pants and headed for the dining room. I asked if I could carry some tea to my room. Mary, a young waitress, handed me a small tray with a white and blue pot and cup, then asked if I wanted sugar or cream or lemon. As I climbed back upstairs I felt happy. When I settled back in bed to write and to explore a few books on Iona I found in my room, I was sad I would only be staying for two days. I had been lucky to find accommodations even for those days.

After making time for writing I took another long soak in the tub. I dressed in walking clothes, went downstairs and found a few tea crackers remaining on the buffet table. Not hungry, I decided to wait until lunch. As I stepped out into the bright sun on the cobblestone street I felt at peace. I passed the miniature post office tucked down several steps from the roadway and stood watching the water lap at the ferry pier. I had traveled thousands of miles to Iona; it was becoming increasingly clear to me that the holy and ordinary mingled there. The island would teach me more about my true self and the "inner wildness."

The gentle morning held a deep happiness that I couldn't remember ever feeling before in my life. Iona was a divine nest for me. Iona was a place I could be at home. I am sure that the intimacy and warmth of the hotel helped me feel safe to live from the inside out. I also realized that the quiet intimacy of the hotel enhanced my contemplation. I felt a turn toward my center, with a new willingness to go into a deeper current of myself.

I set out uphill for the ruins of a 13th century convent not far from the hotel. It was refreshing to be walking in a village with only a few streets. The ferry had just arrived and I joined a group of pilgrims, young and old, anticipating the mystery of Iona. I was grateful for the deep silence, noting that only the residents were allowed cars, which meant no traffic noise.

I entered the convent ruins; small beds of flowers welcomed me. A loving gardener obviously cared for several beds of white alyssum, blue lobelia and other spring blooms. I thought about the women who lived in the convent. What was their life like? The garden also reminded me of my grandmother who had always tended a small vegetable garden behind her home in Philadelphia. I recalled the sweet flowers planted along its edges. I sat on a low stone wall for a moment enjoying the sun and felt the gifts of a pilgrimage dedicated to the heritage of the women in my family. Had my grandmother known Iona or visited the island?

My small paper guidebook to the island told me the convent was built around the 13th century and was dedicated to Mother Mary. I wandered through old stones of grays and pinks quarried locally. As I stood in the open-air ruins I could almost hear the morning prayers of the nuns. Grasses and flowers gave a sense of softness to the wild landscape. Standing in the ruins of the small building, I peered through windowless frames, which offered beautiful snapshots of the distant sea and blue sky. I knew this beauty had been only one lens of the nuns' experience. Harsh cold winters must have been challenging, as were the threats of Viking invasions. The women had to be courageous and committed to their faith.

Leaving the ruins I walked north toward the abbey. I recalled the stories of St. Columba and stood imaging the ruggedness of the island when he and twelve other monks arrived. Celtic Christianity flourished on this small island for years after their arrival. History tells us that the beautiful and famous Book of Kells was in all likelihood written on Iona.

The island often suffered raids; when Vikings raided Iona around 800 AD, the manuscript was taken to Kells, Ireland for safekeeping.

The sun broke out from behind a cloud and a soft wind began to accompany me as I continued north to St. Oran Chapel and the abbey. The chapel was named after a follower of Columba's. I walked the pebbled path to the small grey stone building and then beyond to the graveyard. Short green grasses and rock walls enclosed the area. As I entered the graveyard I truly felt like a pilgrim come to be with the mystery. Certainly the monks, nuns and inhabitants of this island were initially pilgrims.

There were no questions about the riches Iona offered, for over 140,000 people a year traveled to Iona's remote shores. As I stood looking out to the island of Mull, I was glad to know that Iona is held in trust, and since there are few hotels, most pilgrims come as day travelers, returning to Mull or elsewhere for lodging. I felt lucky to be staying on the island, taking time to drink of the beauty. We travel to know ourselves outside the boxes we can enclose ourselves in. Why had I traveled to this island? It was clear that Iona had become a sweet retreat and a mysterious culmination of my journey. Iona was a cradle to hold a new life I had claimed in Ireland. I had been given a primal womb to return to.

Islands are my favorite places of pilgrimage, sheltered places embraced by water. Water holds a pulse; the rhythms of ocean currents give me solace and a deep connection to life. Nature offers us a pattern of harmony, a way to live deeply with ease. What was awakening me to my own holiness was found in landscape, in what are called "holy places." The sacred can be experienced in many ways. Holy places can be sites of temples, places in nature, or a favorite walk. Coming to Iona had been a stretch for me, yet the journey seemed to be necessary, mirroring some essential part of my self. Many pilgrims travel to Iona and return restored, feeling the shining presence of spirit. However, not everyone finds what mirrors that essential self on the island of Iona. The journey leads them elsewhere. Each of us is a unique jewel like Iona.

As I stood in the graveyard on the island of Iona I became aware of our buried lives and untold stories. Suddenly I stood face to face with the reality of my mother's death, and my own as well.

In looking back over my mother's life I had a sense of her being lost, not grounded in her own life nor feeling fulfilled. She was herself very separated from the world about her, from nature and from her true self.

Perhaps my grandmother had felt the same. What were the dreams of the women of my ancestry and was I living out some of them? I felt the luxury of choosing to be fulfilled.

I was creating an evolutionary step for my ancestry. As I stood in the graveyard I felt a passion to continue to unearth the old repressions, the rules, secrets and feelings. I was happy that pilgrimage was also offering my ancestry gifts of healing. I was breaking the silence, daring to be full of both my personal life as well as the larger story. Time to let go of old fears and speak the truth.

I considered my own life as a mother, and the prospect of ultimately becoming a grandmother. Women's lives hold so many unrecognized gifts. Claiming our lives and gifts honors source.

My quest for self asked me to look deeply and honor my unique feminine life. I was in fact following my passion to meet myself through writing. If I was following my passion, writing myself back into my life and claiming the sacred I was also taking back what had been lost. The search integrated all aspects of the feminine. The doorways to recover the divinity of myself as feminine meant stepping into my life, inhabiting my body, tending my creative fires, healing my relationship with nature and with my personal mother. Feelings, intuition, creativity, nurturing and presence were thresholds to step through to meet Self.

Everyday sacred meant bringing every moment of my life through the needle of Her eye. Respect all of life, She called, and be fulfilled in the gifts of Her rhythms.

I approached the small stone chapel and the ancient graveyard, a rather stark and brooding place. I was curious, for I had rarely visited a graveyard during pilgrimage. Death is letting go. I was aware of small deaths every minute. I looked at a modern day headstone of a certain John Smith, a labor leader of Scotland who had been brought to rest there. Yet the mystery of the graveyard was really about the legendary forty-eight or so Scottish kings whose coffins had been brought to Iona for their final sleep.

I had read that thirty headstones, however, had been moved indoors, inside the abbey museum, for protection, and I would need to go to the museum to see them. It was curious to realize these men were brought all that distance from the mainland of Scotland to be buried. Kings from other countries had also found their resting place in this cemetery. Clearly the island had been considered sacred.

I felt a strange wind blow through me, as though I could touch the old stories of these people. Simply walking the ground of the graveyard gave me pause. I certainly would have wanted to be buried in such a place myself, perhaps not for the same reasons as these kings, but perhaps exactly for the same reasons.

I then walked into the one-room chapel, a simple haven of silence. A single candlestick with an unlit candle stood on a small table, but two small windows gave enough light to see. The chapel felt earthen, simple, a vessel which allowed life, provided a womb for prayer, but didn't impose laws or beliefs on those who entered. I offered a prayer up for the pilgrims who came to this place, in both ancient and modern times.

Iona Abbey stood close to the chapel. The original abbey, founded around 1200, was restored in 1910. The abbey stands solitary and vast in contrast to land and low homes scattered about the island. The stone quarried for the building came from the island of Mull. Its proportions seemed out place on the windswept island and in contrast to the earthscape. The abbey church, monastery buildings, refectory and other additions, including a small museum, make up the entire structure. I wasn't interested in exploring so I turned around.

Before walking much farther I felt a gnawing hunger and returned to the hotel for lunch. New guests had arrived and the dining room was bustling with people. I was shown to my small table from last evening. There was comfort in having my own table. It was especially so being single and aging. After perusing the menu, I noticed the young family and grandmother who sat at the next table. I could hear the grandmother telling a story about her cat. Her granddaughter asked her to repeat her favorite part about how the cat disappeared for a day. The grandmother wove a delightful tale about the cat's disappearance and then embellished her return. Speaking of aging, I thought to myself, I hoped I would be as good a storyteller when I became a grandmother. The thought made me smile, since I wasn't sure when that would be. I finished a hearty lunch of barley soup, a salad of fresh greens and a pot of hot tea.

Soon after lunch I headed back outside to explore. I wanted to take advantage of the rest of the afternoon. I considered visiting the abbey, but longed to walk some of the beaches. As I first headed south, wandering the hills among the grasses dotted with small white and yellow wildflowers, I met up with a few cows taking an afternoon nap. The word *bucolic* came to mind, but as I wandered past the homes of the Iona community I wondered what they thought of us travelers. I assumed they looked forward to the winter when few outsiders would risk the harsh weather. The residents of the island would certainly feel hardships from the isolation and wild weather.

Further along a dirt path I stopped at a farmhouse. Outside, sitting on a rough wood table, were beautiful green marble crosses for sale, along with a basket of polished green marble pebbles. I took eight of the pebbles, placing coins in the basket for payment, and then sensed the need to turn around head north instead. The green pebbles felt pure and bright in my hand, filled with the unknown of the *shining* place.

I headed back past the nunnery and walked toward the northernmost beaches. I stopped suddenly to admire a pocket of tall green grasses and wild iris tucked back against a hill. I was certain there was a spring located close by. I hadn't remembered mention of it in my book, but that didn't matter. I stood there feeling a particular kind of joy I felt when discovering natural treasure. I had visited wells and springs in Ireland, but nothing came close to that moment. I felt time open and I returned to a lifetime when I was sitting by such a spring with deep knowing about life. I had discovered my metaphor for Source. A quiet filled me; I had been arriving for years. The moment was about returning to that Source.

Yes, it was a spring baptism. The transformational energies of Iona claimed me. I stood with large tears flowing down my face. I was worthy! My travel in Ireland had showed me my fears, my hiding, my not good enough, my shame. I could let go, and bent down to see if any water lay on the surface. There was some closer to the hill. I leaned into the hill and with grateful prayer took the water, sprinkled some over my head and Pilgrimage had become more than I could imagine.

I was slow to set out after the joy of discovering the spring and seeing the wild iris. I felt cleansed of the past. I walked the road north, which narrowed as I crossed through small gates. The road turned to a dirt path and then disappeared. I crossed the low grasses and stepped down onto a beautiful white sand beach. As I stood looking out on the iridescent blue-green sea, I felt the congruence of land, sky and sea. The hundreds of years of prayer, sacred presence and ancient wisdom sounded from every rock, blade of grass and grain of sand. While I walked I felt the intimacy of the island only three miles long and one mile wide.

I felt embraced and free while pondering the ancientness of the landscape. Geologists suggest that the rock formations of Iona are some of the oldest on earth, over 1500 million years old. I had to take a breath to take it all in. The mystery rolled over me. I was full of the truth of this wonder in a new way. Perhaps the dark cloaks of Ireland had veiled my ability to see the light of such beauty.

Iona offered me a cosmic voice, its peace the true nature of my essence. Hardship, Beauty, and Presence all partnered on Iona.

I sat on the warm sands throwing pebbles and emptying my mind. I listened to the lapping of the North Atlantic waters. I left myself open to listen. I likened my experience that day to other days in the presence of ocean waters. It is said by some that the waters of our planet carry information, and so I stood listening for news of the world. However, my experience was more than listening and opening to the rhythms and currents of ocean waters bringing me peace. The experience was close to "walking in the Great Mother's energy field," a sea of mystery of the outstretched arms of feminine essence. I was able to feel myself being embraced.

I got up and felt gratitude for the magic and transformative experiences of Iona. I would be heading to a place I called home. I knew I wanted to carry the cocoon of peace, the feeling of space. Spontaneously I took a deep breath and opened my mouth. AAAAAAAAAAH. I let the sound flow out of me. It was what I needed to let go into—taking back my voice.

My next thought was to truly forgive mother Yes, it was about forgiveness of her and myself.

I looked out on the vastness of sea and sky and said a prayer of gratitude for being able to come here. Before leaving the beach I picked up a stone with ritual in mind. I wanted to honor the tradition of releasing. I recalled the gift of the fire ceremony at Chartres and tossing the stone out into the blue Mediterranean waters. Again I let go of fear, the fear of being my deep feminine essence; I asked to receive grace.

Iona included my Celtic roots. The island sanctuary had pulled me ever closer to Mother Nature. The whole island was the cathedral. The vast ocean and sky, the rocky coast, light, rock and water were my soul's landscape.

The landscape of Iona poured its wine over me. As a pilgrim I felt the mystery of life as everyday sacred, and engaged the moments of grace and beauty through gentle being. Each of our experiences is different however, coming home to the one heart is revealed to each of us in different places.

As I headed back down the path I decided to stop at the Iona Community Bookstore. While combing the shelves and buying a few postcards I found a book, *The Dove in the Stone* by Alice Howell. Its subtitle, *Finding the Sacred in the Commonplace*, echoed what I had felt on Iona. My quest path seemed to be clearly pointing me to her subtitle, the place where I could find the sacred everywhere. My hearth seeking was part of that everyday sacred. I developed awareness on Iona. I felt peacefulness and a knowing which was hard to describe.

Happy with my walk, my exploration, and my new book, I headed back to the hotel, but then stopped at a small two-room, very old bookstore. I found another treasure which delighted me. The book was called *Saint Bride, the Greatest Woman of the Celtic Church*. James Wilkie wrote it in 1913. This small treasure of a book was inspiring just to hold. The book would be good winter reading when I could sit by the fire. But it was still spring.

It was late in the day when I climbed upstairs to my room and settled into bed under the soft yellow quilt. I was anxious to read Alice Howell. What was delightful about her book was that it was written as a pilgrim would write. She and her husband had traveled to Iona. The book is a weaving of their shared experience, a dialogue between them about Iona, including insights about Sophia wisdom. Her book offered me another lens on the feminine aspect of divinity. I appreciated a statement made by Christopher Bamford in the introduction to her book. He speaks of Sophia clearly when he says, "She is both what is divine in creation and what is created in the divine. She is the great mediator between the uncreated and the created... She teaches us the truth that the entire world is filled with outward and visible signs of inward and spiritual meaning." In reading these words I became a new student of Sophia, learning how the world was filled with manifestations of the inward. Step by step, this understanding would find root and grow in me.

I fell asleep for a short time after finishing my reading and woke just in time for dinner. I dressed and went downstairs to the beautiful roaring fire and a dining room filled with new guests. I happily settled at my table by the fire and ordered my dinner of roasted potatoes with a casserole of lamb and carrots. I felt at home listening to a young French couple at the next table.

After dinner I sat on the closed-in glass porch to have tea and said my goodbyes to the English women I had shared the first dinner with. I felt how the gentle quality of the Argyle Hotel held the qualities of the sacred feminine. It was filled with love, grace, beauty and peace. In the book *The Dove and the Stone*, Alice Howell wrote, "It is this loving intimacy which is feminine in nature, not coming as bolts from on high, but rising up like sap in all things that grow and are alive." I sat enjoying my tea and shortbread cookies until I felt tired.

As I packed my things for my voyage back to Glasgow I knew my short trip to Iona had fulfilled me. The morning brought strong winds and rains but I was ready for the long journey back. I thanked the staff and owner of the inn, then bundled up in my blue coat and headed for the ferry. I would arrive in Glasgow late, stay overnight, and take a flight home to California the next day. Iona was a baptism.

Summer

"When the heart is ready for new beginnings,
unforeseen things can emerge..."

—John O'Donohue

I returned to Mt. Shasta only to set out again. Sonoma was calling me home. Dawn and Matt, along with their family cat Tigger and Sierra their chocolate Labrador, were heading west. Meanwhile, I was packing up, gathering up the elements of hearth.

The evening before I left Mt. Shasta I stepped out on the front porch, remembering the warm afternoon I had arrived. I stood looking up at the mountain and out into the night sky, feeling a deep gratitude. I felt the pulse of the darkness draw me. The miracle of possibilities winked at me from the galaxy of stars above me. I breathed in the crisp night air, standing there in awe. The cool air reminded me of the winter morning I set out on my quest. I turned back into the house, still filled with gratitude, climbed into bed and pulled up the comforter around my chin. Sula settled into the crook of my legs.

It was July when I arrived in Sonoma. Soon after my arrival I met Dawn and Matt for lunch. It was wonderful to see them and I looked forward to a new chapter in family life.

Several days later, after settling into the small cottage I had rented, I set out to walk to the center of town. I anticipated the elixir of our 4th of July parade. Holiday crowds lined the streets, waiting.

The mood was festive. Magic was in the air. I waved as I saw Matt and Dawn across the street with special smiles on their faces. Arm in arm they shared the news. Yes, a baby was on the way! Probably March! I danced up and down.

New life. New beginnings.

My summer was filled with the blooming of a new joy. I settled easily into Sonoma life, planted a small garden, watched fruits bloom. The cycle of the seasons continued. Harvest came and winter brought the dark.

But spring followed with light. Early in March, on a lovely spring evening, the family welcomed Sam, Matt and Dawn's first child. Two years later, Sam's brother Bodey joined us. These were the very best of beginnings.

Deep peace of the running wave to you.
Deep peace of the flowing air to you.
Deep peace of the quiet earth to you.
Deep peace of the shining stars to you.
Deep peace of the infinite peace to you.

--Fiona Macleod, 1895

Resources

"Remember the entrance door to the sanctuary is inside you."
—Rumi

Hal Zina Bennett, *Write from the Heart*

halzinabennett.com—author, writing coach

Christina Baldwin, *Storycatcher: Making Sense of our Lives through the Power and Practice Of Story.*

storycatcher.net

Maureen Murdock, *Unreliable Truth*

May Sarton, *Journal of a Solitude*

CELTIC SPIRITUALITY

Mara Freeman, *Kindling the Celtic Spirit*

chalicecentre.net

John O'Donohue, *Benedictus* and *Beauty*

johnodonohue.com

LABYRINTH
Dr. Lauren Artress, *Walking a Sacred Path*
veriditas.org

SACRED GEOMETRY
Richard Feather Anderson—teacher and facilitator
geomant@ earthlink.net

THE GREATER WORLD
Ted Andrews, *Animal-Speak* and *Nature Speaks*

WOMEN'S WRITING AND CREATIVITY
Emily Hanlon—author, creativity and writing coach
emilyhanlon.com

ART
Kati Siteri, graphic designer, Mill Valley Graphics
Lindsay Whiting, *Living into Art: Journeys through Collage*
lindsay@paperlantern.biz

Iona Gallery—Art of Marianne Lines
www.stoneline.co.uk

CELEBRATING THE PLANET
Eric Allan, *Wild Grace, Nature as a Spiritual Path*

Bill Plotkin, *Soulcraft*

SACRED FEMININE

China Galland, *Longing for Darkness: Tara and the Black Madonna*

Ian Beggs, *The Cult of the Black Madonna*

Jennifer Posada, *The Oracle Within*
jenniferposada.com—healer and writer

PILGRIMAGE

Judith Tripp
circleways.com

Phil Cousineau, *The Art of Pilgrimage*
philcousineau.net

Buy your food locally and visit farmers markets.

Bibliography

Abram, David. *The Spell of the Sensuous*. Random House, 1996.

Arrien, Angeles. *The Second Half of Life*. Sounds True, 2005.

Allegretti, Jan. *Listen to the Silence: Lessons from the Trees and Other Masters*. Tenacity Press. iUniverse, 2007.

Andrews, Ted. *Animal-Speak: The Spiritual and Magical Powers of Creatures Great & Small*. Llewellyn Publications, 2001.

_____. *Nature-Speak: Signs, Omens and Messages in Nature*. Llewellyn Publications, 2007.

Artress, Lauren. *Walking a Sacred Path*. The Berkeley Publishing Group, 1995.

Baldwin,Christina. *Storycatcher: Making Sense of Our Lives through the Power and Practice of Story*. New World Library, 2005.

Begg, Ean. *The Cult of the Black Virgin*. Penguin Books, 1985.

Bennett, Hal Zina. *The Lens of Perception*. Berkeley: Celestial Arts, 1993.

_____. *Write From the Heart*. New World Library, 2001.

Bock, Maryanna. "An Artist's Journey through the Sacred Rainbow."

www.earthcircle.net/bg2.html

Dillard, Annie. "Winter" in *Winter: A Spiritual Biography of the Season.* Edited by Gary Schmidt and Susan M. Felch. Skylight Paths Publishing, 2003.

Freeman, Mara. *Kindling the Celtic Spirit.* Harper San Francisco, 2000.

Galland, China. *Longing for Darkness, Tara and the Black Madonna.* Penguin, 1991.

Hageneder, Fred. *The Spirit of Trees.* The Continuum International Publishing Group, 2001.

Kaplan, Connie Cockrell. *The Woman's Book of Dreams.* Beyond Words Publishing Inc., 1999.

Kidd, Sue Monk. *The Dance of the Dissident Daughter.* Harper San Francisco, 1996.

Matthews, Caitlin. *Sophia, Goddess of Wisdom, Bride of God.* Quest Books, 2001.

MacEowen, Frank. *The Mist-Filled Path: Celtic Wisdom for Exiles, Wanderers, and Seekers.* New World, 2002.

O'Donohue, John. *Anam Cara: A Book of Celtic Wisdom.* Harper Collins, 1997.

Perara, Sylvia Brinton. *Descent to the Goddess.* Inner City Books, Canada, 1981.

About the Author

Joanna Devrais lives in Sonoma, California. Her love of Nature, Beauty and the art of cooking inspire her life. She is co-author of the book *Allergy Free Eating*. Her passion for cooking and healthy lifestyle eating led her to the creation of Heart Cuisine. Currently she teaches the arts of cooking, self care and the wisdom of the sacred feminine. Her newest teachers are the lively spirits of her grandsons Sam and Body.